The
EARLY YEARS
VOLUME II

The
EARLY YEARS
VOLUME II

Jeshua

The Early Years: Volume II

First Edition

www.wayofmastery.com

Published by:
PT. Heartfelt Publishing
PO Box 204, Ubud 80571
admin@wayofmastery.com
www.wayofmastery.com

ISBN: 978-602-9189-20-9

© 1992, 2021 Jayem

Publication or reproduction of this work, in whole or in part, by any means, without the written permission of the author is prohibited.

Jeshua Shares

I promise you this: If you become *wholly committed* to awakening from the dream you have dreamed since the stars first began to appear in the heavens, and even before that, if your one desire is to be only what God created . . . then lay at the altar of your heart with every breath, everything you *think* you know, everything you *think* you need, and look lovingly upon every place that fear has made a home in your mind, and allow correction to come. It will come. Regardless of how you experience it, it *will* come.

And the day and the moment will arise when all of your pain and fear and suffering will have vanished like a wind that pushes the foam of the wave away, revealing the clarity of the ocean beneath you. You will literally feel throughout your being that there never was a dream. Some memories will remain with you and you will know that somewhere you must've dreamed a dream or had a thought of wondering what it would be like to be other than the way God created you, but it will be such a faint echo that it will leave no trace upon you. In your heart you will smile gently, regardless of the circumstances in which you find yourself. There will be peace from the crown of the head to the tips of the toes, so to speak, and that peace will walk before you wherever you go. It will enter a room before you enter it with a body, and those who are becoming sensitive will wonder who has come into their place. And some will even say, "Behold, I believe Christ has come for dinner." And you will be that one, for that is who you are—Christ eternal.

~ The Early Years: Choose to See

Contents

Foreword i

Become the Master of Time 1
Healing through Self Love 43
Teach Only Love 60
Decide to Be Christ 74
Grace As Reality 93
Heaven on Earth 135
Ignorance is Bliss 161
Choose to See 176
Mastering Communication 197
The Meaning of Ascension 209
The Divine Feminine 234

Epilogue 242
The Way of Mastery Outline 246
Shanti Christo 248

Foreword

This book is a transcription of channelings given by Jeshua to public groups from the early years of my work with Him. These teachings are an extensive collection of Jeshua's wisdom, and a vital part of *The Way of Mastery Pathway*.

As recounted in *The Jeshua Letters,* after my more personal initial communion with Jeshua, my studentship and work with Him shifted to a more public stage.

During this period, from 1988 until the time He began the three year course of *The Way of Mastery: The Christ Mind Trilogy,* in 1994, He asked that I remain surrendered to Him. This included stepping into the more public role of channeling for groups, something I was very uncomfortable with in the beginning. Regardless of my discomfort, however, as word got out, groups gathered in increasing numbers at my home in Tacoma, Washington, and invitations, taking me farther and farther afield, came in as well. All this required that I surrender further and further to a process I did not understand at all!

The public phase of my work with Jeshua began with the first group gathering in which He lifted me out of my body (or what I have come to see as 'the' body), and then entered into it to communicate through it to those in attendance. I refer to this stage as the beginning of the 'channeling' phase of my work with Him, although it is important for the reader to understand what is meant by the word 'channeling.'

Here is what would always happen: I would close my eyes and initiate a simple prayer He had given me, and I would feel myself dropping into a deeply meditative space. Then, a peculiar vibration would begin, and as it increased, I would be transported out and above the body; I could see it below, along with the crowd gathered, as well as light beings fully encircling the group.

Things would accelerate, and I would experience a rapid movement through multi-colored light. I could witness the crowd, and then the house in which the crowd sat, and then further, wider, 'telescoping' out, I could see planet earth herself, and then, rapidly, the physical universe itself would vanish, even as the pulsing, vibrating colored light increased.

Then, it would stop, and I would be aware of being with Jeshua, now together with Him in a field of Light. He would teach me while I was there with Him, and yet…while all this was occurring, He was also moving into, and teaching through 'my' body to the group gathered together in my living room in Tacoma.

At some point, He would tell me, "It is finished now." I would then begin to feel a vibrational change, and the reverse of the journey ensued until I 'zoomed' downward and landed – often with a shock – in the body. It would often take as much as 30 minutes for me to be able to move a finger, or begin to make any sound as I slowly adapted to the body. After, it would be so charged with energy that I often would be up for hours, yet in an altered state. Everything shimmered in light, and often objects like buildings, trees, and telephone poles were transparent – I could see right through them! One night, I was very sick with a fever and strep throat and was sure the evening should be cancelled. He assured me there would be no problem, and – to everyone's surprise – as I 'left' and Jeshua entered, I was told later that suddenly there was no trace at all of my sickness!

Indeed, after returning, I experienced the body radiating in clarity and perfect health, only then to gradually feel it 'sink' as the strep throat returned. When I asked Him what had happened, he replied: *"I would suggest that would be a very good question for you to dwell in. Why has what you call 'sickness' returned?"*

This is the type of question He lovingly asks, in this case, to bring attention and contrast to why one might use the body for such a thing as sickness, which, apparently, His use of the body did not include!

The Way of Mastery: The Early Years are transcriptions of these messages, originally recorded live, that capture what Jeshua taught us during these beautiful gatherings. The wisdom, guidance, and sheer brilliance of these teachings are astounding; there is so much in these pages, dear reader, that will help you grow in understanding and support you to truly heal into peace. You might like to know this, as well: Jeshua shared that while this mystical alchemy I was undergoing was part of my studentship, it was also His learning curve in acclimating to 'my' body and learning to utilize the language structure of its 'brain-mind.'

Indeed, the first phases of this period would find Him often communicating in a slow, monotone voice, with no movement of the body at all. Gradually, over time, He could animate it, and seemed to enjoy using American idioms that He had accessed through this process, as well!

Our interactions were varied and amusing. I would often feel His presence as I, for example, watched a bit of television, and he would make comments on the shows and commercials. He said He was learning of my world through the part of my soul that was fixated and operating through the body, that tiny thing which I was still mistakenly thinking of as 'me.'

The Early Years are filled with ancient wisdom, timeless Love, and even prophecy. As you open to this wonderful trove of material from Jeshua, may you enjoy these jewels that He has given us all.

Blessings to you!

Jayem
July, 2021

BECOME THE MASTER OF TIME
July 1993

Now we begin.

Indeed, greetings unto you once again, holy and only begotten Son of God, begotten, not made, and eternally of one substance with all that the Father is—*begotten before time and of one substance with all that the Father is*. Need we say anything else?

Begotten, not born, but begotten before time is. Hmm. And all of you have been led to believe that the body in which you believe yourself to be living came forth but a few short years ago, and you with it. That is an illusion.

Begotten before time is. Your home is eternity. Your being is the Love of God. Nothing has ever changed it; nothing has ever tainted it; nothing has ever limited it except your choice to use your infinite wisdom and power and creativity to create the illusion of limitation. And with it came the birth of time.

Begotten before time is. Have you ever wondered what that must surely mean? For if those words be used as a description for me, Jeshua, the Christ, they can mean nothing in relationship to me if they do not already mean *the same* in relationship to you. Now, how can that be? For well have you been taught that I am something special and you a simple creature. And yet, in reality—not in illusion but in reality—you and I are One, and all that has ever been said about me is *about you*. Every flowery word written in your Holy Scripture is *about you*. Every word that would denigrate you and say that you are a simple creature is not about you at all; it is about somebody else's illusions.

For well have I spoken unto you that you are loved wholly and you have never sinned. You are the Light and the Life of mankind, and wherever you are, the fullness of God comes to be expressed and to be extended unto the one who stands in front of you, and the only thing that can ever create a barrier between you and your brother is *your* choice to believe that you are other than what God created you to be. Therefore, that veil that you would create is only your choice to use the infinite power extended unto you to create a very flimsy screen called separation. In it there is no power. In it there is no reality. In it there is nothing of Truth.

From my perspective—which is the one you are choosing to recognize and reawaken to—that illusion does *not exist*. And when you choose to see your brother through the very eyes that I see you, you will look with the eyes of Christ and you will know and understand that you are born into this world to be the saviour of this world.

Therefore, birth can only take place in time. Birth is taking that which is eternal and changeless and coming down to express in a form that the world can understand—the birthing of a saviour. The Christmas story is yours, the Easter story is yours, whenever you choose to claim the one Truth given you before time is:

> *I and my Father are one. I am Christ eternal. I live; yet not I but Christ lives in me and through me. Though of myself I can do nothing, my Father through me does all things because He is the Light and the Life and the Way and the Truth, and I am one with Him eternally.*
>
> *The world can give me nothing and the world can take nothing from me. Therefore, I live not in fear. I live not in lack and I live not in want. But I live to extend and to share with my holy brother and sister the fullness of my being, and when I do that, I ignite in them the possibility of claiming that reality as their very own.*
>
> *And whenever I choose to come together with my brother and sister and tolerating not a trace of error in me or in them, and they choose to see me through that very same Light, the two have become again as one. Sacred intimacy is realized and the Atonement is completed on Earth as it is already in Heaven.*

That is the power given unto you. It is the power given unto me. It is by that power that I come and blend with this carcass that you think is owned by my beloved brother. And I come forth and I use this vehicle to do nothing else than to make manifest *who you are*, and I will come again and again to serve as your mirror until when you look at even this carcass and hear these words, you recognize that you are looking on no one but yourself, and you are hearing your own voice, that voice that was given you of our Father *before time is*

When you claim those words as your own, then all power is unleashed on Earth in this bodily temple as it is already in Heaven. You think that you are separate from this carcass and I tell you that you are not. If you were to break down your perception and stop looking at the color of your hair and the width and girth of the physical forms, and start to look at what your scientists call molecules and atoms and quarks and electrons and little quantas of light, you would discover that there is not one trace of difference between the body you *think* is yours and this carcass that you *think* belongs to my beloved brother—not one trace of difference.

Ultimately, the perception that bodies abide in space and time and are separate from one another is itself an illusion. And yet, you have the power to see with eyes that are crystal clear, having let go of every trace of illusion of separation, to see not with the eyes of the body but with the eyes of the arisen Christ, to see not a body in front of you but to see the thought of Perfect Love in form that is your brother and your sister. And what power, what healing could you extend unto another if you saw not the body in separation, but if you saw *the eternal presence of Christ* in the one before you? Now, it doesn't really matter if they've forgotten. What matters is that *you* remember.

Hmm. That is why, when in Truth you have awakened and chosen never again to tolerate error in your own perception, when you stand in bodily form in front of another and look into their eyes with the Light of Christ, your simple smile can heal lifetimes. And to the degree that they are willing to receive that Light of the Christ you are, even before your eyes miracles can occur.

Can you come to understand then, that if you are not seeing miracles in *your* life, it is because you are still choosing to linger in a little trace of darkness that says,

> *I believe in God. I believe in Christ, but I am not really quite that Light. If I work a little harder and perfect it, the next time around*

3

> *I will be.*

The most arrogant of acts is to insist that you are *other* than Christ Your world would teach you just the opposite, would it not? For indeed, to say, "I am the arisen Christ," is beheld as the ultimate act of being arrogant.

I tried it and they tried to crucify me. Do you fear crucifixion? Many of you know that what I just said speaks directly to your heart, for you struggle in this world and you run up against your fear and you don't understand its source.

> *Why do I still live in lack? Why do I not manifest the power of Christ?*

And I say unto you: it is because you still carry that trace of fear that the world will crucify you if you truly live in your power. And what is power but the *choice* to rest in the gentleness of allowing your only reality to be lived with every breath you breathe.

> *Will the world crucify me if I let go of every trace of belief that I have ever been separate from God, if I leap off the cliff and trust the power of God to live through me, to throw off my shackles of lack and want and fear? And to let Christ live in me so that I can shout with one of my ancient brothers: I live; yet not I but Christ lives in me.*

And if the world would look upon you and say, "There's goes another nut," can you understand that what you are hearing is coming from a voice of illusion in which *no power resides*? And if that is true—and I assure you that it is—who cares about the opinions of another mind who would insist on illusions over reality?

Many of you know what it means to want to wake up every morning and see your world at peace, to see the complexities of the world healed, to see the chaos ceased, the insanity dissolved. And yet, you arise in the morning and you go out and conform yourself to those very opinions because you still believe that the world can keep you safe, and by conforming to it, you can escape crucifixion.

And yet I say unto you: conformity to the perceptions of your world *is* to choose crucifixion. And as I came forth once before, I come now yet again into this world in many ways. And even in this hour in this evening I am communicating through similar forms in over a hundred locations upon your planet to do one thing: to beseech you to join me, *not in the Crucifixion but in the Resurrection.* There is a Light and a power that is coming to be born upon this plane that is arising from the very soils of this, your Holy Mother, and the time is short upon this Earth. And I ask you to arise with me *to be the Resurrection*.

You know how to be the crucifixion. You have played that one out very well, and all of the gods and all of the levels of this universe applaud you on your ability to put on such a drama. Hm. But the curtain is being raised now. Many in this room are sensitive to the raising of that curtain. You feel it as a quickening that begins to move energy up and down the spine. It creates a feeling at times: "Oh, my God, what's going to happen next?" Open up and let it happen, because the raising of the curtain is nothing more than the death of illusion: because Light is being born because it is being remembered.

Therefore, would you join me and be part of the solution instead of part of the continuation of the problem?

Understand well, fatigue has *nothing at all* to do with the body. It has *everything* to do with the mind. *It has everything to do with the mind.* And when the mind is awakened and chooses only Light and tolerates never again error in its own perceptions and gives every moment over to the Holy Spirit, then indeed, that mind is enlightened because the heart is awakened, and the body will leap up like a bunch of little soldiers that have been sleeping on guard duty and say, "Oh, my God, there's been a change here," and the cells become active. And they begin to realize that you are going to send the infinite Light of God to them and therefore they have to relearn their job. No longer will they be able to tolerate extending sickness to you because you have been sending sick thoughts to them. Do you understand what I am saying? The body is your perfect servant and if you know depression or disease, it is because over a long period of time you've trained the cells of your body to conform to the dis-eased perception held in the mind. And when you have healed that perception, the body must follow suit.

And it is very possible—and you are going to see it happen upon this plane; many of you are going to live to see this happen in these bodies—that when there is a moment's disease or sickness in the body, that very mind will simply choose Light, will transfer Light from the infinitude of Heaven and express it on Earth, and the very cells of the body will instantly be healed. That is what a master can do, and you have come not to be slaves to the world but to demonstrate mastery in *all* regards. And mastery requires utmost responsibility: the ability to respond, and to look upon the whole of this world and say,

> *My goodness, I am the one that made this and now I am going to undo it. Where am I going to start? Right where I am.*

If all minds are joined—and I assure you that they are—right where you, are even in this moment were you to throw open the shackles off of the heart and mind, to open the cells of the body and to say,

> *I am the Holy Son of God and I claim my Kingdom. Let Light descend to Earth now, in me.*

. . . to do that is to have already uplifted the whole of creation.

Imagine that in my Father's house there are many mansions. Each room is a heart and mind, and this mansion has an infinite number of rooms. And you are living in a tiny little closet on the first floor. And you know that above you there are thousands and thousands of floors, and when you open the door of your tiny closet and peek down the l-o-n-g corridor, you know that there are thousands and thousands of rooms on the very floor you are on, and your Father has just said unto you, "I want you to sweep the dust out of the corners of every room." Hmm.

> *Oh, my God, what a task. Whew! How will I ever get it accomplished?*

The secret to the rebirthing of the Kingdom of Heaven on Earth is for *you* to realize that when you sweep the dust out of the corners of *your own tiny closet*, you have done it in *every room* in my Father's mansion, because all minds and hearts are joined. Therefore, receive that healing for yourself and you *are* the janitor that has cleaned every room in the mansion. Makes it much easier.

Does that make sense to you?

Participant: Yes.

While time continues for yet a little while, it is given unto you to make that choice with every breath. This is what I mean by response-ability: the ability to respond in each moment,

> *What thought am I choosing to hold? Am I conforming myself to limitation and lack and fear? Or am I choosing to be the fullness of the Kingdom now because I am begotten before all worlds and am of one substance eternally with all that my Father is?*

That is the choice to be made. That is the choice that is *so important* upon this plane in this time.

In this room this evening there are many, many, many beings who do not at this point associate with physical bodies as you do. They are all around you. Some of you have been feeling that already. Some of you noticed and had thoughts come even while you were whirling around talking and eating,

> *There's something about this room tonight. What is it?*

You could say other guests have been arriving for a while, to help do some things with the energy here. I have said unto you that I am one who likes to have a lot of friends, and this isn't the only plane that I like to have friends on; and this is not the only plane that is available to *you*. Each of you has what you know as guides and teachers and friends on planes unseen with the physical eyes, and *they are there for you because they love you.* They know that you are Christ eternal and they will do anything they can to help you remember, to help you unlock that power to bring the fullness of the Kingdom and express it in *this* world.

Fear not crucifixion. All of you have tasted the illusion of death. Not one of you has escaped being persecuted by others in this drama, and you all carry that fear of crucifixion. Call it rejection. Call it abuse. Call it being put to death. Whatever form it comes, there is a fear that keeps your heart contracted. And yet, the fear itself is an illusion.

That illusion is paper thin, so thin that it only takes one choice to walk through it. And I ask you to join with me, precious and holy and ancient friends, begotten before all worlds, you who are of one substance with all that I am, *I ask you to walk through that veil within yourself and to never settle again for anything but the Power and the Wisdom and the Truth of the Kingdom to be uttered by your lips, to be extended by the movements of your body, that only Light lives in you and as you*—and you will be the Light that heals this world.

The body is nothing more than a tool of communication. And it's not even yours! So what are you worried about? Nobody is going to nail it to a cross this time; and even if they did, it wouldn't matter. From dust the body is created and to dust the body shall return. It is the gift of your Holy Mother, given unto Christ eternal to become as a vehicle for communicating the unconditional Love of God.

If only you could understand what's really occurring on this Earth. Reality is not outside of you. It is not in the complexities that have been brought forth into this world. Reality is *in* you, and all that you have seen and all of the dramas unfolded in this world have been nothing more than you walking into a certain movie house and watching a certain movie. And now the time upon this plane is for you to arise from that seat, to go back out to the center of the movie house that has many little theaters in it, to go back to the center of your heart and to remember who you are, and then to walk into a different theater in which a new movie is about to start—a movie of Light, of abundance, of joy, of peace, of *extraordinary miracles.*

The movie has already started and I come to be your usher to say, "Quickly, quickly, come with me. Tarry no longer. The old movie is already over." You are just sitting in the chair running it through your mind, all of the horrible scenes, and yet the film has already stopped.

For that, we will hold all things up. Indeed. How are you doing, my brother?

Participant: Very well, thank you.

Gone through a few changes in the last few weeks?

Participant: Uh huh.

Hold nothing back! The river is starting to flow in a way that you could not have understood even a few short months ago. Open yourself up wholly every day and tell the Holy Spirit you are ready. Dare your Father to let the fullness of the union of Father and Son to explode through you. Just dare Him to see if He can overwhelm you. Do it every day when you arise. It is very important now because the habits you have known will want to creep back to build little dams. Choose the power of that Light. Choose it with everything you have got every morning when you arise and give thanks for it every night before you sleep.

Fair enough?

Participant: Quite.

Quite a small price to pay for the Grace that heals a hundred thousand illusions.

Participant: I thought it was just one.

One and a hundred thousand are simply two ways to say the same thing. Well then, how are we all doing? It was a bit of a long greeting. I am sorry.

[Laughter]

Participant: It was worth it. It was nice. Wonderful.

You answered my questions.

Ah. What are you going to do with the answers?

Participant: Oh. That is a trick question. Yeah, that is a trick question. Rejoice in them. Take them. Well, you just said about the old habits wanting to jump out of their little corners and grab us again. That really holds true, and it has for me in the last week and I hope it's the last hurrah.

You hope?

Participant: Oh, okay. Got me.

No, I just gently corrected you.

Participant: Right.

Beloved brother, it is *you* that has *me*, and I abide in your heart as the fullness of your being. And the fullness of that being creates the experience of Jeshua so that you can talk with your true Self. Understand well what I am saying unto you because this relates for all of you: inasmuch as you have been as one mind as the ego, or the separate self sense that has created all worlds, you are already of one Mind and one Heart in creating the salvation of the Sonship. As you have created the dramas of illusions of separation, so, too, do you create the drama of salvation.

Therefore, all that I am—and I have said this to you before—as Jeshua Joseph ben Joseph, who came and walked and talked, who sweated, got hungry, urinated in the woods (I'm sorry they didn't put that part in the Bible), all of the things you have ever done and felt tempted by, I, too, have tasted. And yet, understand that *my life is wholly yours.* You are the ones who brought forth the life of Jeshua Joseph ben Joseph, to be the saviour of the world, a mirror that you could look in and be reminded of the Truth of yourself. You could say that you decided to sleep and have a very nice drama, and you scripted that there would be a being upon this plane and when you looked at him, it would trigger a remembrance like,

> *Ah, the bell has rung. Time for me to wake up from my drama. It's been nice but there is a far greater one to be lived.*

You are all that I am and between us there is not anything called separation. Therefore, beloved brother, do not hope that it will be their last hurrah, but *decree* that that is true. Hm!

I would give you a little assignment. Are you ready?

Participant: I am ready.

We will see. Have I not spoken unto you that in each of your days, do something a little outrageous? Anyone hear that before?

Participant: Yes. Yes.

How long has it been since you put it into practice?

> *Well, I think once last week I finally had the time to do something outrageous.*

Precious friend, go unto one of your malls, stand on one of the seats there. They usually put them around those plastic flowers. There's nothing like the aroma of plastic flowers.

[Laughter]

Stand upon the step there or the seat and decree at the top of your lungs,

> *I am the holy Son of God, and in this moment I decree that all of my illusions have just had their last hurrah.*

And look around at those who look at you with their chin on the floor and say,

> *Isn't it great that we are One?*

And then just go about your business.

[Laughter]

Now [breathes deeply]...

> *Holy Father, let these be in me even as I am in You. Let them see the Truth of their being, for I have served them since before the beginning of time and that time is at hand. Father, enter their hearts that they might hear this simple Gospel and see that the time is at hand.*
>
> *Long have I toiled for You. Long have I served the Atonement of Your only begotten Son. And I beseech You, Father, enter these as You have entered me, with the fullness of Your Light and Your Glory and Your Wisdom and Your Power and Your Love. Let them be in me as I am in You, that together the Son might be one again with the Father to express the joy of that perfect union, to blend with the energies of this, our Holy Mother, and to express through these bodies the one Truth of Life eternal.*
>
> *Father, I beseech You, let the time be now and let them awaken to the Truth of our union. Let illusions be ended. Father, let Illusions be ended.*

Would you not receive my prayer? Would you not throw open the shutters of your heart, for I stand and knock, and I beseech you, precious ones whom I love deeply, the time is at hand to put down illusions and join me in the Resurrection.

Very soon now, Easter is upon you. What is it going to mean to you this year? Will it mean what the world wants you to believe it means? That someone in your long, past history finally got the message? Or worse yet, that one was sent by God and was without sin and was perfect anyway. That puts me on a pedestal so far above you that my lifetime becomes totally meaningless. For if I came not and dwell among you as a man, tempted to live the Crucifixion, then my Resurrection is totally meaningless. Look not then upon me with the eyes the world has given you. But please look with the eyes that I seek to give you: to see that I am your brother and your friend. And if Jeshua can awaken to the Truth of his being, then, Lord knows, so can you, *because you are already my equal.*

So, would you join me in a little exercise—rather, a little celebration? Those of you who in this moment feel that your shoulders are a little hunched, throw them back. For God's sake, what are you trying to protect yourself from? What burdens are you insisting on carrying?

Participant: I feel guilty. [Laughter]

So release the guilt and throw the shoulders back. Feel a lightness come to the spine itself. It is the tree of life. Let its branches reach up to the Light of the Father. In the depth of your being, now you can throw open the doorway to each and every cell of the body, your perfect servants.

Block not the angel of air, but feel it ascending and descending along the tree of life. Breathe not only the angel of air but *let each breath be a breath of Light and of power, and of wisdom and of joy.* Within yourself say unto your Father,

> *Yes, I receive You.*

Throw open your heart. Receive it. Dare your Father to send you so much Light that it feels the body might explode. Open yourselves. *Come to where I am.*

Let that little vibration begin. Feel the quickening within you. With every inbreath say,

> *Yes, I accept my Truth. I am the Son of God. I am the Light of the*

> *world. I and my Father are One. I and my Father are One. I and my Father are One!*

Some of you are beginning to see certain colors. Let them come more brightly, more vibrantly. Receive them. Feel the cells all the way down to your fingertips and toes opening. If you begin to feel a little lightheaded and giddy, all the much better. Seriousness has no place in the Kingdom.

> *Yes, I am the Light of the world. I am the birthing of the New Age that is upon this earth. I am all power and I am all Light and I am all joy. I live; yet not I but Christ lives in me, for I am that Mind and that Heart.*

And if you be that power—and I assure you that you are—let not timidity come upon you again. And now, all together, we're going to take one very deep breath, and we are going to inhale the Light and the power of God, and as we exhale, we are going to open our mouths and let sound come out. Take a nice deep inbreath and with all the power of the Christ we are...

[Loud toning, continuing for a while] Not bad. How are you feeling?

Participant: Good. Great. Very good. Energized. Vibrations of my cells.

Vibration of your cells.

Participant: Yes.

Why would you settle for anything less in any moment of your day?

So, you see, when next you are in one of your board meetings and you feel the energy of the world wanting to contract you down so that you are conformed to everybody's illusion of lack and suffering, now you know what to do to change it.

[Laughter]

Participant: Yes. All right. Corporate management will fall down.

It's about time it fell down.

Don't you understand what it's all about? To *be* the Light of the world, not to pray that Light will come. You have been doing that for thousands of lifetimes. Receive the simplicity of the Gospel. If Light is to come, *you* are the ones that have to bring it. Gone is the time of timidity. Gone the time of weakness and lack and frailty. How can you abide in those states and still expect the new world to be born? How can you translate the unhappy dream of the chaos of this world into the happiness of the rebirthing of the Kingdom unless you choose to be that? Not to seek it, not to pray for it, but to decree that the time is at hand because *you* are choosing that *now is the time*.

What do you think, Seedplanter?

Participant: I agree. It's the time. Feels good.

You have a certain song, *The times, they are a-changing*. Are *you* going to change with them? Because, indeed, the time comes rather quickly now that if you choose not to, shall we say, uplift the frequency of your being by declaring that you will never again tolerate the error of misperception that you are anything other than the embodiment of joy, if you choose not to do that, you are simply not going to be able to be on your beloved Earth any longer—because the very heat of joy that will be coming from the very soil, the body of your Holy Mother, will be something that you can't tolerate because you are choosing a heavy vibration that can no longer abide on this Earth.

There are going to be a few that make that choice, to insist on the heaviness. And what will happen when the energy of the Earth becomes so transparent that solid things cannot abide upon it and they simply sink through it? Now, that's a metaphor, of course, but it means that if you truly love your Holy Mother, you had better get it in gear and catch up with the changes going on in Her own frequencies.

Don't let the heart contract with fear; you cannot experience death. All you can ever experience is the consequence of your choice. All of you understand well that what you experience in your life is the *effect* of your *choice*. And a new choice is being born upon this plane, a choice that will tolerate *only* Light, *only* peace, *only* joy, *only* abundance, *only* service one unto another. The time is going to come upon this plane when minds and bodies can't sit still because they are going to be running around the whole time, finding a way to extend service and love to their brothers and sisters, and nothing but service. Gone will be the energy of taking, and it will be replaced by the energy of giving, because being rebirthed is the simple Truth that as you give, you receive.

Give your love away and you will never be without it. Give your vision of One Heart and One Mind away and you will experience it growing within you by leaps and bounds, and you will attract unto yourself other minds and hearts that have been waiting for you to give them the signal to live as unlimited vision. For it is through vision that your Father extends His Love and Creativity into this world. And where there is not vision, what happens to the people? They perish.

All of you know what it means to perish. Some of you are still insisting on perishing. Some of you are yet insisting that lack must be your experience. It's just a chronic habit. Let it go. Insist on abundance. Live abundantly. Live from the Truth that you know there is no such thing as lack. You are here to serve, expressing the unconditional Love of God—and do you think that if your Father is going to ask you to go forth and teach all nations, that He is going to leave you in poverty? Tell Him to get off His can and make sure you have everything you need for the fulfillment of your mission.

Participant: Jeshua, why do you say that? Because there is a reason behind that?

What? A reason behind what I say? Oh! Now I have to think up one.

Participant: Well, those words... you know, that were said that way.

Firewalker, look at the subtleties of your own thought. You are beginning to catch some of the fire you've been walking on. When you say, "I pray for a new world order to be manifested on this Earth," but you, yourself, choose to live in the impoverishment of a lack of energy, a lack of golden coins, in the belief that there is nothing you can do to change your *own* status, you have basically depleted the very life force that is required for the birthing of that new world order. *You* have to be an *example* of that new world order.

Therefore, when you pray unto your Father,

> *Help me, Father, to do your will, whatever it is,*

you come from a place of weakness and lack. That is why I have said that the time of false piety is over with. It is time for you to rise and to stand on the little seats in your malls and say,

> *Father, I have come here to serve the Atonement of Your Son. Now, get off your can and don't forget what we are doing here.*

[Laughter] Participant: Ohhh.

> *Give me the abundance of the Kingdom because I need it to do Your work. Bring it to me. And, by the way, I happen to like nice clothes, and I am not going to drive a rattletrap to do Your work.*

Participant: Oh, God.

The reality you experience is nothing more than the expression of the frequency and the vibration you insist on holding on to. Upgrade your vibrations and frequency daily and the world around you will have to change its shape.

I am calling you not to be meek any longer, but meek in the *true* sense. So meek and so pure that there is not one trace of illusion to be found in you. Allow the death of the world to take place in your own consciousness, that the Kingdom can be reborn in it.

Some of you believe that to achieve great abundance is going to take a lifetime of straining and planning and hard work because it's a tough world.

> *I'm going to have to compete. And if I'm really lucky, in twenty years I'll be able to retire and pay my bills.*

That thinking does not exist in the Kingdom. The only thinking that exists in the Kingdom is that,

> *I am the Holy Son of God and all of the abundance of my Father is given to me now. And I live from it, and I extend it, and I give it away freely and gladly to anyone who would ask. And if my brother lives in lack, I will teach him how to live in abundance because I can't tolerate this any longer.*

> *I am the holy Son of God and I am going to bring the whole of creation with me, and I am not going to stop until it comes to where I am. I am Christ eternal. And even as I manifested Jeshua Joseph ben Joseph and demonstrated the Truth of the Kingdom, I choose now to be the fullness of who I am, and I am going to manifest nothing but miracles until all of my brothers and sisters wake up with me.*

Hmm. Do you see the difference?

Participant: Jeshua, when you talk about abundance, you mostly mention material things. The abundance of love... I have felt a lot of resistance in this community to enacting that. I wonder if you could speak to the higher vision of how we can go about creating trust, safety, for us to do that?

Beloved friend, everything that I have spoken unto you this night addresses that very question. Put it into practice. If there is anyone with whom you are feeling some variance or enmity, then get on the phone and call them and say,

> *We've got to get together. You see, the time is at hand. Let's make sure all of the hatchets are buried. Let's join together and look into each other's eyes and declare that we are the holy Son of God, and we are going to get on with it and manifest that abundance to make this community happen because we cannot any longer tolerate error. We cannot tolerate waiting on the Lord, because we are the Lord.*

How can you manifest that community of trust and safety? By declaring to everyone who is attracted to that community that *you are giving it to them* and you wholly expect that it will be given to *you* because nothing less can any longer be tolerated. Now don't forget to sing and dance and play as you are doing that.

The time is at hand, precious friend. The Father indeed provides all things, and if you would look around you, He is extending unto you many vehicles and many ways in which you can enact the Truth of who you are and bring the abundance to you. But it will *never* happen until *you are ready to declare for yourself the Truth of who you are and to live it with every breath and to settle for nothing less*. Stop waiting for the person to your right or to your left to make it happen for you.

Beloved friend, that is how. How can you create that safety? By declaring and demonstrating and *being* that safety. By *being* that Love that embraces all things. By in your own life cleaning out the cobwebs in your closet, letting the Father manifest all power and wisdom and abundance through you so that you can show your brother and sister how to do it also. This is no fun if you do it alone.

The time is at hand, even as many of you have felt a shift in the way I bring my energy forth to bear through this temporary carcass, and indeed a shift in what I am not so much saying unto you but the way I am saying it. Understand that there is a shift in frequency that has gone on in your Holy Mother, this Earth. Some of you have felt it. Some of you haven't noticed at all because you are too busy keeping yourself limited by the constrictions of your very narrow-minded perceptions. In other words, you are too wrapped up in the drama of the ego to notice what's happening. And those of you that persist in that are going to wake up one day and realize you are not even on the Earth anymore. You are somewhere else.

What happened? Did the New Age pass me by?

Yes.

Participant: But you get to come back, don't you? Choose again to come back?

[Laughter]

Participant: Well, you do. You never get left out. It's just a matter of when. I don't know if I am using that as an excuse or anything, but I'm just wanting to say that we are all going home. We are all going to make it. I'm not trying to negate anything you're saying.

Firewalker, you *are* trying to negate something that came out of an impulse of your own thinking that wants still to have a trapdoor to escape through. If we are all coming home, that means that for you—this is not at the conscious mind, it is at a slightly deeper level—you are hoping that you will still have time to make up for it if you don't choose it now. That is where those statements came from.

The mind and heart that chooses the Truth of the Kingdom does not even entertain the thought that maybe later the choice can still be made anew. It is too busy choosing *now*. Contemplate that well within yourself. For though you would look around you and want many to catch on fire and leap ahead, there is still a part of you that has the rope tied around the end of the dock, and your own ship is not quite yet sailing freely.

Participant: That's true.

I know.

I have news for you. None of this is going to happen until you choose it for yourself. The whole of creation is *on hold, waiting for you*. Now, that's responsibility! But guess what? The whole of creation is on hold waiting for *each and every one of you*. *That* is your responsibility: to be the Light of the world with every breath you breathe. You don't have time for the drama of separation. You don't have time for the drama of indulging in the whimperings of the ego. All of that is an illusion. You don't have time for it.

Will you not join with me and truly come to where I am? Come to that frequency or that vibration that cannot tolerate error in your own perceptions any longer, to see that there is but One Mind and One Heart, called Christ, and all of these little bodies are nothing more than vehicles through which that One Mind and One Heart can express the Love of God.

Wherever you are, whether you are in a grocery store, and someone else in this room tonight is in an office, and somebody else in this room tonight is in a garden planting seeds, can you remember fully that you are One and you are united and you are together all the time? You are never alone. You can't be alone.

And if all you did was to think on the energy in this room and the little exercise we did and allowed that power to come forth through you, wherever you are you would know that the power of the one Mind of Christ is moving through you. And when you extend love unto anyone on this plane, once it is done, you could just that fast, [snapping fingers] move to that plane of reality in which everyone in this room is abiding as if you were sitting around a table watching a movie, and you could step into that frequency and say,

> *Ah, I've just extended some more Love into the world. How did you do over there?*

It's all available to you. You have never been separate one from another, and those of you that are attracted to the expression of *community* need to start putting that Truth into practice. You can join with any mind of any brother and any sister anytime you want, if only to extend power and love to them.

You don't have time to stare at your soap operas any longer. You don't have time to sit in your easy chair, lamenting how tough your life is, because your life and your world will be transformed when you learn to do nothing but extend the Love of God with every breath you breathe. Whenever the mind knows heaviness or doubt or loneliness, think upon your brother and sister who has come with you to extend the Love of Christ into this world—and empower them.

Guess what happens when you do that? As you give you receive. As you empower your brother or sister, you will feel that power coursing through *you*, and you will wonder what happened to your depression and your doubt and your fear and your loneliness. It's all just an illusion, anyway.

Do you understand what I am saying to you?

You've learned to contract yourself, to separate yourself from the power of Christ. How, then, do you find it? By giving it away.

Salvation can only be known by sharing it. So when you think you are bored, you've washed all of your dishes, you've cleaned the cobwebs out of your closet, you've washed the filth off your automobiles, you've put the food into the belly of the body, you have paid all of your bills unto Caesar and you think you've got nothing to do— Saturday night and nowhere to go—think about your brothers and sisters, and do nothing more than play with *empowering* them. Play at it and *love* it. Pretend like you are the controller of the universe. Send the power of Christ to your brother and your sister.

Hmm! Hmm.

Participant: Jeshua, I am answering your very joyful call. You showed up in a session I was giving this afternoon and it was quite clear that I would move my day and my evening a lot in order to come and be with you tonight. So I am just here, and open to your reflection.

[Short pause]

I am with you always. Join with me until you see and hear me as easily as you hear the voice that you are now hearing. Join with me so fully that there is no longer a trace of distance between us. Time to upgrade, shall we say, the frequency or power of the work that you do. But it's going to take leaps and bounds! Hmm.

Participant: Well, I have been feeling that. My daily awareness is to release, release, allow. Really allow the lightness to come, the movement to move. It feels so large at times that I keep wanting to damper it or contract or take a breath, and basically I am daily just breathing through and expanding.

A rather good idea.

Precious friend, have you not carried with you, even in the beautiful work you do, have you not carried a chronic thought,

> *Am I truly worthy of total union with Christ?*

Know you that feeling?

Participant: Yes.

Let it be gone. Well have you known that I have been knocking upon the door of your heart for a very long time.

Participant: Indeed.

Sometimes you let me come in and have a little cup of tea. But then you say, "Oh, you have to leave now."

Beloved friend, from this day, more powerfully than ever in the past, when you do the work you do in what you call the initiation, you are going to feel me standing next to you. And when you do your little ritual, there will come a day when you will literally see me standing on just the other side of the one you are doing your ritual with, and I am going to join with you.

In other words, we are going to be working together at a new level to increase the power and the transformation of that initiation.

What do you think?

Participant: Oh, I welcome it. I have actually been inviting you clearly in every circle.

You have been inviting me but there has been this little shadow over in the corner of the mind,

> *Well, could I really take it if he truly showed up?*

Know you the trace of that feeling?

Participant: Oh, yeah.

Yes. [Chuckles]

Thank you for receiving my invitation to come to this gathering.

Participant: Indeed, it is my honor. My joy.

Yes, as it is mine. I have known you for a very long time, and you know that.

Participant: Yes.

And you know that you are in Truth involved in your life's purpose and function in the work that you do. If you want to call it work. And you are going to see it begin to accelerate.

Participant: The room is very full tonight.

Standing room only.

Participant: Floating room only.

Indeed.

Participant: Jeshua, I notice when you have been using the word "time," you have a different tone. I'm wondering about that. It feels different when you use that. You are doing something with your frequency. I was curious.

Anyone else notice that?

Participant: Yes.

Precious friend, you have perceived well. There is a shift of what you perceive as frequency when I use that word tonight because it is a way of intoning a certain power that can begin to actually break down the perception or the limitations of time that seem to enshroud the mind and the heart.

Participant: You are doing that with more than just that word.

Yes.

Participant: Especially that one, more than others?

Tonight, especially that word. You could say it's the lesson for today.

Time is a very important barrier that has been created in the mind that is inhered in the illusion of separation. Time is the very thing that needs to be transcended. Become the masters of time and you will remember that you abide in eternity. It is going to be very, very important in only a little bit of time. Are you truly choosing to master the illusion of time? Or are you letting it continue to master you?

Remember always that time is given you for one reason and one reason only. Does anybody remember what it is?

Participant: To extend Love.

Which is to do something I have stated to you probably thirty-five times or more. To use it constructively. To construct, to let the creative thought of God flow through you, so that what is created in the illusion of time sends a message to your brother and sister that time is an illusion and that only eternity is real; that time cannot be a barrier or limit you in any way from communication with all of the gods and goddesses that you have prayed for the opportunity to communicate with. Time is an illusion that has been translated from a limitation to an opportunity to express what is *unlimited*. Own it. Use it constructively, and your constructive use of it will translate it into a vehicle through which *you* become the Light of the world.

Does that help a little bit? It is time.

Participant: That's rather a paradox you've given us.

Yes.

Participant: Thank you.

What you experience *is* a paradox. Don't try to make sense out of anything that I come to teach you. *Just do it.* And in the doing of it, you will witness miracles extended through you. And when you have seen them extended through you into the life of your brothers and sisters, you will have to finally admit that they have already been done to you.

Please, never, never, never, never in any moment of your day, never choose to limit what I can do through you. If you could give me but one gift, give that to me. Give to me your solemn promise that you will never limit what I can do through you.

Participant: I promise.

And you are going to see the fruit of that promise.

Participant: I have.

Yes. Are you ready for it to expand exponentially?

Participant: Yes.

Thank you, Father! How are we all doing?

Participant: Okay. Time to stretch a little, I think.

Then, do so. No one is stopping you.

Participant: Yes, I am.

How about the rest of you?

Participant: Stretch time.

So, go ahead and take a short little break if you want. I am not going to do what you would perceive as depart from this blending with my beloved brother. But rather, instead, I am going to quicken it a little bit. If ever you want to know what *you* have to be willing to release, willing to release in order to join with me, have a little chat with my beloved brother. Many of you have no idea what it takes to blend with me like this although you would pray for it, and some of you have known jealousy. Are you willing to let everything in you that is false *die*? Are you willing to experience the pain of a thousand little deaths within you as the ego becomes ashes? Why not give it a try? Hm. Indeed.

Are you truly willing to realize that throughout thousands of lifetimes you haven't known what in hell is going on? But you have judged the world as though you did, because you have judged yourself as being separate from God. That illusion is the cornerstone of the separate self. Are you willing to loosen your fingers from it and let it become as the dust of the ground? *That is death.* But from that death the fullness of life can be born and you shall become the perfect servant of the Atonement. The form may differ but the power of the miracles wrought through you is the same. Become the one who allows only miracles.

Remember always that the purpose of the miracle, you see, is to shorten the need for time. Therefore, use time constructively to allow miracles, and miracles will shorten the need for time. Do you see how it all works?

So, take your short little break. If you want to leave, by all means do so, and do so with my love and my blessing. If would like to remain for yet a little while, then please do so and we will see what happens.

I love you and I give you my peace, and until your strength is the same as mine, please *use* mine. You can't use it up and it's freely given. Therefore, never allow yourself to feel weak or frail or fearful. All you have to do is to reach into your heart and pull out a handful of my strength and my certainty until you've learned that that strength and that certainty is yours and it cannot be taken from you.

I love you, because you are the Light of the world.

Peace be unto the only begotten Son of God, and I'll be seeing you very soon.

Amen.

[Break]

Participant: Jeshua I have a couple of questions. I am new and I have been enjoying this evening very much, and I appreciate the reflections that you give us of how to be, how to perceive to attain mastery of the self and peace in the heart and quiet in the mind. I get to see all the ways that I don't do that, which is wonderful.

I have a question about a reference that you do make and I... how do I say this? You had said to all of us to... When we are not feeling strong to turn to you for our strength. Yes? Okay. And I have a question in turn because I use a different terminology. The strength that you are speaking of is the strength, of course, that comes from God, right?

Yes.

Participant: Okay. My question is, I guess, why the need to go through you, to get your strength, because I see your strength as the strength of God Almighty moving through you, moving through each of us, and I have a question about that. Do you understand what I am saying? I'm sure you do.

I do, but do *you*?

Participant: Yeah. I think I do. Yeah. I just wanted to get clear. Do we need to go by you or can we... you know ... I feel like the Source is one and the same. Is there a reason that maybe those who need to lean on you were in that way because of whatever relationship that they might... because they are connected to you... they see you on these weekends and get a deeper connection. Is that like a stepping stone or what are you saying when you are saying that? Now I'm clear.

And you actually are giving the answer.

Now, first of all, I would say this: I am the Way, the Truth and the Life and no man comes to the Father but by me. So if you haven't done it yet, learn how to pronounce the name "Jeshua," because no other name under heaven can bring you salvation!

[Laughter] Participant: I'm leaving!

Now, what does all of that mean?

Well have you spoken that there are some that come not only to these Friday night gatherings and, therefore, see me as the vehicle through which they come to remembrance of the holy union of Father and Son, but indeed many who come unto these gatherings have known me throughout what you would perceive as lifetimes.

There is something called holy lineage that is extremely important. Imagine that a child sleeps in a meadow and begins to dream dreams of many journeys and forgets that he sleeps in his Father's arms. And he begins to believe that the nightmares he is using his own creative power to create have a power in themselves, and he learns the complexity upon complexity and world upon world, and comes to actually believe he has been separated from his Father's Holy Kingdom.

Now, somewhere along the line—he might be a cobbler; he might be a Roman soldier; he might be a member of the Sanhedrin; he might be working in a court in Egypt—somewhere in one of those journeys he hears a message. He sees someone that others call "Master." And though he does not know it, he has heard this message before and he is seeing those who are its masters walking with him upon the Earth. Yet, for some reason in this moment something is different. And as he hears the words of that master being spoken, something begins to vibrate in the heart and a little door opens and for just a moment he sees the union of Father and Son. That is the beginning of a holy lineage, and though he might close that door and say,

Oh, not yet,

and go back to being a cobbler or what have you, and though he might choose to travel through another hundred thousand worlds, when it is time for the soul to take its final journey home, that soul shall make sure that it comes back into contact with that lineage because it becomes the doorway home.

I am the lineage for many and, therefore, especially in *this* work that I do with my beloved brother because I am *his* lineage, I come forth and use a certain language that identifies me as the one who walked and talked as Jeshua Joseph ben Joseph. I talk about Abba, I talk about the Holy Mother, I talk about the union of Father and Son, because this is a language that those entrusted to me of my Father have known very, very well. Most of them have known many incarnations within what you would call the Judeo-Christian tradition. It is a language that vibrates within their soul, and so I come and I use it yet again. It is not, as you know, the only one that could be used.

But those who come and resonate with what I say unto them, there are many in this room that would nod their head and say,

Oh, yes, I know Jeshua is my lineage.

Your lineage is a little different but you appreciate the universality of the Gospel that is expressed in these words, do you not?

Participant: Yes, very much.

Therefore, do not see it so much as a stepping stone but see it as the enactment of the awakening of the Sonship. This same Gospel can be given in many forms. As you know, yours is a bit different. And yet, when I say that I am the Way and the Truth and the Life and that no man comes to the Father but by me, I am speaking a Gospel that has been given in many forms to any heart and mind that must come to realize that you *are* Christ eternal. You *are* Jeshua. You are the power of the Light that is the offspring of Light Divine. You are the Daughter of the Goddess and, therefore, when you come to be fully identified in the core of your own being as that same Love and Power and Wisdom that took form as Jeshua, then indeed you have become the Way, the Truth and the Life.

Does that make sense?

Participant: That is wonderfully clear for me, and I really appreciate the recognition, because I was aware that I had a different lineage and I just wanted to get clear for myself and understand what was really going on here, and what you were referring to, so that I could remain in honor and love—my love for your words and your works that have been so vastly written and talked and preached about. So, I thank you for that very special message.

I do have a question that is personal. Is that okay to ask?

Oh, of course not.

[Laughter]

Participant: No. This year I decided that I am... what you were talking earlier about lack. I really want to be done with it. I mean, clearly done with it and really trust. And as I have been declaring that I wanted to trust God more in allowing that flow to happen with not so much fear coming in, of course, fear comes blasting in my face—and I got ill from it and I had to go through that whole recognition of letting go to another level of vibration so that I could receive more, understand more. And there is a part of me that recognizes there is a way I am blocking my abundance. And I really want to be able to... I know that I will be able to move it out of the way. However, I am not really clear on what it is that I need to move, unless it is the big issue of totally trusting and just having faith in every single moment of every single breath that I take that all is well. My mind gets in the way. I don't know if you have any insight to share with me on this?

None. I haven't the foggiest idea what you are talking about.

[Laughter]

Participant: Okay, I'll rephrase that.

No, you don't need to.

Participant: I know that you know and I would like some help with this! Thank you.

Beloved friend, you have already given yourself the answer but you have not understood it. Indeed, your mind gets in the way and the obstacle that blocks it is the belief that there is an obstacle that *you* must remove *before* you can receive the abundance.

Participant: Oh. Okay.

Beloved friend, do what I am about to suggest to you. Do it daily for a period of twenty-one days. Fair enough?

Participant: Uh huh, fair enough.

Now, this is going to require that you do this twenty-four hours a day and you do not eat or drink in the meantime.

[Laughter]

Just kidding.

Now, when you arise in your morning, sit up, throw the shoulders back, feel the spine lengthen, block not the angel of air, and say unto that One who is the Teacher who teaches without error—the One I have called the Holy Spirit—and ask Him to correct the *only* obstacle in you: ask Him to correct the perception that an obstacle exists. As you breathe the angel of air, let the body soften. Let it feel as though the cells are becoming Light itself. You will feel that softness, and over the course of these twenty-one days you will feel that state and know it very well. And as that softness comes, simply say,

Thank you, Holy Father, for I am *healed.*

Participant: Yes.

Then go about your day. But as you go about the day, within your mind ask that a higher vision be born through you. That's all you need to do. Do it with innocence, not trying to let the mind get caught up with wondering what the vision might be. Just ask that it born through you. In twenty-one days you are going to know that a deep healing and shift has occurred. A certain perception will no longer arise and you won't even have noticed at first that it's not in you any longer. And on around the twenty-second or twenty-third day you are suddenly going to be startled to realize that you will notice a certain weight is not with you, and you won't even know where it went.

Fair enough?

Participant: That is great, yes. Thank you.

You have much to do upon this plane and for you to move into the fulfillment of part of your purpose is going to require that you become a demonstration of one who is a teacher of God and one who lives in unlimited abundance.

Somebody has to do it. What do you think?

Participant: That's pretty awesome.

Don't fear abundance of any kind, even of golden coins. But when they come to you, remember what they are really for: to give the Love of God away. Keep that in mind.

Participant: Okay. And my second question is personal. I came to a decision just today, and I feel like it's clear. I just want to ask you that I am not copping out on part of . . . I'm not copping out. Okay. Go forward and do it. Is that what you are saying? Okay. Thank you. That's all, and I appreciate your graciousness.

I appreciate the Light and the clarity and the power and the love and the demonstration that you are about to bring and give unto this world.

Participant: That makes my palms sweat.

Jeshua, this woman started her question with a proclamation that was quite profound, I thought. She said, "Jeshua, I'm new." It is the first thing she said, and I rather liked it. So, can I say I am new, too?

Are you ready to be new?

Participant: I think so . . . Okay, I am ready.

There. All that "I hope" and "I think so."

Participant: Great.

Yes. Indeed, beloved brother, is it not true that all things *are* being made new for you? Is it not true that the perceptions have been dropping away almost constantly, and that even in the midst of your day you sometimes stop and realize that you are seeing things in a wholly new way? Is that not true?

Participant: Yes, energies are changing.

Yes. Allow, allow, allow. Do not strive. Do not make. *Allow.* You know what I mean by that?

Participant: Yes.

Had any nice conversations with deceased entities lately?

Participant: I started to. I tried, but they weren't very willing to listen.

That doesn't matter. Talk to them anyway.

Participant: Okay.

What you perceive as their unwillingness means that you are just getting caught up with the superficiality of their drama. Speak to the deeper part.

Participant: You said... when you told me that there is a teacher that would help me... can you be a little more specific about that? No? Let's not. Okay.

I could, but I love you far too much to do anything which is a disservice to you.

Participant: Right.

Allow, allow, allow.

Seems like such a simple message, and yet in this year you have realized through revelation after revelation of the depths of the meaning of that teaching: to allow. Is that not true?

Participant: Yes.

Continuing to learn it, aren't you?

Participant: Uh huh.

It is the most important of Keys to the Kingdom, and because you've begun to master the use of that key, it must necessarily come to pass that you will quickly come to the completion of your journey and reside where I am. The end is certain now. Allow it to be.

Surprise!

Participant: I have to hug the trees, huh?

Yes. You don't *have* to hug them. You get to hug them. They are waiting.

The day will come when you will understand the power and the significance of doing just that. You will come to understand what it really means in and for the depth of your soul.

Ah, nothing like enjoying the journey that another is taking in their choice to awaken from dreams to reality. It brings *me* great joy to watch each of your journeys, journeys no longer to spin in small circles but journeys to awaken from the soil of separation and to burst forth as the fragrance and the flowering of divine remembrance. Because well do I know what is going to transpire upon this plane when the Sonship chooses to be the flowering of awakening. It's something worth working for, throughout all of time.

You are all so very beautiful. In you there is so much Light, so much love and so much radiance, so much wisdom and so much beauty that you cannot contain it in the vessel of the human body. And when you choose to let it shine fully, when you decide just to throw caution to the wind—which is what I would call casting aside the belief in limitation—so much Light will radiate through you that the time must surely come to pass when the choice to manifest physical bodies will have served its purpose and you will have moved beyond it. And even what you call your world will dissolve in Light. Is that the end of creation? Hardly. But it is the transcendence of one form of it. Let your Light so shine before men that it is unmistakable—and you are the Light of the world.

Many of you would do well to call your mothers and your fathers and your brothers and your sisters and your children and say,

> *Guess what? I'm the arisen Christ. How are you doing today?*

[Laughter]

Because, you see, when the thought comes,

> *Well, I couldn't do that*

it means you just identified yourself with the illusion that *is* the world. That's how close you are in every moment.

Participant: I would rather say it in person than over the telephone.

Very good.

Participant: What would we do with the aghast responses we would get?

Love it. Because you will see they will say, "Of course you can't be that. What's the matter with you?" And you sit there and smile back, giving nothing but love because, you see, a master returns *all* responses in love.

A master takes attack and returns love. A master takes condemnation and returns love. A master takes disbelief and returns love. And sooner or later they will stop and go, "Oh, my God, you are serious." And then you can smile and say,

> *Oh, yes, I am quite serious.*

Participant: And let them know that they are the same?

Exactly. Tell them that you are not going to stop loving them with the Light of Christ until they remember that they, too, are that Light. Let them know that you will be with them throughout the next one hundred thousand incarnations if they so choose to do it that way, and *you* will be the one who is with them always, even as the master Jeshua said, "I am with you always." Take the love that I give to you and give it to your brother and sister. "For he that drinks from my mouth becomes as I am and I shall become he or she." That is what I mean when I say, "Take my strength and use it until yours is as certain as mine."

Need that take a long time? Time is an illusion. You can choose it now. When you walk out of this building tonight, you can say,

> *Oh, Jeshua is my brother. We came from the same lineage. We have the same divine parent. What is in him is in me also. Therefore, I am going to love all others as he has loved me.*

If you believe and feel that through my presence in your life, not just this life, that the grace of our Father has thrown open the shutters of your heart, then simply be as I am. Become the perfect servant of the Grace of God. Lay down the dream of the dreamer and awaken as the saviour of the world. Then my life has not been lived in vain. My death, my burial, and my resurrection will have truly been filled with meaning, because until *you* pick up your cross—which is made of Light—and follow me, all that I have given unto you remains in vain.

If, therefore, you would love me, if, therefore, you would extend your appreciation and thanks unto me, speak not in words to me, but go and do likewise to your brother and your sister. For only in honoring the Son within your own heart can you in Truth honor me. And when you have extended that love unto your brother and sister, indeed, you will feel me rejoice and you will know that, in Truth, I am with you always. And we shall walk hand in hand as equals in the Kingdom of our blessed Father, doing nothing but serving the Atonement because there is nothing else to do. Join with me by being what I am. Of myself I do nothing but my Father though me does all things. And my Father is *only* Love.

Therefore, be that which you are and you are the Love that my Father has given to the world through me. Be, therefore, that which I am and *you* are the Light of the world. Great is my love for you. Great, *great is my love for you* because I know who you are even when you choose not to believe it.

I cannot find words in your language to express the love I feel. Though many of you forget about me during the course of your day, I forget you not. And I look upon you in this illusion and I see naught but myself. For have I not tried to teach you that the only thing you need to learn is that there is nothing outside of you? All of creation is contained within your Heart because you are the only begotten of the Father, begotten before all worlds and of one substance eternally with all that our Father is.

Oh, how can I not love you? How can I not love the Light of the world? How can I not love the only creation of my Father, that which is eternal and changeless?

Pure is your heart. Pure is your heart. You have never sinned. You are Love in form. Give it to the world even as I have given that love to you. Give it with every breath you breathe and gone will be your depression and gone will be your doubt. Gone will be your lack. There are no limitations in you. You can do it all because of yourselves you do nothing, but your Father through you can do all things.

The body that you have thought yourself to be is *only* a vehicle of communication.

Stop identifying with it, and identify with the Truth of your being. You are Spirit and you are Divine. You have never known birth and you will never taste death. This illusion is a game. Play it with the *infinite joy of Christ*. Wherever you are, you are only there to be a demonstration of what transcends the world.

Short is the time that I am given to be with you in this way and yet, eternal is the time that I am with you. And though this world arises and passes away in the twinkling of an eye, we are together throughout eternity. Join with me; play with me.

You are already a master. Claim it. And when you are in a grocery store buying the food that you would put into the body, take pause and remember,

> *Ah, this mass of flesh that seems to be handing golden coins to the one who seems to be separate from me and who seems to have a frown upon their face and depression in their countenance because they do something they hate, this little body is nothing more than a vehicle to extend the Peace and Love of God.*

Send that beam of Light through the heart of your very body and join with the heart of the one across that little stand. Look them in the eye and say,

> *Thank you from the bottom of my heart for the service you give me. I love you for your willingness to do the work you do.*

When they've picked up their chin, you will feel their countenance shift. And though you may never see them again, they will remember you always. And you have no idea of the seed you will have planted, because they, in their turn, will begin to be quickened by your love. And it may be the next day, it may be next week, they, too, will remember that they can extend the love of Christ unto another. You will have started a string of miracles, and there is absolutely nothing worth doing than being the initiator of the string of miracles that awakens the Child of God.

Would you do that with me? Would you choose to play in each day as the one who can bring a miracle and give it to another? I need you as much as some of you have believed you need me. I can work from planes unseen but I can only join with so many bodies to do this kind of work. But wherever you are, you can join with me and say,

> *Jeshua, I'm going to extend the love of Christ. Are you ready? Here it goes.*

And trust this: when you call upon me in order to extend that miracle, rest assured I *am* with you. Some of you have already begun to see me, even though your eyes are open, in the midst of other experiences because you are beginning to get the message.

I am not limited by space and time. Nor are you. Join with me and play. Play in the Spirit of Light of being the saviors of the world.

Would you please do that for me? Would you please promise to join with me? Would you please in this moment let your decree be heard by your brothers and sisters by just saying,

> *Yes, I will join with you in the salvation of the world.*

Participants repeat: "Yes, I will join with you in the salvation of the world."

Ah, nothing like having some help!

[Laughter]

Now, that means tomorrow when you arise and lift your head from the pillow, leave your past behind you because it doesn't exist. Let your head rise and your body rise and say,

> *Oh, boy, what a great day this is going to be because I am going to give the love of Christ to this world. I am going to be vigilant in every moment. Who can I give it to? What do you think, Jeshua? Is that a good candidate?*

And I'll say, "Oh, yes, indeed. Go and do so."

Begin to play with it. Let the seriousness go. It has no place in the Kingdom. Play with me! Dance with me! Sing with me! Rejoice with me! Begin to have fun pushing buttons and blowing cobwebs away. So people think you are a little crazy. So what? If the world is crazy—and I assure you that it is—what will be perceived as *your* craziness is actually a demonstration of sanity. There.

Contemplate this well tonight: "Into thy hands I commend my Spirit." Treat it well and give it away with love. Into thy hands, my brothers and sisters, I commend my Spirit, and it is finished—whenever you choose to be the Light of the world. And indeed I *am* with you always.

Go in peace. Remember this day to keep it holy. Remember this day to keep it holy. Remember this day in every moment, and you are the Light of the world.

You are my brothers and my sisters and you are my friends. I will never abandon you and I will never forsake you; and even if you are not quite of my lineage, sit down and have a cup of tea with me now and then.

Let it come to pass that in *this* hour and *this* day you shall go out no more from our Father's holy place. And indeed entrust your heart to the Truth of your only reality.

Ask now and *receive* the fullness of that perfect wedding between our Heavenly Father and our Earthly Mother that you might extend it as far as from the East unto the West. Be the Light of the world. Go in peace and *always* take me with you, because I have no other desire than to be where the awakened Son of God is.

Peace be unto you. Amen.

HEALING THROUGH SELF LOVE

October 1993

Now, we begin.

And indeed, once again, greetings unto you, beloved and holy friends. As always, I come forth to abide with you, not from a place that is apart from you, but in Truth from that place that forever we share as One. For the Mind of Christ *is One*, and only that Mind is perfectly sane; only that Mind is perfectly awake.

Understand, then, that I come forth to you not from a great distance. I come forth to abide with you because we are already One. I come forth because I love you, for you are indeed the first-born of the Father—*you are indeed the first-born of the Father*. You are, as I am, Christ Eternal. The only difference then that can seem to remain is that, occasionally, you use the very power of the One Mind that we share in order to dream that you are something *other* than who I am, other than who you are.

I have trained my part of the Sonship, my part of the Mind, to remain steadfast and vigilant for the Kingdom. I have trained my mind, what you might think of as the soul, that spark of light that shines forth as a great Ray of Light in the Mind of God, I have trained that part of the mind to remain steadfast in and as the sanity that Christ is. I have no choice but to come unto you in whatever way you will allow. I have no choice, for where Love has truly been awakened as the essence of all that the Self is, that mind no longer dwells in authority over itself, but it serves first the Will of the Father, that which I have termed as Abba. That Will is that the Son of God be returned to perfect wakefulness in the Mind of God. I come, then, not "freely" as you would perceive freedom, I come forth as a choiceless choice which is the *only* freedom. And again, when any mind has truly chosen to awaken and embrace the truth of its only Reality, there is nothing left but the extension of Love. And Love heals all things, Love embraces all things, Love forever transcends all things, and returns all things into the hands of a perfectly loving God.

When I look upon you and, rest assured, I can do that at any moment . . .

[Laughter]

Hm, no sense in closing the blinds.

[Laughter]

. . . When I look upon you from the place in which I dwell and from the place that I never journey forth—that place which is so intimate with your soul that I can hear your thoughts, that I can feel your feelings—when I look upon you from that place, I know Love. For the recognition of Love comes when you look upon another and see God's only Creation. And when I look upon you, regardless of how you may be choosing to look upon yourself, I see the first-born of my Father, I see the radiance of Light that Christ is, dwelling ever perfect *within you*. Yes, I see the temporary illusions with which you are choosing to remain identified for yet a little while. I cannot take those illusions from you, for healing truly comes forth from the depth of the soul, for if it did not, then the perfect freedom given of the Father to the Son would be a lie. I cannot give you the healing that you seek but I can love you until you choose it for yourself. I can express it to you and I will do so in whatever way that I can find, in whatever way that I can devise to bridge the gap between where you are as Christ and where you *think* you dwell as a separate self, because of an ancient thought of guilt.

I am indeed only your brother and your friend. I know no limitation. In truth, neither do you. 'Tis only the thoughts that you choose to be identified with that create the perception that shapes what you call the world, the experiences that you have, that seem to mirror back to you that you are not yet one with God. The retraining of the mind is all that there is, until the mind thinks perfectly with God—and *God is but Love*.

Love does not punish and Love does not condemn. Love allows all things. Love trusts all things. Love rests in perfect quiet. Imagine then, if you will, in a distant meadow on a beautiful spring day a small tiny flower opens itself to the rays of the sun. No one is around to notice and not a sound has been made. The petals of the flower open and willingly receive the light that is there to nourish it. Such is Love, such is the love of the soul that releases its illusions and opens its petals to simply receive the light that is always there. And even in the midst of your world, where yet you seem to be identified with the body that passes through many, many changes and seems to express the very epitome of limitation, even there, *even there,* you can be as the petals of the flower in the meadow, unseen and unheard. You are that one with the power to open your petals, to let the heart open, to be the one who will choose to be the presence of Love. You have that power to open to the rays of Light coming, streaming forth eternally without measure from the Mind of the One that has sent you forth in Her image, in His image, as the thought of Love in form. You are that one that can open the petals of the heart and say,

> *Father, what is Your Will in this moment? What needs to be spoken? What course of action would You have me take so that You, through me, awaken the Sonship?*

You are that one who is the gentle flower living in the most beautiful of meadows. You have been placed there by Love Itself. You are the one with all power under Heaven and Earth to open the petals of your own heart, to receive the rays of Light shining upon you from the One Who loves you and then to allow Love to guide your words, your gestures, the movements of the body, the place that you will live, the work that you will do. All is provided for the one—*all is provided for the one*—who will open the petals of the heart and be nourished by the light of a perfect Love.

There is, indeed, no power created from the illusion of separation that can begin for even an instant to take that power from you. There is no one that you have ever known that has had the power to cause the petals of your heart to contract and to wither. For it is indeed in the very choice *for Love* that healing is restored.

I would not say these things unto you if I did not know that they were true. I learned that these things are indeed true when, as a man, I walked upon your earth and chose to take my Father at His word: "I am His beloved Son and in Him do I dwell." And my life became *my* way of coming home, even unto what was called the Crucifixion. Yet again, and though I have said this to you many times, rest assured, I have gone nowhere. And those that sought once to get rid of me have only discovered that in the very attempt they merely created a resonance between themselves and me and I have become the guest that came for dinner and never left!

[Laughter]

What, then, did my life teach me, if not that *God is Love*? God is not judgment; God is not spite; God is not punishment. God is Love. And each time you dwell in a perfectly loving thought, you are the presence of God: you *are* the presence of Love. That very thought is sent as a blessing that shines forth from the heart of your flower as the petals have opened and receive the light of Truth, *that* truth radiates out and touches the farthest of stars. And each time you love, the whole of creation has been uplifted to the open arms of God, the whole of creation has journeyed forth in its remembrance of what is true.

Are you then powerful? Oh yes, beyond measure! For from you comes forth *whatever you choose*. Nothing can arise by accident. Each event that you experience can come to you *only* because you have called forth for it. It is indeed an answer to your very prayer for a perfect and consummate awakening. It is the answer you seek as you make the transition from one who is journeying *to* the Kingdom to one who journeys *within* it. Please listen well: the egoic mind would have you truly believe that the only purpose is to journey *to* the Kingdom—but rest assured, beloved friends, *that* journey is an illusion. That journey to the Kingdom has already been taken care of by the Grace of Love that restored you to perfect union in the very [snaps fingers] moment that you dared to dream the dream of separation. It's already over! There is only the process whereby you give yourself permission to receive the Truth that is true always.

But the journey *to* the Kingdom, the remembrance that the journey is complete is not the end, it is a return to an ancient beginning.

For you were birthed to create: not to make, not to do—to *create*. Because you were birthed in the image of God, you *will* step into the Kingdom wherefrom *you will create without end* the good, the holy and the beautiful! And each time you smile upon your brother or sister, each time in the temple of your own heart you extend forgiveness, each time you rest in the perfect appreciation that your brother or sister has brought you a gift, even if it's a memory from three thousand years ago—when you abide in a loving thought, you are creating, you are extending your perfect treasure and in its extension, you are remembering ever more deeply the Truth that is true always.

The journey within the Kingdom is a journey without end. The journey *to* the Kingdom has an end and that end is perfectly certain. Within your Holy Mind you have the power to delay the completion of your journey to the Kingdom, but you have no power to renounce it. You have no power to usurp the Will of your Father; it failed in an ancient past and it fails now.

In the journey *within* the Kingdom there is ceaseless creation, and yet that mind that abides awake within the Kingdom merely comes and goes thus. That one is like the wind, indeed. And when the past is gone it is not carried forward, and the future has not come and it is not of a concern, for that one abides in the holy and perfect eternal Now, resting in union with all that God is. And it no longer matters where you find yourself, for you can be found nowhere but with*in* the Kingdom—and the Kingdom *is* joy, and the Kingdom *is* creation and creativity. The Kingdom is compassion, the Kingdom is Love, the Kingdom is *about this much willingness* [demonstrates with finger and thumb]—that's all. A pinch of willingness can work miracles. And indeed, I say unto you: You have heard and answered the call, and though some of you have not yet totally received it, your journey is indeed over and from the depth of your own being, from the depth of your own perfect union with God, you are calling forth precisely the events and the moments and the experiences that are growing the soul of Christ within *you*.

You are therefore the Light that lights this world. Never—in fact, I would ask you to make a promise—*never from this moment allow the mind to compare your journey to another's.* For only the egoic part of the mind compares and contrasts. Does that make sense for you? How many times have you suffered and not realized that the only reason you're suffering is because you've used the power of the mind to compare yourself to another, so that you could have the experience of believing that you were "less than"?

[Audience agreement]

Cleverly done! Hm. Nip that one in the bud, hm? *Never* compare your journey to that of another. Your journey is in God, your journey is with God, your one relationship is with your Creator: that's the one that matters. And as you cultivate that as being your sole, your primary, your only value, you will discover that your cup shall overflow and you will discover many brothers and sisters with whom you can have the most loving, the most holy, the most pure relationships that the mind could possibly comprehend. It comes forth not because you seek it, not because you try to grab another and bring them into your sphere, *but because you love God above all created things.*

There is no quality of relationship like a holy relationship. And a holy relationship is one in which two minds, two souls, two beings have truly looked within—*truly looked within*—and acknowledged that there is no lack. Those two then choose freely to join together for one purpose only: to create, to extend the good, the holy and the beautiful. And if at any moment there is a fear that someone in your sphere might leave you, rest assured that there is yet a small kernel of specialness waiting to be healed within you. How do you heal it? With Love! With Self-Love, by simply being vigilant for the Kingdom and re-committing yourself to your relationship with your Creator.

What freedom, then, awaits you, what joy awaits you, what power and light and truth await you to flood forth from the petals of your flower. For all true things that are coming from God, the good, the holy and the beautiful, come forth not from the mind that analyzes and plans and compares and contrasts, but from the Awakened Heart that rests in perfect meekness and knows of its perfect union, that it is indeed nurtured in each moment by the rays of golden light descending upon it from the Mind of God Herself. It is from the heart that all good things issue forth, it is from the heart purified of one thing—fear, contraction—through which the Father extends Himself.

What freedom, then, awaits you! It is closer than the palms of your hand, waiting on your welcome, for you to close your petals around this great gift of perfect freedom in which fear holds no power. A perfect freedom in which you look upon your brothers and sisters and your love for the Christ in them is so great, so overwhelmingly great, that you know that there's no place they can go and achieve separation from you . . . that your love, the perfection of your desire to love as your Creator loves you, has become so grand and so great that it reaches out to embrace all—all of creation, every illusion, every hurt, every fear, every planet, every universe, every dimension! Your love is so grand that it embraces all things, and knows—*knows*—that *separation is not possible, that death is unreal and that only what God creates is true.*

You are free. *You are free now!* You are free to live even this life that you seem to be having on your planet *in such a state of knowledge.* And that is what knowledge is. It has nothing to do with belief, it has nothing to do with hope, it has nothing to do with theology, it has nothing to do with spirituality; those are words, those are ideas. And the grandest of ideas do but one thing: they point to that knowledge *that transcends all ideas.* The grandest of words that mankind has ever come up with that can somehow signify *that* Mystery, *that* Truth, *that* Knowledge—is Love. God is a four-letter word.

Love: the simplicity of making a decision to want Love, and learning that there is nowhere you can go to seek it. There is absolutely nothing you can do to *bring Love to you.* Nothing! No amount of accomplishment restores the Son to the Father. No amount of manipulation or seduction with the body brings Love to you. In truth, the body can never be used to *get.* It fails miserably. It *can* be used to *give*. And as you give, you *do* receive. And as you give perfect Love, the remembrance of the perfect Love that you are is restored in your soul. Give you therefore without measure, without ceasing, and you will *receive ceaselessly* that which you truly desire.

I once made a decision as a man, and rest assured that is the only reason that I come forth to communicate with you, for if I have not experienced all that you have experienced, nothing I say to you holds any value or meaning. There is no substance to the words of one who speaks without having experienced. Hm. But because I, too, took on "the sins of the world," the misperceptions of the world, I came to learn all that I could learn of this dimension, which is merely a temporary thought, and I learned it because I loved my Father and I wanted to discover the way to bring the truth of my Father's presence into the deepest and darkest pits of hell, might be one way of describing it—to bring Light into darkness. There is no greater, no greater task for Christ but to bring Light to darkness. That's what you were created for, to bring Light to darkness, to extend the Father into illusions, thereby transforming them, and returning the energy that makes up illusions into the sanity of the radiance of the union of Father and Son: the Christ Light.

Nothing, then, prevents you in any moment from choosing for Love. Nothing is unworthy of your love, and as I say that, I watch many minds immediately begin to think of things that seem to appear outside of themselves, but rest assured, nothing is outside of you. Every memory that you have, every choice that you have ever made for which you yet feel ashamed or guilty, is worthy of *your love,* and that is the only thing that will heal the burden that perhaps yet weighs upon you. Seek, therefore, for that which is birthed from illusions of fear. Search your own mind, search your own beingness, discover the corners of the basement, so to speak, and bring the radiance of *your love* to it. Look upon each and every experience that you have ever had that seems to create the petals contracting in your heart. Bring the Light of that heart and say within the mind,

No! I will not deny Love here.

Bring forth that memory, wrap it in the petals of your *own Self-Love*. See it as having been absolutely perfect, for I say this unto you: each experience that you have called unto yourself, *you have done from your greatness*. You have done it because you, as a soul, have come into this dimension to discover what it is that got so crazy. You are the one that has stepped forth out of compassion, to understand and know the sins of the world in order to bring the Light and Love of Christ, that illusions might be healed.

Look, therefore, not outside of yourself, for the journey to the Kingdom takes you eternally within, ever deeper and ever deeper. Hold nothing back, *hold not one illusion back from the greatness of the Love that dwells within you as the Heart and Soul of your true Self*. For God, Who is but Love, *is the essence of your Self*. And if you think for one moment that there is anything too grand in your experience for That One not to heal, please choose again.

Time can indeed be wasted, and all of you have known the experience of how much time can waste. And yet given unto you time is, that it might be used constructively, and there is no greater, more constructive use of time than to look within and bring Light and Love to anything yet dwelling within you that has been devoid of it.

Nothing in your illusions is true. You have never sinned and you have never failed. *Never have you failed!* You have in truth hurt no one at any time, for nothing can come to any soul that it does not call unto itself out of its belief about what it is worth, or out of its desire to learn. Although you are Christ, please hear this well: *you are powerless to usurp the power and freedom of another*. And any drama that you may have been in, rest assured, it was by agreement.

"You play Romeo, I'll play Juliet." Hm.

"Okay! Excuse me: as we go into this incarnation, do I need to be what you call in your language the "bad ass"? Hm? Hm?

[Laughter]

"I had that role last time. Must I do it again?"

To which your friend says, "Well, yes, I haven't quite learnt the lesson I want to learn. I just can't get it! I want to really learn what it means to feel like I'm a *victim*."

[Laughter]

And *Love* allows all things. Love is the willingness to show up in the way that can best serve the growth of another soul; and the wise teacher learns the language of the student. What is the language? Not the words. It is the predilections, hm? The patterns within the soul, the vibratory quality, if you will—and Love adapts itself endlessly and ceaselessly, through you and as you, to serve one another. That service may be nothing more than finally helping to get your brother or sister to the point where they're sick and tired of what they've been trying to create, to do—to make, that is. You may be serving a function by being such the "bad ass" that it forces another to relinquish control of the soul and cry out for God,

> *Surely there must be another way, and I am determined to find it!*

Have you ever noticed that when you really release your illusions, the other players in your drama seem to change? Have you noticed that?

[Murmurs of agreement]

Suddenly they seem much softer than they were before. There's been no communication in the third-dimensional way but it's because communication is ongoing and it never ceases at the level of the soul, and each and every one of your moments—*each and every one of your moments*—is not unplanned by you. Hm. And you have heard it said, and it is a simple but very true analogy: you are the director of the play, you are the actors of the play, you are the scriptwriter, the choreographer, *and you are the critic who writes the review!*

[Laughter]

Hm! Oh, you know *that* role. Hm. Ahh. So the next time you are critical of yourself, go ahead, be critical, and then appreciate yourself *for doing it so well. Love yourself for judging and loathing yourself!* It is only Love that heals. How do you get out of the awful feeling that self-judgment brings? By loving yourself for being so capable of doing it so well.

[Laughter]

Hm. Indeed beloved friends, it is your own Love of Self that heals you. *It is your own Love of Self that heals you.* No one can do it for you, for no one has ever had the power to take your Self-Love away from you. You have called certain players to yourself in order to give it away, and they have been your saviors, hm?

Self-Love, then indeed, is the doorway to Wisdom Divine. Bring love, then, to each moment. Learn to cultivate your ability while yet you remain in this plane, to feel Love of Self prior to every breath and with each and every step. As you make your tea in the morning, *love yourself* for the very experience that you are creating. When you rile a brother or a sister, love yourself for it, for they have merely agreed to play a role that you have asked for, because your deepest desire—understand this well—desire is the root of all things. Without desire you would not be in existence, for the Love that God Is desired to extend Itself eternally and (what is your term?) the "Voilà! There you are!"

Love! There is no other message, there is no other Truth, there is no *magic* whereby you can get it right. *There is only the decision to love* and yet the mind has been trained,

> *"Oh if I'm going to love, I'd better run out there into the world and find somebody to give the love to."*

That's not up to you! The only one you are required to give your love to is yourself and as you choose to do so, your cup begins to overflow, And rest assured, That One That created you, Who sees you choosing again to receive the Light that touches the heart of the flower that you are, looks upon you and is well pleased and then says unto you, "By the way, I could use a little help. Would you love that one there? Ah, very good. Now how about making a right hand turn, there's another one at the end of the next street."

Hm? And you show up, wherever you are in the dimensions of Creation, to be the extension of Love—but *only, only, only* to the degree that *you* have allowed yourself to *love your Self*. No amount of sacrifice, no amount of doing, no amount of *anything* restores the Son to the Father *but Self-Love*.

I and my Father are One is an extremely powerful expression of Self-Love. And your world would teach you that such love is blasphemy against God. Your world would teach you and try to have you believe that such love is arrogant and selfish—but that's how God loves you. And you cannot know the Father without loving His Creation. No attempt has ever worked to restore your union with God while holding some small part of yourself away from your own love. That is like tying weights around your ankles and then trying to jump to the moon. Even if you succeed in getting the feet and the weights up off the ground for one little moment of freedom [claps hands], you know the crashing feeling? If you're crashing at any moment, *stop* and ask only this question,

> *What within myself am I refusing to love in this moment?*

Stop what you're doing, discover what it is, and bring love to it. You will feel the headache go away, the eyes clear up, the stuffy nose be fixed, if you will. You'll feel your energy of your auric field be restored to perfect balance, the colors of the trees will be brighter. You'll be returned to peace, for Love heals.

Self-Love. You are Christ, and the one being that some of you *have yet refused to love*, through all of your practices of forgiveness, through all of your great community service, and all of the rest. These are good things, by the way, when they flow *out of* the perfection of

Self-Love, for no one can bring peace to the planet who is not at peace within themselves. And no one can bring that Love that heals all things to the planet, unless they have first loved themselves.

I was looked upon as a miracle-worker. I am still looked upon as a great teacher. And yet I say unto you: all that has flowed forth and will continue to flow forth, without ceasing and without end, *does so because I chose to love my Father's Child, my Self, Jeshua ben Joseph. That's all.* I dared to receive the Truth and give it to myself. It was the height of perfect selfishness, but *that* has made all the difference.

If you so desire—and I say those words carefully, for rest assured, no one can desire for you . . . you are the one that must decide what you will desire above all things, what you will value above all things . . . and if you desire (and many of you have this experience anyway; I'm not telling you anything new)—if you desire it, I am indeed available as your friend and as your brother. Not as your savior, not as the first-born of the Father sent out of the clouds to save all of you wretched fools that were somehow birthed from an unloving universe—no. But you are free to *invite* me to enter into the mind, into the depth of your own soul and to help gently bring back to your conscious mind what is yet crying out for *your Self-Love.* Do you see? I don't bring it up so that I can reach in and get rid of it for you, that terrible thorn in your side, I merely bring it back to your consciousness where you are free to choose again, *with Love.* This means that your perfect Christedness is never outside of your reach: Love waits on *your welcome.*

Ahh, Love! God is Love and when you open the petals of your heart to receive Self-Love, you've said unto your Father,

> *Come forth and re-enter my soul. Make my being* Your *dwelling place.*

And you become the Most High and you are free and you are awake and you are One with God. And you have indeed completed the journey *to* the Kingdom and are living now the journey within it. *You are free as the result of your decision to receive and love your Self.*

Nothing else works—*nothing else works*. Everything else that can be used by the Holy Spirit *will* be used to gently move you in the direction of discovering that the doorway to the Kingdom *is Self-Love*. And then, and only then, will you love all of Creation as your Father loves you. And often the great pain, the great loneliness that you feel still within the heart, indeed at all times when you feel it, is *the soul's longing to love as God loves. That's what you want!* That's what all your seeking has been about: to love as God loves. For such Love is perfectly free. It will never happen (for you have the power to delay it indefinitely) it will never happen until you have turned to love your Self. Let *you* be your priority. Learn, then, well to love the holy Child of God that happens to be right where you are. Hm.

Well there, once again I have said something to you that is not new. What can be new? Illusions can appear new but they are merely the same old stuff playing out in a temporary different form. Hm? And Love is not new, Love simply is.

I love you because I am eternally in love with my Self and I know that I am the first-born of the Father, and I know that you, too, are That One. And in our relationship, there can only be one who doesn't know that—and it's not me!

[Laughter]

So in any moment that you think you lack, in any moment that you actually believe that God doesn't support you, in any moment when you think that you are alone, in any moment where you think you're confused, simply ask,

> *What is it that I'm thinking about myself that Jeshua never thinks?... Oh! Now I remember!*

and choose again. Stop what you're doing; don't try to fix the problem. What you think is the problem is merely a lack of Self-Love, that's all. Bring your attention back to Self, wrap yourself in the petals of your own Love, for they have been warmed by the rays of Light descending from the Mind of God. Those petals' warmth, brought back in and wrapped around yourself, will bring the soothing touch that you so desperately desire and so often seek in the touch of another. It is truly only the Self-Loving who can enjoy loving another, even in your physical dimension with what you call the groping of the bodies, hm?

[Laughter]

Who can enjoy that, save that one that loves him or herself? And where can such communication find its perfection, save in the joining within Holy Relationship, where there is no trying to get, for there is no lack? There is only the celebration of God's Beloved. And then you merely get to romp for a while, trying to outdo one another in loving the Beloved of God, without one thought of needing to get. This may sound sacrilegious but I would say give it a try sometime. Or perhaps a holy hug will suffice for you.

So. It has been but a simple message of this hour. It is a message I never tire of giving, and I will continue to give it in whatever way I can, and through whatever mind will open itself to me, in whatever creative way I can reach across the gap that seems to exist in another mind between itself and myself, between itself and God . . . For my desire is that the Sonship be restored and I will not cease until that moment occurs.

My offering to *you* is simply this: *Would you, therefore, choose to join with me in healing the Sonship by accepting that healing fully for yourself?*

And in that moment, you are returned to an ancient beginning and you become free to extend your treasure. Your cup will overflow in ways that you cannot comprehend and the support of many brothers and sisters and friends, unseen by physical eyes, will be there to surround you, to uplift you, to carry you. And not one thing will be left in your pathway. That is how powerful Love is. You can be moving full steam ahead, right at a brick wall, and where you rest in *knowing* that *God is but Love,* that you have one function to serve, [snaps fingers] that wall will vanish just before you reach it, and not one obstacle will be left for you to trip on, to fall over.

You cannot fail to accomplish what the Father gives unto you to do—and the only thing worth doing is what That One gives you. And what That One gives you is Love, that through you might be extended the good, the holy and the beautiful. And what is that but a reflection of yourself? You *are* the good, you *are* the holy and you *are* the beautiful.

So! Hm. I have a plane to catch.

[Laughter]

There are times I have done what you would perceive as sitting on the wing and looked in the windows to see what everyone was doing in there. Hm! Why do you eat that food?

[Loud laughter and clapping]

Ask for a few figs or dates, you'll be just fine. Hm.

You are indeed unlimited forever. The greatest use of your perfect freedom is to embrace the place that you are and bless it with the Love of Christ. Rest assured, if you need to be somewhere else in the next moment, the Holy Spirit will let you know. The tickets will be given, the bags will be packed, the limousine will arrive and you will not fail to be taken to the place where the Father asks you to go, and all will be provided, for you are loved above all things. And the Father's great joy is to extend unto the Son the *whole* of His Kingdom. Why settle for a crumb when you can have the whole cake?

When will you make the decision—*when will you make the decision*—to love *your Self,* that all things might come unto you, that through you they might pour forth to embrace the whole of Creation *and restore it to perfect union with God?* . . . *Now* is a very good time!

And so, tonight we will entertain no questions, for questions are only entertainment.

[Laughter]

And I look forward to that moment when because of *your decision*, we come together—and I speak not just of this temporary way of coming together; this is but one small ripple on the wave. There is nothing that obstructs my coming unto you or your coming unto me in perfect immediacy [snaps fingers] when you choose it . . . I look forward to the day when you come unto me and say,

> *I have no questions, only knowledge.*

So with that, indeed, beloved friends, love you one another as you have first loved your Self. Close the gap between one another by *loving away the gap* between yourself and your Self. Indeed.

Be you therefore at peace this day and always.

Be you in perfect knowledge that Love lights your way.

Be you in perfect knowledge that I am but your brother and your friend and I am indeed with you always, for I love you—and there's no gap!

Peace, then, be with you always.

Amen.

TEACH ONLY LOVE
February 1994

Now, we begin.

And once again, and as always: greetings unto you, Beloved and Holy Children of God. Indeed greetings unto you, my brothers and my sisters, for in truth I look upon you and see no distance between us. I look upon you only with Love, I look upon you and receive the blessing of your countenance, your perfection, your radiance, the unique gifts of your own unique journeys.

Can you, then, well receive that I come forth to abide with you as a *friend*, and as your brother and, as long as you desire it, as a guide and as a teacher. But my teaching is never designed to have you *lean on me*. It is not designed to have you become dependent upon me. But rather, I seek, in whatever way I can, to teach you that which is beyond the teaching itself; to teach you that you are the one that you seek, that you are the one who is already equal to all that I am or ever could be, for well there is within you the *power* to be the Truth that sets the world free.

You do not need to climb a high mountain in order to bless this world. You do not need to accomplish anything that the world can see. Rather, that one that is awakened to the Reality that only Love is real, that one that is awakened to the Truth that "I and my Father are One," seeks not to ascend the highest peak but to *descend*, to take up a rightful place at the side of those who journey still through the labyrinths of illusion—for illusion is the cause of all pain; illusion, the source of all suffering. And because your brother and your sister is yourself, that one that truly loves God seeks not to ascend in the clouds, as they once said of me, but rather to discover a way in which to impart the simplicity of the lesson of Love and seeks ways to be seen, to be noticed, to be heard in such a way that those who are calling for Love can receive it. Teaching, then, is an art, and not a science, and as you teach, you *must* learn. It's the Law of Consciousness, the Law of Spirit. What you teach, you learn instantly, and what you teach consistently, you learn repeatedly, until what you have learned permeates the field of your awareness so completely that no shadow can steal across the vast expanse of that which you are.

Here, then, is the great glory and the gift of your world while time seems to remain for you—and, indeed, it will remain, until you've forgiven the past and released the future and have chosen to learn to abide where God is. Now, as you abide in that place and realize that time, the experience of this world and each and every form of relationship that emerges in the field of your awareness is a perfect and divine gift given unto you *for you*, the Holy Son of God (being neither male nor female) to learn ever more deeply to teach only Love. That is the only purpose time has. For when you choose to be that one who teaches only Love and embraces each situation—not as the world would teach you to embrace it, but as Truth teaches you to embrace it; not as something you're doing in order to survive into tomorrow, but as an opportunity to seize with the fullness of your spirit and your consciousness to learn to be the embodiment of Love—to realize that *you*, you are the one for whom the stars have been set in the heavens, you are the one for whom your planet spins, you are the one for whom this universe has existed for a very long time, you are the one for whom all appearances have been given to you to create the opportunity for *you* to accept the gift God has given you—your existence as Christ—and to choose to put that reality into practice: to learn in the field of time that which directs you to what is timeless and, indeed, what comes from what is timeless. For here is the great completion of what some have called the mystical ascent of the soul; here, the completion of all spiritual unfolding; *here* is the culmination and the secret of what you would hear termed in your world 'ascension,' for ascension is merely the remembrance of what has already occurred by Grace. You cannot achieve it; it's been done for you by the Love and Grace of God.

Ascension, then, is completed when you allow the depth of your identity as a unique individual to settle into the Heart (with a capital H), that Heart through which the Holy Spirit speaks, through which Love is extended, through which Kindness flowers forth, Freedom radiates, and Peace is given to the world. When you indeed come to rest in that Heart, the mind will become your perfect servant and it will never be filled with conflict again, period, at any time. And when you abide in that Heart, you will know that the great culmination of this remarkable process, this journey from the dream of separation to the dream of awakening into the Reality of what has always been, is not the end of time but the *transformation* of time, for Creation will never die. Creation is extension, and extension requires some quality of time.

Rather than an escape, then, rather than a completion of some sort, as you come to rest in that Heart, to live peacefully and fear-less-ly, whole and complete in your perfect union with God, the unconflicted mind serves you perfectly. It will always know where to go, what to do, what to say; no big deal, no effort. Then, you have become the Cross of Light. The vertical axis means merely that which connects the things of Time to the things of Eternity; vertical axis. And because you abide at the Heart you extend that recognition as far as from the East to the West in the field of Time itself, and you are liberated—you are liberated *right where you are*, even if it seems to be that you find yourself in a body upon planet Earth. For the body is not a barrier to Truth and the world cannot imprison you. This would be to give illusion reality.

Come to understand then, that what I sought to teach—not through necessarily my words, but through my life, my experiences, including my death, and my willingness to remain with you always—is to teach only Love. And Love embraces all things, trusts all things, enfolds all things in wisdom, and thereby transcends all things without ceasing. When you fully awaken to realize you have nowhere to go and nothing to achieve, and this moment, just as you find it, is the perfection of Heaven, you will know the freedom that I have sought to guide you to. You will have come wholly to where I am and you will recognise that you are in perfect communication with me at

all times. Seek then not to journey some*where*, but seek to embrace the place in which you find yourself in each and every moment. For the body being what it is, for the physical dimension being what it is, you will be in flux and flow *constantly*. Just try to sit down in a chair and see if you can stay there for three days.

> *No problem, I can do that, all I have to do is ignore my bladder ... or hunger.*

So understand that while this body lasts, you will be in ceaseless motion, you cannot be in any other way. But freedom comes when you are willing to embrace the body *as the body*, not to deny it, not to hate it, not to feel imprisoned by it, not to place your happiness upon its losing ten pounds, or changing the color of the hair, but rather the body becomes exactly what it is: a temporary neutral event, which *you can choose to use as a means* for teaching only Love in a way that can be seen by the world. And what is the world but the perception that the body is real? And that if there's something called Spirit, we haven't been able to find it yet.

When you come to rest in that Heart and abide *as* that Cross of Light, fully aligned and in union with the Mind of God, the Heart of God, and freed from your resistance to time, to embodiment, so that you are constantly extending your creations in the horizontal plane of time—when you abide in that place you *will know* what Eternity is. You will be Eternity embodied. And though others may look upon you and think, "Well, that's just Mary, that's just Jane, that's just Fred. Hm, I've known them for my whole life," rest assured, the same was said about me: "Is that not the son of Joseph the carpenter? What wisdom could possibly be coming from him?" The same wisdom that can flow through you, the same Love given of my Father to each of us equally, the same wisdom that flows from the Holy Spirit, the Comforter, and will speak through *any mind* that simply releases the delusion of believing that this world means anything, and all appearances, all relationships, all moments have been given over entirely to the purpose of the healing of God's Son. Please remember: "son" simply means "offspring of," "to spring forth from."

Time then, is no longer a prison and Heaven comes to be perceived as spread across the face of the Earth. And each step you take, you know that you walk in the Kingdom; every breath you breathe is sanctified by your holiness because you have received it without resistance. And each relationship, each moment of each relationship, has been sanctified by the holiness of your commitment to teach only Love. And perhaps above all, each moment of relationship *with yourself* has become sanctified so that in each moment of relationship with yourself, you are teaching yourself only Love. You have begotten many worlds, you have begotten many universes, and verily I say unto you: each time you think a thought, you have set into motion a web of energy, a web of relationships that is Creation Itself.

How important then is your thought? You need only look around yourself. For everything that your physical eyes show you, whether you're sitting in your living room, in your automobile, in this room with these friends, everything you see is the direct result of the thoughts you have been willing to give permission to make a home in your mind. Everything that you have ever experienced has come not because it was forced upon you, but because you called it to yourself, just as you have called this very moment to yourself. By being in this room in this hour you have collapsed all webs of relationships that could have had a different conclusion, a different completion or effect. You have done that. Your birth into this world was the effect of your freely chosen, your freely made decision to attract, to coalesce around you, a certain field of energy: you call it your parents, your culture, your time-frame, your planet, your universe, your dimension. You remain for ever more perfectly free Spirit, made in the image of God, given the self-same power to create. And you've never, ever once succeeded in ceasing to create—it's not even remotely possible; you don't even get to take a break! You are always creating and you always will be.

The only decision then is,

What do I want?

That sounds rather selfish, I know, in your world, you're not supposed to talk that way. "What do *I* want?" I speak not of the egoic mind that is reacting from fear and then seeks relationships to console itself: relationships with persons, relationships with substances and all of the rest. Hm. Everything is relationship. But I speak of that "I" that is the focal point, the essence of your consciousness, the essence of your being, that spark of Divinity, that ray of light that is as a sunbeam to the sun, that cannot be destroyed, that is made of the same substance of that which birthed you—that which I have called "Abba."

How will you choose to become familiar with, to be in relationship with, that ray of light that is the power of your very consciousness? How will you utilize it in each moment? For in each moment you are literally birthing your experience. And it's all okay. Any experience you have ever had is perfectly okay. In no time and in no moment have you ever failed. You have created, you have added to the Creation that is the universe. You have *never* failed! Can you hear that? Can you really, honestly, truthfully *hear* with your Soul that you have never failed? It's impossible! Now, it's not impossible for someone else to *judge* you as having failed. That's their free use of consciousness and in that moment they are like one that has held the guillotine above their own head and judged you and dropped it upon themselves. That is what judgement does. *You* have never failed and you never will fail. The only thing that it is wise to consider is this:

Do I wish to continue this creation? Or do I wish to choose anew?

Do you see how different that is from those that would teach you about sin, and about guilt, and about failure, and about wretchedness, and about unworthiness? ... Hm ... powerlessness? Who can take your power from you? No one! You can only choose how you will use it. So in your most wretched hours, you have been a perfectly powerful creator. And you are free to continue that line of creation as long as you want, to extend it on the horizontal plane of time for *lifetimes*, if you wish. You could be what you call in your world (what is your saying here?) "crying in your glass of beer" for ten thousand lifetimes, and never leave the bar. Hm! Do you know that there are many beings, sparks of Divinity, what you call souls, that are not currently in embodied form as you know it, who are exactly living that experience, who have been locked into some perception and have been there for eons. They even show up in your physical dimension sometimes: they're called ghosts. Locked into some tiny little place of creation and they've been there a *long* time, but Love can release them.

Recently, I suggested to this my beloved brother, and indeed unto his mate and friend that it would be wise to journey to a certain state they call the Kansas, and I suggested to them that it would be good to drive, although they didn't quite realize it was me mentioning this. I wanted them to experience something . . .

Recently you had what is called a bit of an explosion in your Oklahoma that destroyed a large building, and many beings died. The vast majority of them are still there because no one has taken the time to go to that place, to contact those souls, to speak to them as though you're right in front of them, to let them know a transition has occurred and it's okay; that if they will only look above themselves they will see a Light and that it's safe to journey to that Light; it's safe to release and to entrust their family, their friends, their children, their co-workers, their pets, to the care of those still embodied; that they are safe and free to release this dimension. I sent them there because I wanted them to feel palpably, as you would say, the reality of that: that a soul can be locked in an experience at the moment of death and stay that way for a very long time—until what happens? Someone who has awakened to a deeper understanding, who wants to teach only Love so that they may learn it, reaches back, metaphorically and allows themselves to become a channel for that wisdom that knows how to release the soul from its bondage. So I want to suggest to you this evening that all of you, before you rest your head on the pillow, say one thing in your mind:

> *I am not just this. It's only the body that is resting in this bed. It emerges out of my Self, out of my Divinity! I am free to go anywhere at any time [snaps fingers] that fast!*

How long does it take to think a thought? And I want very much for you to have the experience of putting yourself in what you call the Oklahoma and go to that place— and you'll know you're there, trust me, you will feel the pain and the sorrow, the depression, the sadness, the fear, the anguish—and simply say within yourself,

> *Father, who would you have me help in this moment?*

And then observe what comes into the field of your awareness: it may be an adult, it may be a man, it may be a woman, it may be a child. [Snaps fingers] Be right there! It's that easy. It's that quick. And as you abide with them, let that image of whoever that is be there. Don't let the mind say,

Well this is just hogwash, this must be imagination.

There is no such thing as imagination; there is only awareness of what you are creating and experiencing, whether it be in this dimension or another. Therefore, be there, and simply look upon that one, surround them with Light, and speak to them as though they were right in front of you physically. You can even open the physical mouth if you wish to, to help kind of ground it. Let them know that they are pure Spirit. Let them know that it is safe to release the world they knew and that if they will simply turn their gaze skyward, so to speak, they will begin to see a pin-prick of Light far above them. If they give themselves permission to let go—for they have not failed— they can begin to move to that Light and there will be someone to greet them, to help them understand what has occurred, and bring them into a deeper dimension of knowledge. There are by the way some of you in this room who, you could say, this is your night job anyway. You do it in what you call your dream state. Sometimes you awaken and you know who you are, and you realize you had a dream about someone, but you can't for the life of you figure out where on earth *that* connection ever came from. Hm! You're already doing it! This is just the process of *deliberately* doing it.

Please, help me release my brothers and sisters who are yet standing on floors that no longer exist, of a building that was shattered by one insane thought. That is what you're here for: to teach only Love, to participate in the healing of the Son. And if you think for one moment that your life is too ordinary, stop fooling yourself! You can be a street sweeper and in the middle of your eleven o'clock appointment to sweep up the papers in front of the court house, you can be healing the mind of that which your world would call the criminals and the judges who are meeting on the tenth floor of the building, by simply allowing yourself to be with them, in just the way that I've described.

The body never imprisons you! Only *you* can imprison you, by choosing to think that you are less than what you are created to be. The body?—a temporary teaching and learning device. It arises in one tiny corner of an infinite number of dimensions, in which you are already having complete experience now. How many of you have thought, well, it would be really nice to journey to Tahiti for a vacation and also be in Paris at the same time? You can do that; you are doing that multidimensionally already, so why not embrace this tiny, little, minuscule corner of your creation, see how utterly harmless it is, and yet see how rich it is in the potential for you to deepen your knowledge of what Love is. Stop believing the mumbo-jumbo of the world and start using your time to extend and teach Love.

You have an interesting word in your language: boredom. Boredom can only be the *denial* of the truth of who you are, and you can heal a multitude without ever lifting your buttocks from the chair. You are not ordinary, and *no life is ordinary*, or belittling. And why? Because there's only One Life: a life lived in the Light of Truth. That's all there is! Why not get on with it? So when next you watch the mind trying to seduce you into believing there's something you must do to get closer to God, drop it immediately and ask,

> *How can I serve—right now—the extension of Love? Who needs to be blessed? Who needs to be thought of? Who needs to be held? Who needs to be called?*

If you start giving yourself to the extension of Love, your days will be so filled that you won't even notice time at all. You won't be harried or stressed; you will be fulfilled beyond measure. And conversely, or paradoxically, what will occur in your consciousness, your experience of time, is that you are living in timelessness. Why? Because you're so committed to teaching only Love that you know you're in the right place at the right time and this is the moment in which I can relax into the Truth of who I am and remember my purpose:

> *I am the extension of God's Love, the thought of Love in form. I have no needs, I have no lacks, I have no past and I have no future. I am now forever one with God. Who can I love? ...Who can I love?*

> ...*Who can I love?*

I would not say these things to you if it was not so. I would not say these things to you if they did not come from the depth of my own experience, learned while yet I lived in and as a body. It was that learning that carried me through the dimension of death into a deliberate and conscious knowing of my absolute unlimitedness, so that I could experience the great delight of blessing the whole of Creation in every moment and being in loving relationship with *all* dimensions at once. The only thing that therefore is preventing you from knowing that is that you're still letting yourself use the power of consciousness *to waste time* by perceiving yourself as unworthy, in lack, not knowledgeable enough, not the right connections—do you see? Every time you let your mind wallow in that, you have your reward. Whether you like it or not is another issue.

Seize time! Every moment!

> *How can I teach Love, right now? Well, I'm in the middle of the desert and there's no one for miles...*

Hm. Perhaps it would be wise to go to a different dimension, and just shift your thought. Why look for someone that's linked to a body? Is that the only way you can teach Love? Those grand brothers and sisters, whose bodies were destroyed as the result of one insane thought in your Oklahoma, would deeply appreciate it if you would look beyond *bodies* to find someone to bless and love. There are beings around you right now in this room, around what you call the body; there are an infinite number of dimensions. And this room is filled, there's no space left: filled with souls, consciousnesses, sparks of Divinity, intelligence. Not only are you never alone, but you never have anything called privacy.

[Laughter]

Hm. So what are you trying to get away with in your "private moments"? Hm! Comical, sometimes: "I'm *sooooo* alone. Nobody loves *meeee*, I could never bless the world how *Jeshua* does it."

[Laughter]

Verily I say unto you, you have your reward; you've created it in that moment. And you can live in what the world calls squalor, you can live in what some would call here your little houses of cardboard in the alleys of your big cities, and there, with the rain hitting the top of that cardboard and leaking down through the walls into the concrete and making your butt feel a little cold and wet, *you* can know perfect peace and be totally absorbed with extending Love to the fullness of Creation. And that means that there's no excuse for waiting until tomorrow, when a better job comes along, or—oh, here's a good one in your world—if only my *soulmate* would show up!

[Laughter]

You want to find your soulmate? Open your eyes and look around! Hm. Or perhaps a new wardrobe would do it. How many ways have you cleverly created to delay putting into action the Truth of what you are? Quite a few of them, isn't there? And in any moment, when you believe that you are bored, when you have what you call idleness—there's no such thing as idleness: you are totally constantly involved in creativity, in creation. You're a non-union worker who gets no breaks.

[Laughter]

Hm, hm. And you are paid immediately for every creation. Immediately! The only step that remains is simply this:

> *What do I want? What will this moment be for? I decree it, I create it, I bring it into being and I reap the harvest.*

That's all there is. There is nothing else. Why? Because you are a perfectly free being, abiding in the free Mind of God, Who places no demands upon you *whatsoever*, though the Mind of God would ask that you consider being happy. That's all! To consider being happy. And to lay up your treasure, not where moth and dust corrupt and thieves break through to steal, but to lay up your treasures which are of Heaven. And what is Heaven? Consciousness, creativity, the extension of Love, the decision to heal, to dissolve into peace. That is the great gift of time, the perfect freedom in which you abide. There is no such thing as prison; there is no such thing as separation. And as my sister said unto you earlier today: *When will you believe?* Hm.

I love you, because I know who you are. I love you because—and listen well—I love you because *I learned to love myself, unconditionally*, which can only take you into unlimitedness. You—you are that one for whom all things have been created, set in place. You are the one supported by your beautiful and precious Mother Earth, who gives you the very body that you utilize, and let us hope you utilize it well. You are the one for whom the bird sings each morning, you are the one for whom the clouds dance in multicolors at your sunsets. You are the one for whom the one known as my Mother continues to teach only Love to anyone who will listen. You are the one— you are the one for whom each blade of grass grows from the soil to remind you of the beauty of Life, *to remind you that that same beauty is in you, now*! Claim it and own it, nurture it, treasure it.

Learn indeed, beloved friends, to love yourself as your Father has first loved you and always loves you. See your innocence in your perfection. See the totality of your incredible creativity in each moment and with each breath. And when you have truly loved yourself wholly and *unconditionally*, so wholly and unconditionally that you will not tolerate holding onto anything unlike Love in your consciousness at all, and you will do whatever it takes to dissolve it (and you'll have a good time doing it) ... When you've come to wholly love yourself, you will be where I am—instantaneously. No, the body may not vibrate into Light and the sixty thousand people that live in your Santa Fe won't go, "Ooh, aahh." You'll get no press; no movie will be made about you for the television. You will simply be free. And you will walk in the world but not of it, and only the perfectly enlightened will know the truth of who you are. But you will know, and you'll never be without the bliss of knowing that

I and my Father are one and all that I do is my Father's Will.

... That where my mind ends, His begins, and the created and the Creator are so intimately linked that one cannot tell where one begins and the other ends. And yet you will always know the humility of knowing that you are the created by something so infinite and vast that I could only think to call it Abba.

Be you therefore that which you are and begin your ministry now. Bless this world with your holiness, shine the Light of your truth upon it, be the one willing to lead the way, in *your* relationships, in *your* life, *right where you are*—and you may rest assured that if something needs to change, when you are abiding in that place you won't be able to prevent it. It will come like a miracle borne on the wings of a dove, dropped into your lap, effortlessly. Effort is of your world and has no part in the Kingdom. And if you're struggling to leave something you don't like, perhaps that very struggle is chaining you to it. Turn again and embrace it with the fullness of Love that you can bring in each moment, and you just might find that what seemed to be your prison has been the pathway that has set you free. And where you will go, you cannot know, but there are many, many, many, many mansions in my Father's Kingdom, worlds without end—and already, let us say, you've been assigned and there are a multitude of beings who are waiting for *you* to lead them, and as you claim the Atonement for yourself, they will find you. Just as you have found me, perhaps through this my beloved brother. I did not have to seek for you; because I have awakened and grown in the fullness of my Father's Love, you have found *me*. And just in that way there are many that are already assigned to *you*, waiting for you to welcome Love into and as the Truth of your Being.

What is your work in the world? To awaken. To accept the Atonement. To surrender the illusion that there is anywhere to go. To accept that not of yourself but of the Father's Love you can do all things, and your pathway will be set before you.

I come to bring my friends to myself that they might know the truth of who they are and stretch their arms and heart wide to accept those friends waiting for them to lead them. Where, then, can you teach Love? *Open your eyes* to the place in which you find yourself and just do it. Hm!

[Laughter]

So, in closing then, understand well that I keep my word. I once said,

> *I am with you always.*

There is no room for conjecture, doubt or argument. It is simply the way it is. And that which you have called the Shanti Christo will indeed know the touch of my hand —and not just mine. For we come to serve and to support and to join with any endeavour to extend the Holy, the Good and the Beautiful, that miracles might be seen by those who don't believe in them and by so seeing them, their hearts can be touched, and their minds awakened, their souls uplifted and their journey home can begin. So rest assured, you will indeed see miracles through this expression. Not because I demanded it of you but because a vision was received; and because it was received and planted in good soil, I have come to play with you. And I will play without ceasing, until Heaven is spread across the face of this most precious, precious planet, even this planet that I was once taught to call my Mother.

Therefore, indeed, know I am with you always. Laugh, sing, dance, play, celebrate, love, hug, caress, kiss, touch, remind, speak the Truth, and support one another, for without relationship there is no Kingdom.

Thank you, then, for your time. Thank you for your willingness to heal the Son of God. Rest assured, I am going nowhere because you are where I want to be, because you are my Father's Creation and I love you.

Be you therefore at peace always; embrace this world and thereby heal it.

Amen.

DECIDE TO BE CHRIST
March 1994

Decide to Be Christ

Now, we begin.

And indeed greetings unto you, Beloved and Holy Children of God. Indeed greetings unto you, beloved brothers and sisters. Indeed greetings *unto* you, the embodiment of all that Love is, the embodiment of all that Wisdom is, the embodiment of all that Simplicity is. Indeed, greetings unto *you, Holy Child of God.*

For I come forth not from a dimension apart from you, but I come forth from that place which we have shared together as One, since before the beginning of time. I come forth, then, to abide with you *because I love you.* For I look upon you and I look beyond your illusions of suffering and strife, I look beyond the temporary illusions that *seem* at times to cloud your perceptions still—and *I see only the radiance of that which my Father has birthed and has sustained forever.* For *in you* do I see the reflection of the Truth that *I Am*, and in seeing Christ in *you*, I know Christ in myself.

And the only difference between you and me may yet be that there are a few moments when you make the decision to see yourself other than Christ, and therefore fail to see Christ in your brother and sister. And likewise, there may be a moment when you choose not to see Christ who dwells within your brother or sister, thereby convincing yourself that Christ cannot dwell within you. For remember always that it takes One to know One. And if you see Christ in me, it can only be because *you* have acknowledged from a place within yourself that you *are* the One that you've been seeking. Only Christ can welcome Christ, as only Love can welcome Love. Because you are that Love, all power under Heaven and Earth is given unto you, without measure, consistently—there is not a moment that it is taken from you—and from that power you *choose to create* what *you* have chosen to perceive.

Therefore, the only journey is a journey without distance to a goal that has never changed. It is a journey from the decision to see yourself as separate from God to the decision to see yourself as One with God, and to become entirely vigilant for the Kingdom. And the Kingdom is simply the eternal union of God and His Holy Child, of Creator and created. Like a sunbeam to the sun are you, and nothing you have ever dreamed about yourself has changed for one moment the Truth that is true always.

Therefore indeed beloved friends I *never* come to instruct you, for what could I possibly teach you that you do not already know? And in any moment, if in your dreams, in your prayers, your meditations, if temporarily through the domain of the mind of this my beloved brother, there are words uttered—caused, if you will, by an impulse of my Love for you—that sound true to you, that touch your heart, that heal the mind, that awaken you, that restore your peace ... rest assured, I have done nothing. For of myself I can *do* nothing, but the Father through me can do all things. For it is the Father in *you* that has activated your awareness. That Truth has been heard. Therefore, when healing comes to your mind it is because *you* have healed it.

And you have chosen the context, perhaps, just as some of you in this very hour will choose this context in which to heal an ancient wound, in which to awaken ever more deeply into the Truth that is true always.

Some of you will insist that I have done something to you. But rest assured, *I have no power* over the Holy Child of God: you. I can love you, and I indeed do. I can join with you in the space between your thoughts, and I do—not because there is something amiss with you but because I see in you *everything that is good, everything that is holy, everything that is beautiful, everything worthy of Christ's Love*; that is what is true about you. Therefore I enter into your dreams and into your meditations and into your prayers, I enter in wherever you would create a space for me *because I love the Child of God who radiates the truth of my Father's Presence and reminds* me *of who I am*.

You, each of you, I see as my savior. Just as when I walked your planet as a man, I learned to look upon everyone as my savior, to see in them the Light of Christ beyond all illusions and it was in seeing that Light that I finally learned that *it must be in me*. This is why relationship *is* the means of your salvation. No one can awaken alone, for there is no truth behind the illusion of separation. There is only One Mind dancing in a myriad of forms, dimensions, layers of consciousness, layers of potentiality, but behind it all *you* are the Shining One sent forth from the Holy Mind of God, at one with that Mind always. And in Truth, only that Mind is Real, for Christ is God's *only* creation.

Therefore, beloved friends, in this hour I am going to ask you to do something that is actually quite important for all of us. If you would indeed honor the Son—the Christ—that dwells in me, then choose from this moment to use the power of choice given unto you to decide to *be* Christ. If you would honor me, then in this hour truly decide to honor *yourself*—to look beyond the illusions that seem perhaps still to govern the mind; to become so arrogant that you take God at His word and simply begin to entertain the thought:

> *I am That One. I have always been That One. I could never succeed in being* other *than That One. It is I who have come to bless this world with the Love of Christ. It is I that find myself temporarily embodied upon a certain planet in a certain solar system in a certain dimension among infinite dimensions. Here, I bless this world. Now, in this moment, Love restores all things, for I am the Redeemer of the world. And as I bless the world, I bless myself. And as I love the world, I have loved myself. And as I see Christ in my brother or sister, I merely reinforce the reality that That One is who I am.*

This is how close the Kingdom is at all times. This, how close the Kingdom *is*—*now*. What is the width or the distance of a thought? Hm! And yet I say unto you, all that you behold from your perception, even the very body, the trees that bless this planet, the bird that sings at dawn, the wind that whispers gently across the flower bed, the fragrance of that flower—all things that can be perceived exist nowhere save in the distance between the beginning and the ending of a thought. *That* is how powerful you are.

Therefore dare to think the thought of Truth,

> *I and my Father are One, here and now; I cannot change it. I can delay my recognition of it, for I am given infinite freedom to do so, and perhaps I've been doing a very good job, but nothing I have ever dared to believe about myself has ever been true, except the Truth*

> *that is true always: I am That One. I am the One shining beyond all stars. I am the One through whom Creation has flowed. I am the One who blesses Creation with the Love of Christ.*

There may yet be some of you who think that that is arrogant, but I say unto you: the only thing that is arrogant is to insist that you are less than you are created to be and then to try to enlist others to believe it with you. Hm? Hm! Hm. You know that one, hm? How much time and energy have you spent—and rest assured, time can waste as well as be wasted—how much time and energy have you spent trying to convince others of your unlovability? How much time and energy have you spent enlisting others to believe *with* you that you are unworthy, that you are weak, that you cannot find peace? How much time and energy have you spent manifesting worlds in which separation seemed to be a success? How much evidence have you amassed to prove it? And yet I say unto you, all of it is your creation. It exists nowhere except between the beginning and the ending of a choice, a thought. And yet the Father waits silently for His Holy Child to awaken from an ancient dream and choose again. The very same power that you have been using and investing in proving to yourself that you are yet separate from God is the *very power* that must come to be used to acknowledge the Truth that is true always. And this *is* being vigilant for the Kingdom.

It is not necessary, then, to seek for Love, for Love is the Truth of your Being. It is, however, quite necessary to seek out the ways in which you have invested time and energy into the birthing of perceptions and beliefs that seem to be other than the Truth—and then to choose anew. All purification, then, is of the mind. And I speak here not of what some would call the lower mind that is engaged in the activities of the body. I speak of the depth of the Mind, or what I often refer to as the Heart—the Heart, the Sanctuary in which Christ yet resides within you: unchanged, unchanging, unchangeable forever.

Please, waste not another moment, for you are worthy of Peace. Please, waste not another moment, but *arise now* in the Holiness of your Being by simply entertaining this one thought *right now* in your Being:

> *I and my Father are One. I am as I am created to be. I choose to accept the Truth and to live it—not by my power, for I have none, but by that power that has birthed me in this moment. I am* the savior of the world.

So how does that feel?

[Indistinct reply]

Hm. Is that ok? For, you see, here is the question you must come to answer for yourself. You must be able to answer this question:

> *Is it okay for me to be God's Holy Child?*

Hm! The only reason you've birthed ideas of separation is that you've answered that question in the past by saying,

> *Well, not yet. It's okay for Jeshua ben Joseph, and perhaps a few others; I'll select them out and give them permission to be awake.*

But if you would honor the Son that dwells in me, *please* honor the Son, the Christ Light, that dwells within you.

Does it feel, what did you say, the pretty darn good? Hm! Trust me, beloved friend, as you live in that decision you will experience an unending expansion of the depth of that goodness and you will discover that your Father's Kingdom has no end and is extended without end in you and through you. And just as you can come to be the master of the domain of your body-mind and of your world, there will then come a day and a moment when you will play as the master of universes, just as you are now beginning to play with the mastery over your mind that seems to be limited to one body.

In my Father's house are many mansions, many dimensions, worlds without end, and you, because you *are* God's Holy Child, are free to open and receive all that has been prepared for you—and if you would well receive it, the whole of Creation in its infinite glory and its unending extension is given to *you*. That is God's delight. Just as a child turns to the father or the mother, and the father and mother feel such love for the child that they would give all things unto that one, likewise does your Father prepare all things for you; and therefore Love merely waits on your welcome.

> *Father, I would receive the Kingdom You have prepared for me since before the beginning of time. I have dreamt long and hard and I have discovered that in separation and limitation there's something lacking: You and me in our perfect and holy Union. Therefore now do I choose to open and receive all that You would give me, gladly. Press it down upon me without measure—let it rain like the showers from infinite, infinite heavenly skies—and I will never cease in my receiving, for I know that I am the one birthed from Your Holy Mind and I am the one whom You love above all.*

That is the Truth, and frankly, though I have tried in a million ways, there's no better way to say it than that. That Truth is true about me *because*—please listen carefully— because and only because it is true for *you*. Hm? If it were true for me and not true for you, then God could not be God, because something would have been created in inequality, and something given would also be withheld—*and God withholds nothing.* Therefore that which God is, is pressed down upon you like a gentle spring shower without ceasing and with perfect equality, unto you and unto me, unto every saint and every sinner. And the shower that falls is the power *to choose.* That's all, that is what the Kingdom is: the power to choose what you will be aware of, how you will use the power of mind to create the thoughts that you think and thereby create universes of experience.

Now, here is a simple question that you can ask if you want to find out if this is true. Do you find yourself existing right now? Do you find yourself existing right now? What's the answer? Hm?

Participant: Yes. Yes.

You're using it. You're using the power of God's Love that is showering down upon you to be aware of your literal existence as a sentient being. Hm? And you are just as free to decide what qualities you will experience, right here, right now.

So take a moment and make what you call eye contact—the eyes are the window to the soul—make eye contact with someone in the room, some perfect stranger, existing in an infinitely far space away from you, locked into another body, painfully imprisoned just like you are [laughs] and simply decide that you are Christ and that you would do nothing else in this moment but bless them. Transmit the Love of God *now*.

[Short pause]

No need to tighten the jaw and furrow the brow, the Kingdom is effortless. Hmmm. There, I believe some of you are feeling that shift in the room. Who's doing it but you?

Now within your own mind gently say, as you continue that eye contact,

> *I behold my beloved Self in whom I am well pleased. As I bless, I am blessed. As I love, I receive Love. Therefore in my giving do I find that which I would receive. Therefore my giving will be without ceasing, that I might give all, to receive all.*

Good. Was that pretty darn good? Hm, hm?

[Laughter]

How did that feel? Was it difficult? Did you go through any gyrations in order to do it? The Kingdom is the simplest of the simple. It requires literally no efforting, for effort is of the world, not of the Kingdom. Love is eternally present, waiting only on *your* decision to have vigilance over *your* Kingdom, which is your power to choose. Nothing outside of you has caused anything at any time, for all that you experience flows from within you. And no one has the power to dictate your choice, for no one can usurp the free will of the Holy Son of God.

There is a necessary step in anyone's spiritual journey and that step has just been described for you. The journey *to* the Kingdom truly begins when you completely decide to assume complete responsibility for exactly what you're experiencing in any moment—without fail, without justification, without explanation. For until you choose to claim such power, you cannot truly make the decision—except for momentary glimpses—you can't make the constant decision to be the embodiment of Christ. Why? Because you're constantly giving your power to an illusion outside of yourself. Does that make sense for you?

So the whole of spirituality, after all is said and done, rests only in this:

The Kingdom is at hand. It is spread across the face of the Earth and mankind sees it not because he fails to look into his own consciousness, his own Mind, and *claim* the *power* that is going on all the time: the power by which that Mind creates and experiences its creations.

So we have that settled. Hm? Good.

Now, remember that at any time that you notice yourself entertaining an insane idea —and what is an insane idea, except the idea that,

> *Something out there really is causing my experience. I'm not really the awakened Son of God.*

Those are insane ideas. When you have them, realize that you have just freely used the power of your sanity to simply entertain an insane idea. For no other reason than to have the experience. That's all that's going on. That's it! And you are just as free to choose again.

Guilt is a very clever illusion. With it, you have decided that since you once held an insane idea, you've taken away from yourself your worthiness to think sanely:

> *And now I must strive and work. I must prove myself worthy and hope that God in His Grace will finally have mercy upon me, a poor*

> *wretched sinner, and take my burdens from me, and allow me to be healed. Oh Father, don't You hear my prayers?*

Frankly, your Father is not even aware of your illusions! He's too busy loving you as you are and giving you the very power to *choose* illusion.

So, understand the great temptation of guilt and how you have worn it like a cloak in order to avoid being what you can't help but be. You're then trying to shake your hand off of your wrist and you can use the same power to use that hand to bless Creation. On or off, Love or fear, there is no gray area. There is only the power of Mind given unto you freely. There is only the opportunity to choose again and again and again and again and again, until the bliss of choosing *for* the Kingdom finally out- values every other possibility and the mind becomes consistently anchored in the sunbeam that has come forth from the Sun of God and streams forth only Love. Rest assured that as you cultivate that in each present moment, the power of your own beingness will carry you far, far, far beyond the need for a body, the need for time, definitely far beyond the need for, shall we say, dramatic learning experiences.

Is it, then, possible to truly awaken while yet in the world of illusion? Of course! Awakening can only occur *now* and because Love is real, because you are who you are always, nothing in any moment has the power to obstruct you from being awake— except the power of your decision. That's all. That is the one thing that in this hour I'd wish to express to you. If you can get this, you've gotten it:

Nothing holds power over you and nothing creates your experience except the decision, the choice, that you have used within the power of the Mind.

That's all that's happening, in all dimensions. It's what's happening in the dimension where I hang out—which by the way is not quite accurate, since I hang out in all dimensions, and so do you. The only difference is: I'm perfectly aware of it, while some of you are trying to be perfectly unaware of it. Where I abide, with a multitude of friends, it is quite true that there is no valuation of the body, therefore no need to manifest one. There is communion and communication. It is immediate, it is more like a frequency that passes unobstructed through a solid wall and we are engaged in ongoing creativity without ceasing, for what can Creation be, what can the very purpose of existence be, if it is not to extend or create the good, the holy, and the beautiful as a way of celebrating Divine Union with all that God Is? This is why I once implored you:

Remember only your loving thoughts, for only they are true.

And each time you entertain what was once an insane choice, you're actually saying,

> *I, by the power given unto me of my Father, choose to imprison myself in an illusion and to suffer the guilt that comes with it. Now let me do it really well.*

When you remember only your loving thoughts, you are thinking with God. That *is* the Mind of God because only Love is real. The Kingdom is immediate and at hand. Nothing can obstruct it, nothing can limit it. Perception can be corrected so that you see the real world right here, right where you are. Where there are seemingly chairs and bodies and rooms and lightbulbs and all of the rest, and funny little wires that go to funny littles keys so that the master can make beautiful music come out of them, right here, the real world abides and it is what is perceived when *you* choose to see only through the eyes of Love.

I chose a very dramatic way to learn my final lesson. I invite you to learn your final lesson with ease and gentleness. When I said, "Take up your cross and follow me," I did not invite you into a realm of suffering and strife and sacrifice. Rather, the cross that you crucified yourself upon so many times is merely the illusion of guilt, the insistence that you have actually succeeded in separating yourself from God. To take up your cross is like packing up your tent when it's time to go home: you don't trudge with it on your back, you throw it in the trunk, hm? You get in your automobile and you step on the gas and you have a nice cup of water as you speed down the highway, saying, "It was a nice camping trip, but it's done."

Therefore take up your cross and follow me please, please, please, for the world is crying out to see again the embodiment of Christ. And just as once as a man I chose to take my Father at His word—to choose to embody Christ, that I might learn what Christ is—so, too, you are given the opportunity, in each moment, in each situation, to be the hands of Christ, to be the feet of Christ, to be the voice of Christ, to be the gentleness in the eyes, the laughter, the embrace, the tear. *You* are the one that your brother and sister can see because they yet believe that only the body is real. And I can be walking (or shall we say gliding) down the street next to them, shouting in their ear, "Beloved friend, I'm right here, I'm right here, I'm right here," and they can have a thousand images in their mind,

> *I just had a thought of Christ, I just had a thought of Christ, but that can't be real, because only bodies are real.*

I've been shouting till I'm blue in my non-physical face, but *you* cannot be denied, *you* who have yet a little while in the experience of embodiment, *you* are the one who can stand before a brother or sister as the embodiment of the Truth and teach only Love.

Nothing can be received until it is offered and that is your only purpose. You are not responsible for the reception of Love but for its extension, and by extending it you keep it for yourself. And it grows and it grows and it grows and it grows and it carries the very spark of Divinity that you are, beyond all worlds, beyond all dimensions—which are, by the way, infinite, so I hope you hear what I'm saying to you—your own Love will carry you beyond what is infinite and is infinitely created, that makes you pretty darn good... Hm?

And I come not alone, for there is one that you have known who also comes with me whenever I join to do this work through this my beloved Brother, who comes with me wherever I go, in whatever creative work I seek to ease illusions from the minds of my brothers and sisters. That one that you have known as "Saint" Germain—I do not give him such honor, he is just my friend Germain—rest assured we are what you call bosom buddies, though we have no bosom!

[Laughter]

Therefore nothing gets in the way. And he is here now. Well, after all, levity is good in the Kingdom. It's made of light, so how could it be serious? Indeed, this is just to let you know that that one is indeed my brother and friend. I met him once a long time ago, while he was in body and I was in body and I have spoken of that in another time and place, but rest assured, let us just say for now that he was present at what you call my Crucifixion, though you should be able to tell by now that the world failed to get rid of me. He was present and he was not on what you would call the "good side," until in a moment we made eye contact and he used that context to awaken. And from that moment he went on to create several incarnations to learn mastery of many things and is indeed my equal in all things. And from that moment, in an ancient land far, far away and long in the past, we have been joined as loving brothers and that bond will never be broken.

The point of sharing that story with you is this: Where Love has been allowed to join two minds, or souls, separation is no longer possible, for Love has healed the illusion. Bodies come and go but Love joins you with the beloved. Because this is true, waste not a moment, those of you that long to join with your brothers and sisters. Love in each moment and you have healed the gap and restored the perfect remembrance of what is true always. And you will transcend the great horror and suffering that the illusion of separation is, and you will know that when you have loved, wherever that being goes through infinite dimensions, *you are with them and they with you* and no gap exists. And after all, isn't that what you try to do with your bodies? Get so close there's no more gap, and you call it "making love"? Hm. *Would you choose to close the gap between yourself and the whole of Creation, so that in your consciousness constantly there is only the revelation of Oneness?* Take my word for it—it's worth it. For nothing can elevate the heart and the soul into such celebration as the experience of living Oneness! And

Oneness comes when *you* close the gap by blessing the one in front of you with the Love of Christ. They're stuck with you forever!

Therefore when I said, "I am with you always" . . . you get the picture!

[Laughter]

Some of you have occasionally wished that I wasn't.

[Laughter]

And some of you have argued with me and said, "Where did you go? Where did you go?" Beloved friends, I have gone nowhere, it is you that went—into fear, into contraction, into drama. Perfectly okay, if that's what, shall we say (what do you call it?) lights your fire. But rest assured, I retract from no one who has ever once prepared a place for me, which simply means: I loved them and they received me. [Snaps fingers] Separation gone, unity restored, never to be broken again.

If you could say that there may yet be something in me that I long for—it's not quite accurate, however we'll use it—what I long for is for you to give yourself permission to experience yourself as I experience you. That's all. For then, O beloved friends, then *what we can create together knows no boundary or limitation*. What we can experience together in the fields of creativity, in the dimensions of Creation, is pure unbounded, unlimited, ongoing, deepening bliss. We can create together the good, the holy, and the beautiful forever and ever and ever and ever. That's the meaning of "singing God's praises in Heaven."

If you will join with me by recognizing that you are Christ, if you'll join with me by blessing me, by loving me, by being the one who looks upon Jeshua ben Joseph and says,

> *Beyond your dumb ideas of crucifixion—why you ever did that I don't know—but I know that you're Christ and I love you anyway.*

When *you* make the decision to turn the tables and be the savior who comes to heal your brother Jeshua ben Joseph, when *you* come to look upon *me* and realize you're Christ looking at a brother who longs to know Christ, O my friends, then we can join!

When I am your Beloved, as you are mine, the sacred dance of unity will carry us far beyond all imagined worlds and together we will create that which extends the good, the holy, and the beautiful, so brightly, so creatively, so magnificently, so simply, that the hour and day must certainly come when every mind in every dimension has perfectly awakened.

You, then, are in charge of the Atonement. And frankly, I think God has given the assignment to someone perfectly capable of it: you, all of you. How could it be? *How could it be that you are here now if you did not already know the Truth that sets all things free?* What could have the power to make you be in this room, hanging out with an old brother who has no body, unless you already knew? How could you recognize that I am who I say I am unless you were already awakened to the Truth that is true always:

> *I am that Shining One.*

If you weren't awakened to it, rest assured you'd be somewhere else on this planet, simply because nothing happens by accident. It could very well be that at some level of the soul you've already been in communication with me and said,

> *You know, I would like to hang out with you and I'm going to use this context to choose to be awake. Why not? Tried everything else!*

So. By the way, just as an aside, there is no one in this room that did not also know me in that incarnation that has become so famous. I'm not saying that you were in embodiment at the time. You'll have to figure that one out for yourself. But there is no one in this room who did not know me in that time frame in which I was embodied, went through some learning lessons and got famous.

[Laughter]

Participant: Are you saying you're.... [then indistinct]

Indeed. I'm also saying within the great stream of the dream of Creation everyone in this room, shall we say, at least had their attention turned to the events that were unfolding, were quite aware of what was going on, whether you were in body or not. A few of you were looking through the window, but *all of you* have known me before. Not just as this soul or this spark of Divinity but you've known me as I took on the embodiment and became the man known as Jeshua ben Joseph. So here we are again, family gathering.

And all of you abide within what I'll describe here as a stream of energy that I like to call "the Lineage," a specific kind of strand, if you will, that carries a certain vibration, certain characteristics, certain beings that are within it, that have actually created it. That lineage goes back a long ways. It involves myself, it involves you, it involves— no I won't do it!—Germain . . .

[Laughter]

. . . it involves the one that was known as Mary, many countless others, all have awakened to the vibration of Christed Consciousness within themselves and realized that there's nothing else to do but extend Love to any mind that will receive it, thereby giving them the invitation to step into the remembrance that they are Christ. There's nothing beyond Christed Consciousness; it already enfolds all things, and you are That. Hm. There . . . Good.

Beloved friends, turn gently then, from the roar and din of the world that you believe you have made in error and know that you have never been capable of error, but you, out of your Divine greatness, have chosen to take on the sins of the world. That is, you've chosen to experience what it's like to perceive oneself in separation in order to understand dimensions of illusion, dimensions of suffering; to enfold within your being all possibilities. Why? Because your compassion is infinite and unbounded.

And you have not suffered because you've failed. You've suffered because you looked upon a tiny little planet, floating in a certain dimension, in which separation was being played out and your compassion brought you here, to learn of this world, to master this world, to take it in and know what it's like so that when you look into the eyes of a brother or sister and say, "I love you," they know that you know what you're talking about. No one can fool you, can they? When another says, "I'm suffering," you can say,

> *I know. I took it on once myself. I know that dimension and* I am arisen—*and because the ascension has been completed in me, the same power is in you.*

It is only by taking on "the sins of the world"—perceptions of separation—that you become the vessel, the vehicle, that is large enough to embrace any suffering that comes along the pike. And at a soul level, when you look into the eyes of another and say,

> *Yes, I know that you're suffering—and I love you. I know the Christ lives in you,*

... at a soul level *they* know that you're not what you call "talking out of your hat." They know that you know because you've been there; and that is why I did what I did. Anybody can hang out in seventeen dimensions beyond this planet and talk about Love. And those that have fallen into illusion say, "Well yes, well come down here and try it out." Hm?

I came down here for the same reason you did: out of the infinite compassion of Christ, so that I could embrace all of my brothers or sisters and help them to uplift themselves back to the place from which they've never fallen. You're doing it, right now—*you*, in the very life you're living! You, out of *your* Christedness, out of *your* compassion, have opened yourself and called forth all manner of experiences so that *you* could wrap yourself around this dimension and enfold it in your love. That's all you're doing here. So give yourself some credit. Never again entertain the thought that you have failed! You are the one that looked with tears upon this dimension and said,

"I'll go." I mean, after all, I'm not even willing to do that again! You are! You are that one! You are the embodiment of the Savior! You are the one sent forth from the Mind of God, you are the one that has been willing to feel it all, to experience every dimension of suffering *just so you could heal it*! And thereby demonstrate that *the Truth is true always and only Love is real.*

So there, now you know what you've been doing! Give yourself some credit, for though through the eyes of the body it looks as though things may be hopeless, rest assured, the heat has been turned up by all of you and there's a point where the water has no longer a choice but to boil and turn to steam. Hm? The train is pulling into the station because *you* have been willing to wrap yourself around this world in your own beingness and heal it with Love—you, just as you are, right where you are. Everyone in this room is actively fulfilling their function.

So before you go to bed tonight, go to a friend and simply say,

> *What a good boy am I—or girl. I'm doing such a marvelous job, and now I'm going to go to sleep and just go off in my dream and see who needs a touch of Grace. I'm not going to go to sleep to try to dream and solve my problems—I don't have any! I'm going to go to sleep and deliberately choose, by intention, to let this body sleep and allow my spirit to find a heart that needs to be blessed.*

Do that and you might find yourself having some interesting conversation over breakfast.

So. Therefore, indeed, we have babbled at you long enough. The message has been given. Has it been received? So, we're going to do something we've never done before. Since you now know that you are Christ and I'm just your brother, put it into practice and take a moment and think on the one you dare to call your friend, Jeshua ben Joseph, and in your own mind, and in your own being, simply say to me,

> *Jeshua, I bless you with the Love of Christ that I am.*

[Short pause]

Rather fun, isn't it? Don't you immediately feel lighter? More expanded? Isn't there a part of you that knows that's the Truth? Therefore when next you set up an altar, whether individually or the next time some of you will choose to gather as a group, make it a point to *also bring a picture of yourself*. And if you really want to have some fun, cover up my picture with yours. And start your morning meditations by honoring those pictures. Indeed.

And if you can convince those that run the big stone buildings and brick buildings around the planet that have this funny emaciated image of me hanging on a cross, would you *please* tell them to take them down? I find them to be rather embarrassing. So it was a learning experience that may not have been necessary—it was my choice! Don't need to make such a big deal of it! I suppose every Christ must have a flaw.

[Laughter]

So, I long for the day when beings gather in those brick and stone buildings and sit there and say,

Why are we here? Well, since we can't remember, we might as well have a good dance.

[Laughter]

Then I will know I've succeeded. Indeed!

So, how are you all doing? Has it been worth your *time*? It hasn't been worth mine; I don't have any.

[Laughter]

But rest assured, the opportunity, *the opportunity* to think up a creative way to join with you, to be received by you, to have an opportunity to love you by activating thought that vibrates vocal chords, that transmits something to you that allows our hearts to join as they have countless times, in countless other ways... Indeed, beloved friends, oh yes! It has been worth my while, for you are my treasure, you are my joy, you are my blessing and my beloved. *You are the one who shows me my Father, and how can I do less than love you forever for what you give to me? And indeed, I am with you always.*

So, there are a few of you that feel a question *burning deep in your soul.* This is what we're going to do: I'm not going to engage them right now. I want you, whether you believe it or not, to accept that you are Christ. Therefore, just before you lay your head on the pillow, begin by acknowledging:

> *I and my Father are one, there are no barriers to the depth of wisdom within me. Therefore now, in this moment, I ask this question and I receive the answer. So be it.*

See what comes. Then tomorrow, we will set aside just a short time, and I would be most pleased to, shall we say, pop back into your presence and we'll see if there are really any questions left that still require that the answer be given through something and someone that seems to be outside of yourself. Fair enough?

[Audience agreement]

Good.

Therefore love you one another, as the Father has first loved all of us. Look with graciousness and gentleness. Look with appreciation upon the mystery of the moment in which you find yourselves with one another, for it is the power of your Love that brings you unto one another. *Love you one another and you are the Light that lights this world and redeems it from all illusion.*
Be you therefore at peace this day—be you therefore at peace eternally—precious and holy and ancient friends.

Amen.

GRACE AS REALITY
May 1994

Now, we begin.

And greetings unto you, beloved and holy Children of Light Divine. In truth it is with great joy that I come forth to abide with you in this hour, even as you have chosen to come forth and abide with me. Know then, that always I come forth with great joy and I come forth from that place that is of Light and of Truth and of Joy, a place of unconditional Love beyond all boundary, beyond all limitations. I come forth from the place that is already prepared for all of us, given lovingly by the One Who has sent us forth, and that One I have called Abba, or Father, and that One—and that One alone—knows you and holds you, embraces you and feels thankfulness *for you*, because you are indeed the Creation of God.

You are the offspring of Light Divine, and if you are that offspring, and I assure you that you are, the reality of the essence of who you are *is but Love*. For if you are made in the image of our Father, Who Is but Love, then surely you too are that Light and are that Truth and are that Presence, and you are therefore the Word made Flesh that has come to dwell among mankind—not to judge mankind, but to look lovingly upon all illusions, and by taking the hand of your brother and sister, to gently lead them from darkness to Light. Not because *you know* where Light is, but because you have become willing to *allow* life to be lived through you with every word and every breath, with every action—so that life becomes translated from a struggle to survive, from an attempt to work out your salvation, or what some would call your karma (I believe the word is), and to begin to embrace that life is given unto you freely and completely and wholly, and if it were not given in this way, in this moment *you would cease to exist*.

Therefore, if you find yourself listening and hearing words spoken now, rest assured, it is because life is given to you—not *earned,* but *given*—given with perfect freedom from a Love beyond comprehension, a Love that knows no boundaries, a Love that was there before time began and will be there with you long after time has ceased to be. Here and now, as we gather in this moment, the same opportunity is given unto us that is given unto the creation of God—His Children,

His Son—in each and every moment. In each and every moment of experience, the same opportunity is given to you as was given to me then, when I once walked upon this Earth, and *is continually* given unto me.

What is that opportunity? Is it not to set aside the perceptions born of the illusions of this world, born of fear and doubt and guilt and judgment, and to embrace with great simplicity the only Truth and only Reality that has ever been? And what is Real cannot be threatened and what is unreal does not exist. And that which alone is Real is the Love that God Is, and the Love that brings you forth as a great Ray of Light that would shine in what could be called darkness, which is only a temporary forgetting of Truth. Therefore, understand well that while we gather in this one little building, in this one little town, on this one speck of earth, which is but a small spinning sphere in a grand universe (and this grand universe is but one of many upon many, upon many, in a multitude of dimensions)—*here* we have an opportunity to choose to set aside all judgment and to hear only the Voice of Love that unites us as One, as brother and brother, as brother and sister, as sister and sister, as the only begotten Child of God.

That is the opportunity that I came, then, to extend unto mankind. It is the opportunity that I ceaselessly extend to every mind that would but turn from the roar and the din of the world for just one Holy Instant: to seek the place of quiet and calm inside in which there is laid upon the altar of the Heart your judgments, your fears, your ideas of what the world is and what it is for; to surrender all things and to throw open the shutters of the Heart to once again become vulnerable and open and to merely ask of me,

> *I have prepared a place, come and enter therein.*

And indeed I will do so, not as a saviour above you, but always and only as your brother and as your friend.

I am your friend, because a friend in ancient times was not a word, you see, taken lightly. A friend was one who was committed to seeing past any illusions, any doubts, any fears; not to not see them, but to see through them and beyond them to the great ray of Light that shines forth from the mind of Christ that dwells within you as your only Reality, and to abide with you and to hold you in that Light until you have the strength to hold yourself in it as well. Therefore when I say I come as your brother and as your friend, rest assured, I come to celebrate the reality of your Beauty, your Joy, your Truth, your Radiance, your Wisdom. I come forth to *join* with you, never to be apart from you and never, certainly, to be above you. And those of you who have felt some kinship with me, some devotion to me, rest assured that I am worthy of it only to the degree that I am devoted to you. I am devoted to you always and eternally.

I love you. I love you because I know who you are. I know that within you that great Ray of Light shines eternally and has never been dimmed by the experiences of the world. I love you because in you do I know that which I am; and when I look upon you and see naught but the face of Christ, I realize that Christ is the essence of my own being.

I came into this world as a Light unto the world. Does this make me different than you? Some of you in your religions have been taught that I came forth from the Mind of God to save you, that I was the only begotten Son of God—and I guess that makes you His adoptees if you choose Him.

[Laughter]

Nothing could be further from the truth. I came forth from the Mind of God exactly as you have come forth, and the life that I lived then, in all essential details, is the same as yours—for in the field of space and time, given a body that knew hunger, that had to deal with cold and all of the rest of it, I experienced everything that you have ever experienced, just as each of you have experienced everything that the one sitting next to you has experienced. You all know the same fears, you all know the same doubts, you all know the same visions, the same dreams. All of you know that somewhere within you there is a Grand Being who rests in perfect innocence.

I came forth to celebrate the Truth and to demonstrate it to a world that had seemed to have forgotten it; to demonstrate that life is eternal and that death is unreal; to demonstrate that in all situations— *all* situations—all power is given unto the Holy Son of God to choose the Voice for Love over judgment and fear; that there is a place within all of us, a place of purity and innocence, a place that remains perfectly guiltless, for God creates only in His image and what He creates reflects the purity of His eternal Love forever. I came forth to extend my hand and to say,

"Come. Come to where I am. Join with me in becoming the demonstration that there's another way of looking at everything. Join with me in the demonstration that Love heals all things. Join with me in being willing to be in the field of space and time and yet to hold vigilance over the mind so that you do not allow it to become absorbed by the energies, the frequencies, the thought patterns, the perceptions that make up this world… To instead, through vigilance, to learn the power of choice can never be taken from you and that no matter the circumstances, you hold the Light in you to choose the Voice for Love, to choose peace instead of turmoil, safety instead of fear and insecurity and doubt that within you lies a wisdom so deep that already it outshines all worlds and looks far beyond this mere body, and that there is indeed within you the Light that knows that you've not come to suffer the world, you've come to be joyous, to express the joyousness that Love is, to look into the eyes of your brother and sister and to see that they are your savior! They are the ones who have brought to you the opportunity to look past the thoughts of the world and to see the face of Christ. And the great thing is, of course, that it takes one to know one."

[Laughter]

And many of you, many of you in your journeys through space and time—and tonight we won't resort to talk of what you would know by the term of reincarnation (it's really not essential to the process of waking up) but all of you, even in this life, know the feeling of feeling separate from God, all of you know the feeling of *searching*,

Perhaps if I go just to that other workshop over there,

and then when a group of friends come and say it was the most incredible experience, you feel lost, you go,

My God, I should have gone, when's the next time?

[Laughter]

Is that really much unlike friends who come and say, "Have you been to the new pizza diner down the road yet? It was so incredible."

Oh my God, I have to go and have that pizza...

[Laughter]

All of you know that energy of seeking, and doubting that you have the power to find. But always and forever, the truth remains this: The Kingdom of Heaven is within you. Will you then dissect the body to find it? Of course not. For if you would well receive it, the body you seem to carry does not house you; you house the body. It arises from within you and within the choices you have made in your access to the infinite Mind that Christ is. You have chosen, therefore, the body, this time frame; you have chosen it. It has not been forced upon you by any means.

The Kingdom of Heaven is indeed within you. It lies as a jewel, placed gently on the altar of the Heart—with a capital—the Heart whose first beat came from the breath that God breathed into it, long before there were ever such a thing as a body. The Kingdom lies within the 'you' that you have constructed out of your experiences and out of all of the beliefs and ideas that you have garnered in your journey through time and space. Within all perceptions, within all constructs that the mind holds, the Kingdom is found. Silence is the threshold to this Truth Divine.

How then to come to silence? Some of you know well what it means to master the flow of the breath, to chant little words in your mind.

Some of you know what it means to take substances called drugs to try to make yourself silent, or perhaps enough food and television might do it. Hm?

[Laughter]

The Soul yearns for silence, because the Soul knows that silence is the doorway, the threshold, that merges you with the Kingdom of Heaven. Silence is the threshold in which the voice, the guidance of the Holy Spirit comes, perhaps as a voice, loud and clear, perhaps as an intuitive nudge, perhaps as a quiet knowingness—and you all know that place.

But how to come to silence? In the end there is no technique that accomplishes it; that would make silence *conditional*. Does that make sense to you? If it takes a technique to become silent, it means that without the technique silence is impossible, and therefore silence is conditional; and what is conditional has no part in the Kingdom.

Silence waits, just as Love does, on our welcome.

It is a silence that is not artificial. It does not simply mean that the heart slows down, and the breath slows down and you don't move a muscle. It doesn't mean just turning off the television or putting the book away. Silence, the silence that speaks of the Divine and whispers it gently to the part of you that has always remained Divine, that silence requires only your willingness to lay upon the altar of the Heart every perception you have ever held about anyone or about the world, every perception and belief that you cling so rigidly unto, thinking that it's going to keep you safe, that it's going to show you how to get through this life. Silence comes when the mind is truly willing to relinquish its attachment to the world that it has made, the world of its experience, the world of its thoughts. Silence comes, then, always as the result of a simple choice, and the more often that choice is made, the simpler it becomes, and in the end, silence becomes what you could call pervasive in the mind, so that although you walk and talk seemingly in this world, there is a core within of Perfect Silence, of Perfect Light, and though you speak and hear others speak to you, though you get up in the morning and make the breakfast so you can feed the body, though you do all things, there is a place of perfect Peace and it comes as the result of being willing, over and over again, to relinquish your beliefs and your perceptions about the world, to look upon the body and say,

> *I don't know what this is. I don't know what it's for! I've certainly known how to misuse it, but I don't know what it is.*

I look about and I see this world with buildings and what you call your automobiles. I must admit, they're a little better than walking on foot and riding on donkeys. But do you really know what these things are, and where they've come from, and what purpose they *can* serve? You know well what the world would ask them to serve but what purpose can all these things that have been manifested, what *can* they serve?

I say unto you that those very questions are not unlike the questions that I, too, as a man, had need of coming unto—to look upon my brothers and sisters, to look upon the great teachers and the friends that I was blessed with, upon even the parents that I was blessed with, to look upon the tumult of the time frame in which I walked upon this earth, to journey into the desert, to get away from all the noise, even the noise of my own thoughts, and to ask of my Father,

> *What's it for? How would you have me use it? What purpose would you extend unto me?*

And I was taught that the body itself has been created in error. It is—in a sense—it has been created to house the ego, to create and to give forth the symbol, and therefore the belief, that separation exists, because (everybody knows it) if you look upon another one as a body, you *know* there's a distance between you. That is evident, through the body's eyes.

But there is another eye, another way of seeing that looks well beyond the body and sees that all minds are joined eternally and that you've never looked upon a thing called a stranger. Know you that word?

Eliminate it from your vocabulary because it is a lie. You have never looked upon a stranger, for you see reflected only yourself. And as you see your brother or sister, you will see yourself and as you know them, you will know yourself. To look upon another with judgment means that you have judged yourself and created separation from God. To look upon another with forgiveness, with softness, with gentleness, and with love means that you are willing to look upon that truth in yourself. The body, then, becomes translated into this and this alone. The body becomes translated through the choice of relinquishing your own perceptions of the world into only this: a means for communicating Love, and that is all.

Now, that's a little different than what the world would teach you. Your world would teach you that the body is something that you can gather to yourself joy, pleasure, fulfillment, you name it. I want to share with you this night that if you take but one thought with you and make it your own, carry this thought:

The body can bring you nothing. The body cannot bring you what you seek, because it is not found there. It cannot bring you intimacy, it cannot bring you union, it cannot bring you Joy with a capital J. It will bring what the body calls pleasure, perhaps. The pleasure arises in time, and what starts in time ends in time—and you all know what that feels like. The ice cream is delicious until you realize that the container is empty.

[Laughter]

The body... The body can bring nothing to you. But thank God, through Grace, the body *can* become the means through which you learn to extend what you possess eternally—Love. So that each gesture, each touch, each smile, is a very conscious and deliberate choice to be the one who allows Light to shine forth and to enlighten the world, to allow your brother and sister to become your savior and your salvation, to begin the practice of realizing that every opportunity you see is given to you so that the Holy Spirit can ask you,

> *Well, what choice are you going to make this time? Love or fear, peace or judgment, extension or contraction, giving or the insane attempt to take?*

The body is either the symbol of separation and pain or it becomes the temple of the living Spirit. And that is all that little phrase once meant. It's where the body becomes solely the means for communicating Love, and nothing else; it becomes the servant of the awakened Heart and the enlightened Mind. Now I know it's probably true that no one in this room has ever misused the body...

[Laughter]

Would you be willing to lay even the body down upon the altar of the Heart, to surrender it back to the Source of your creation, and to hold the thought,

> *You know, I really never have known what this thing is or what it's for. I pamper it, I feed it, I do what I think is going to get me some pleasure through it. I clothe it in the winter and I unclothe it in the hot heat of the summer. But I've never known how to truly use it, how to bring peace to the cells of the body, how to allow an integration of the body, the emotions, and the mind. Perhaps there's another way of looking at the body itself.*

And there is. The body will reflect for you always the choice you are making between Love and fear, between joining and separating, between forgiveness and judgment.

Know you that experience where you walk into a room of perfect strangers and something somewhere in the room just doesn't feel very good? It's like you're picking up a little vibration and you turn around and there's someone standing on the other side of the room. You've never laid your physical eyes on them but somehow you know that you'd just as soon avoid them? Have you had that kind of experience, feeling the energy of someone and feeling repelled by it somewhat? They haven't said a word, they haven't even *looked* at you yet, but there's a *knowingness*—remember, you never look upon a stranger!

And have you not also had the experience of being around someone who seems to radiate light so much that, no matter what's going on, just to *think* about them seems to *enlighten* your spirit, to bring you a sense of joy, and when you lay your physical eyes on them, somehow the weight of your daily life is suspended and you feel joy. Have you had that experience?

To the degree that one's mind has become corrected so that the body is not used to house old judgments and old fears and old angers, and it is not used to look upon other bodies as having something that this body can gain, but as correction comes to the mind and the mind becomes enlightened, so too must the body follow. The cells of the body begin to vibrate in a different way; emotional and even physical toxicity is released; the body becomes clearer and clearer and clearer. It becomes a vehicle that radiates Light to various degrees, and that is what you're feeling. What you're feeling through the body of that one is really the reflection of what has occurred in the mind. And the body of one who, shall we say, is what you might call a master is simply the body that has become so perfected that it becomes *as Light* because there's no trace in the mind left of judgment or fear or doubt, there is only the unconditional Love that God Is.

And what I want to share with you is—as you look down at your thighs and your feet and your hands—that bag of dust that you have identified with as being you, is not you. It comes to you from the dust of the ground, it is given to you by your Holy Mother, this precious Earth, and its one purpose and function—its *only* purpose and function—has been to be the vehicle through which Christ extends Light and Love; that's all. It has never been designed to bring pleasure or joy to the mind who thinks it is separate from God.

So you see, that is why I said: If you just take one thought home with you tonight and make it your own, you'll find that it will present a pathway for you of much learning and much revelation. If you hold the thought, as you wake up in the morning, and you raise your hands up and look at them, go, *these are only for giving Love and extending Light.*

... and as you walk with your feet upon this Earth, each step you take, you simply hold the thought,

I step so I that can carry this body in its journey in which Light and Love are extended, and that is all.

... what you'll find is that a myriad of things will begin to crop up in your awareness, and you'll see how the mind has been utilizing the body, at least at times, in error. And as those conflicts come up, your awareness brings Light to the conflict and correction comes.

To give you an example: You might be feeling just a bit depressed, or down or lonely or whatever, and so you call your best friend and say, "Let's go to that pizza diner down the road."

And of course what you're really wanting to do is to escape the feeling of conflict that's going on in you. And so you call your friend and they say, "Well, really I was kind of busy, right..."

"Oh no, please. Please come, please come!"

What you're really saying is: "Look, I need you to come fill my hole, okay?"

So you call your friend and they go, out of guilt they say, "Well okay, I'll come, I'm not really hungry. I just got done eating, but oh what the heck, what's another pizza?"

Because you see, you've also learned in this world that you always have to *accommodate*. It's not okay just to say no and stand in your own truth. So you get together and you go to the pizza diner and you're feeling better because now you've been able to kind of cover up that inner feeling, and after three or four slices of pizza, you're becoming numb to the whole thing anyway, and you raise a bunch of conversation with the friend.

And then you remember,

> *Wait a minute, when I got up this morning, I held the thought that this body is only for the extension of Light and Love.*

And if you're quite clear and honest and innocent with yourself, without judgment, you look and you see the whole pattern of thought that brought you to the diner, sitting across from your friend, ostensibly wanting to be with them when you know darn well that there was a conflict, something going on in you, an energy that you didn't want to feel, didn't want to deal with, and you needed it to be masked. And you look upon your friend and you realize,

> *I've just abused them.*

And you look in their eye and you say, "You know, I need your forgiveness. I didn't come here to be with you. I asked you to come here to save me from something that's going on in me. I just was feeling really restless and out of touch and alone. Help me."

Now, two things have just happened. You've allowed correction to come back to your mind; you've brought honesty to what's really going on. And that's good, because you can't transcend what you fail to embrace; it goes on and on and on forever. And the other thing that happens is this: You've relinquished the pattern or the energy in the mind, you've laid it out on the table, you're not hiding anything; you've made yourself vulnerable to your friend.

And now something very special can happen, because you have provided your brother or sister with exactly what they're looking for, whether they know it or not: the opportunity to join with you in Holy Relationship. For you have extended unto them the opportunity to give forgiveness, to relinquish any feelings or judgments or resentments (because, remember, they were already full anyway)— to set it all aside, to smile, to join with you sitting across the table in a pizza diner of all places, it becomes a sacred temple in which the Holy Children of God join together and look innocently upon one another and laugh at the ego. And perhaps you extend your hands to one another, and you clasp your hands and you look into their eyes; and suddenly the very energy that was going on in you, that seemed to compel you into the whole series of events that got you and your friend at the diner, that conflict dissolves.

What's occurred? A miracle's occurred, the miracle of a Holy Instant that corrects all things. And you realize that your brother and your sister is indeed the means to your salvation. And in each moment that you are willing to set aside the masks, the ideas of yourself, the fears, the judgments—all the momentums of the mind trying to find its own way in this world and just lay it at their altar, and join with them, and see only Love—to become wholly vulnerable, you begin to see that,

> *My God, this isn't just my friend who I happened to meet three weeks ago. Christ is in front of me! For Christ's sake!*

[Laughter]

And you see in that moment the miracle of the Atonement has occurred, you have been lifted out of the perceptions of the world and a very ordinary occurrence has become extraordinary and blessed forever. And you have joined with your friend in a way that no physical intimacy has ever gotten anybody. And all it took was the willingness to look with the eyes of Christ, the willingness to be vulnerable, to set aside all perceptions and judgments, to just be straight and honest.

It's very much like saying, "You know, I keep having to face the fact that I don't know who I am or what the world is for."

And your friend says, "Oh thank God, I can relax now! 'Cause you see, I don't know either!"

[Laughter]

And then you can join together, and then you can ask, in your momentary prayer—and if you don't quite have the courage to be outrageous, you won't stand on the table at the diner yet—you'll just sit there quietly looking at each other and you'll simply ask the Holy Spirit to bring that correction to the mind so that it becomes more firmly established.

And in this way, almost unbeknownst to you, miracles come to replace the struggle and the strife of life. You become very, very humble because you realize none of your perceptions have ever been true or accurate, except the ones inspired by the gentleness of Love that is totally inclusive of all of Life and embraces unconditionally everyone and everything.

In that moment—and you've all experienced at least a few of those moments—Peace comes. Peace, a peace that passes all understanding and could never hope to be explained in the languages of this world. And that Peace bespeaks a way of living that is available to everyone at all times, a way of living that requires no planning in the way the world would think of this, no striving, no doubt, no anxiety; a way of living that flows gently, in which you smile a little bit more often, in which you talk a little bit less; a way of living that is marked by Grace. And Grace that is lived will reveal to you your true reality. Grace, when fully lived, reveals to you that *you* are the only begotten of God, Christ Eternal, unbounded forever, and that you participate in that Mind, in that Energy, in that Love—call it what you will—with me and with every mind, every brother and sister who's ever chosen to set aside the world and to allow the Kingdom to be lived from within.

Grace. The word itself is so powerful. It speaks of something that comes, it is wholly given, and can never hopefully be earned. No dance you could ever dance could ever earn you a smidgen more of Grace, and Grace descends gently upon you even now, fully in every moment. Grace is available to every mind and every heart that would but choose to receive it, to remember the truth of the Kingdom and to set aside the beliefs of the world:

> *Love is the nature of my being; Father, I receive it. Do with me what You will; I've never known what to do with me anyway!*

Grace As Reality

Grace. Grace brings a gentleness to all of your activities. Grace brings a peace. Grace brings that Light that can flow through you in this moment, if you would but allow it. Grace, given fully by God unto His only creation: *you*! You are the one in whom the Father remains well pleased. You are the one—*you* are the one—who has come forth into *this* time frame, just as I came forth into a different one, for only one purpose: to demonstrate the truth that the world is *not real* and holds no power over God's creation; that the world that would try to get you to judge, try to get you to hold on to ideas and beliefs about what is and what should be and what shouldn't be and what ought never have been, all of that stuff, the world will try to get you to believe that judgment is justified, that forgiveness must be given cautiously. Hm! It is not forgiveness when it's given cautiously. Grace is the truth that will completely reverse the ideas that you have held in the mind and bring correction completely unto you. It cannot be earned, you cannot strive for it, you can only be willing to allow it...

> *To allow it.*

I've said before that there's really only one curriculum that anybody ever needs to learn, and quite frankly, you don't have the freedom to decide not to learn it. You *do* have the freedom—and this is the freedom given unto you since before time is—you have the perfect freedom to decide *when* to learn it. Does that make sense to you?

> *Ha! Well, not today, Father. You see I have this gripe to pick with my brother. I'll get back to the curriculum tomorrow.*

And the Holy Spirit stands just on the other side and goes,

> *Huh, I thought you wanted to learn the curriculum, so I helped set up this whole affair so that you could extend Love to your brother with whom you think you have a gripe. Oh well, I'll just bring another one.*

[Loud laughter]

Do you know that experience? Something's repeating in my life—what is going on here? What have you not brought forgiveness to? What fear do you still hold on to? What judgment or perception are you unwilling to let go of, so that correction can come and you can be taught anew?

> *Ah, the curriculum. I and my Father are One, the Kingdom of Heaven is within, that which is real cannot be threatened and that which is unreal does not exist. The ego, which is my drama that I've been playing out and out and out, is nothing more than an illusory thought; it is like a gnat floating in the vastness of space. It holds no power, no function and no reality, but each time I listen to its voice I have left the Kingdom.*

That fast! And so the only curriculum, you see, is to choose to hear the Voice for Love, to be the vehicle of forgiveness.

The curriculum ends where the dream of separation began: as a thought. Now, think about this, as a *thought* held in the mind of the Son of God, one thought,

> *What would it be like to experience myself as separate from my Father?*

Voilà, the world!

[Laughter]

Hm! And you thought you had no power to create? Hm! I'll share another little thought, just to plant a seed, something to think about: God creates only what is changeless and right now, look around and see if you can see one thing with the physical eyes that is changeless. Hmm. Come up with anything?

What have you ever experienced through the body's senses, through the thoughts of the world, through all of your worldly experiences, what have you experienced that is changeless? Isn't that part of the frustration of the world—just when you think you've got it, it slips through your grasp? You meet the grand lover at a dance and three weeks later, they don't know your name.

[Laughter]

You sit down to the most scrumptious dinner you could imagine only to wake up the next day with a stomach ache, constipation or what have you, a headache. Or you embark on a career that you know:

> *This one's really going to give it to me. I know exactly what I want and this is gonna do it.*

And every time, or every so often down the journey, you realize somehow it's not quite taking you where you thought it was and other things are popping up instead; and sooner or later the career ends. The mate leaves, the cat or the dog dies, you *all* know these experiences, you've known them countless times. How often, when you've been met with that frustration that somehow you've tried to make something work and it hasn't worked, how often have you just run out and tried all over again?

> *That must have been the wrong choice. It must be this tree over here; I'll eat the fruit of this tree.*

Hm! Know you that experience? Some of you have done that very well with what you call your significant other relationships. You would change them as often as you would change your socks.

[Laughter]

All of it—and do continue to laugh, because all of it is an illusion. All of it emanates, if you would well receive it, from one thought held in the Mind of the Holy Son of God:

> *What would it be like to experience separation from God?*

With that thought, a dream began. And why is it a dream and not real? Because God only creates what is changeless and it is not possible that the Holy Son of God ever *be separate* from God—except in your perceptions and in your feelings and beliefs; it's the only place. Likewise, only in the thought held lovingly in the mind can your union be restored.

And with that one thought—of course this is a bit of a metaphor but it's rather effective—imagine a Light, shining forth from all eternity. It has no beginning and it has no end and you cannot see its boundaries or its end, And into this radiant Light, one mad idea crept: *separation from God!* And the Holy Son of God forgot to laugh and took on seriousness, and seriousness *empowers* thought. Know you when you think a negative thought? When you take it seriously, you are empowering that thought to manifest its reality. It is called fear.

The Holy Son of God chose not to laugh and in that moment [snaps fingers] what your scientists would call the Big Bang occurred and in which that Light exploded into seemingly an infinite number of points of light, all quite identical under the cosmic microscope but seemingly separate one from another. And each of those points of light, out of fear, and out of holding that one thought within itself, began to proliferate the fields of experience. It created *unlike* God, creating things that are forever changing, that forever slip through the grasp, and the most prime example is the body. It begins to sag no matter what you do. No matter how often you fast, you still need to eat. You can't seem to overcome the body's desire, the need for food; hunger always seems to come to it. It shudders when the temperature becomes too cold. It sweats when it gets too hot, it gets dirty and smelly. Know you those feelings, those experiences? The body is a prime example of a creation that is *unlike* God's.

And so it continued, dimension upon dimension. Time began, and out of the field of time continued density, and density is separation—the appearance of it—and eventually this physical world was made manifest. And upon it you've enacted countless journeys. Huh, my goodness gracious, the dramas that have been acted out! You've all been crucified a thousand times, you've all been the crucifier a thousand times—and why? Because you never look upon anybody but yourself, and if you look into the past of your history and you see a grand tyrant, rest assured that you are looking upon an aspect of that mind that was fragmented at the beginning of time. You are therefore looking upon an aspect of your own dream. Not a pleasant thought, is it? But it is very true. And that is why only Love heals. It is only Love that restores the Son to His rightful place. It is only Love that corrects the misperception of separation. It is only Love that corrects the uses of the body. When you look upon this world, and you see mirrored to you what can be called ego—but it's just called the ego as the perception of separation from God—when you look upon it in any of its aspects, when you look at, ahh what was the one... Saddam, hm? Now there's an aspect of ego, no sense denying it. When you look upon it with judgment, you have only ensured that it will continue. And you are all quite free and quite capable of thinking up a million other examples of expressions of the ego mind's living in separation. If you're really honest, I'm sure you can look inside yourself and come up with a few examples.

Love alone heals, and the way the ego, the way the dream, begins to dissolve is through the relinquishing of the power that you've given unto it, And when you look upon Saddam and feel angry with him, when you feel fear at what tyrants seem to be causing in the world, you have just decided to take it seriously and you believe that something in the field of ego—in my day it was called the 'evil one'—you believe that there are demons out there that can get you. And *you* are empowering them to continue, because all minds are joined. You have told them that their experience is real. Love heals and Love is extended through forgiveness, in the choice the mind makes to look past appearances and to see only the Light that shines there, waiting to be remembered and restored in the one before you.

Now, that sounds like a nice lofty thought, but is it true? I once chose, as a man, not because I was ordered by God—God doesn't order anyone to do anything—*I* chose to bring upon myself a demonstration that death is unreal, as a way of teaching my brothers and sisters that if you think of the most extreme circumstance you can, the opportunity to choose Love is always available. Rest assured, and I know perfectly well, that even if a tyrant ordered someone to strap you to a heavy wooden beam and to pound nails into your hands and feet, the power within you to choose Love has not been taken from you, in any stretch of the imagination.

And paradoxically, in the midst of even your most painful circumstances, when you make the choice to allow Love to descend first into your own being so that it can radiate out to everyone else concerned, you will feel the nails as though they were being withdrawn from your hands and feet. All of you know what it is like to be crucified in some way or another. All of you have felt that. All of you have had glimpses of the power of forgiveness and Love. When you just relinquished your beliefs, your anger, everything about a situation, what comes? Peace comes back. There have been times in some of your lives when some rather dramatic things have happened and it's got your kettle boiling, and all of a sudden you said,

> *Oh, the heck with it!*

And you changed your attitude and you actually *laughed!* What happened? You used the power of choice given unto you to remember the Truth.

Grace. Grace descends gently, like a soft spring rain, so gently that you don't even feel or hear the drops. There's no breeze, it just falls gently, so gently that you don't see it, and yet you are bathed in it constantly. Grace waits, as Love does, to be received by a heart that is finally willing to say,

> *You know, no matter how hard I've tried, I still find myself judging my brother, judging my sister. I still think I know what the world if for and how it ought to be. And I admit that—you know something?—I'm really not happy yet.*

Do you know that feeling? Something underneath that tells you:

> *Happiness is really not established in me yet. What still needs to change? Ah! A different relationship, a different career, a different pizza!*

[Laughter]

The world—all things that begin in time and end in time and are therefore changing—the world has never, ever, ever offered you anything that can restore you to the happiness that is rightfully yours. What would it mean if you were to go and sit on the corner of your street and just look at this town as a symbol of the world, look at the buildings, look at the automobiles, and just say,

> *This world means nothing. It gives me nothing, it takes nothing from me.*

It would begin to bring about discernment, the discernment between Truth and falsehood. And as you relinquish the value you've placed upon the things you hoped would bring you happiness and safety, you will discover that the place of safety is still within you and has been there since the moment when the Holy Son of God first held the thought,

> *What would it be like to be separate from my Father?*

Correction comes with relinquishing the world. Relinquishing the world does not have anything to do with living in caves and eating a grain of rice a day. It has everything to do with relinquishing your perceptions of what the world is for and allowing it just to be as it is, while you focus on choosing Peace, so that you become the center of Light that seems to walk around in a body. Do you know what begins to happen when you do that? You will quite literally open up what can be called an inner eye, and perception will be healed, and it feels like a very literal physical shift. You are taken away, if you will, from identifying as the body, and you literally see the body for what it is: a nothing, a momentary device through which the Light of Christ can extend Love; it's not even yours any more!

Yes, you'll continue to feed it, do the little things you need to do so that it can function as long as it lasts, but something quite literally shifts: it's not you any longer. And you'll look upon your relationships and upon your careers and they'll all be different! The world will have been swept clean from your mind. That will be replaced by the perception that you're the Holy Son of God, and you're here for a very short time, and each opportunity, each moment, is given unto you because the world is crying out for your blessings. Not the ego's blessings, "Yes, I bless you, my child." Hm. The world cries out for the blessings that you can extend to it by choosing peace, by smiling at the ego and the ways of the world, by being the demonstration that there is another choice, another way, another path.

Ahhh, Grace! Does Grace set the mind and the heart free? Oh yes! It has already done so. Salvation has already been completed and the Son is already restored, and time becomes translated. It becomes translated from your insane attempt to seek the happiness, the union with God. It becomes translated into the gentle explanation, if you will, the gentle demonstration that peace *has* been restored to you—and how do you know? Each time you extend peace to another, you must then understand that peace must have already been restored to you, for you cannot give what you do not possess. And so, by giving we receive.

I learned, just as each and every one of you are learning, to give all that you have received by Grace; and when you know that you are giving all, you will know that you have received all, and you will know that your Redeemer has awakened and arisen within you. And right where you are, Heaven is. For Heaven is not a place and it is not a condition. Heaven is the Real World in which the Son abides eternally with all that God Is—and *God Is but Love*.

Hmmm. Grace... Grace. There is a choice that each mind, each soul in its journey comes to and I've called this coming to the threshold of the Kingdom. How do you cross into it? Not by accepting me as your saviour, though I would be honoured if you accepted me as your friend and your brother, who would walk with you to God; frankly, because I see no point in walking any other place. Each of you has come to the threshold of the Kingdom of Heaven a million times—a million times. If you've chosen to set aside learning the curriculum, you've taken a detour. Hm? You said,

Oh yes, there's the pizza diner I want to get to...

and you made a right turn.

The way that the threshold is crossed is by laying aside your perception of yourself as a separate one who is *seeking* God, along with every other perception of yourself you've ever held, in which you become finally willing to acknowledge that *you have found*. Think about it. To acknowledge in your own mind,

> *No. No more games, I know the truth. I am the Son of God, I am therefore here only for the extension of Love and the world's games mean nothing.*

Think what it would mean to acknowledge that within yourself:

> *My God, I have set up a drama so that I can pretend to be a seeker again and again and again, so that I can avoid finding.*

And some of you like the game! That's okay, there's nothing wrong with liking it, and I hope you enjoy it. But in the end, seeking becomes like a weight upon the heart, and the soul in its weariness drops to its metaphorical knees—because obviously it doesn't have any—and it just says:

> *I'm tired.*

And it sets aside the weight of the world, and a Light begins to be remembered. Hmm. The echo of an ancient melody, at once so familiar but it seemed to be forgotten, begins to arise in the soul that has relinquished the world and returned to silence. And the thought comes to replace the one thought of separation—for upon it all worlds have been built, and all subsequent thoughts and dramas are nothing more than expressions of that one thought of separation—and an inner voice speaks these words:

> *You are my Beloved Son in whom I remain well pleased. Arise, for you are Christ.*

And then perception is healed and for the first time a major shift has occurred in your mind. And you know that it's time, and before the altar of God that rests in the silent sanctuary of your Heart, you have the audacity in the eyes of the world to finally exclaim the truth,

> *I and my Father are One and of myself I've never done anything, but now through me my Father will do all things. I am home and I am at peace. Truth is restored and I will go out no more from this holy place, for the light of day has come and all darkness is vanquished. I and my Father are One and it's never been any other way.*

Does that bring responsibility as long as you seem to live in time? Of course it does! It is a responsibility that the world has taught you not to take on. The world has actually taught you that *I'm* the only one who had the strength to assume that responsibility. Now isn't that a clever device of separation?

All power is given unto *you*, as the Holy Son of God, all power under Heaven and Earth to hear only the Voice for Love. It's a delightful voice, it speaks gently and it shows you the humour of your illusions. And if you would hear only that voice and acknowledge that you are One with God, that you're not sent to suffer the world—to live in lack, to live in poverty, to judge the world—you are sent to be a Light to the world, to show the world that its perceptions and beliefs don't cut it, to allow miracle- mindedness to descend upon you so that miracles can be lived and extended through you, given unto your brothers and sisters who have been given unto you that they might look upon the face of Christ and remember that they see only themselves.

Who, then, has ever honored me? Only those who have honored the Son that dwells in their own heart. Who honors me is the one who chooses to be joyous at all times. Who honors me? The one who laughs and sings and dances and plays and brings a new vision to this plane: a vision of *one family* under God, healed and restored, in which no one is left outside. Who honors me? You do, each time you choose to acknowledge,

Grace As Reality

> *Yeah, I know the truth. I hear you Jeshua, I know, I know, yeah. Okay, alright already— I get it!*

[Laughter]

And then you see, I *do* become your brother and your friend—because all minds are joined and that means *I am not unavailable to anyone in any situation.* I'm not limited in who I come and talk with. I'm one who likes to have a lot of friends and I will come into any mind and unto any heart that prepares the place for me. Does it take ten thousand lifetimes of flogging the body and fasting it, beating yourself up with guilt? *No!* It takes a simple choice:

> *Look, Jeshua, I too am the Son of God… uh, let's be friends!*

That's how the place in the heart is prepared: by acknowledging the truth! And when the door has been opened, just a crack, I will no longer need to knock upon the door but I will enter therein and take up my place with you—not as your savior, but as your friend and your brother who would only play with you joyously—and join with you in your willingness *to teach only Love,* because that is what you are. Each time the mind brings up a thought of judgment, you have separated yourself from God, pure and simple! There's no gray area there at all. Each time you look upon a judgmental thought and say,

> *Ha! Voice of the ego. Let it go. Look at your brother and extend only Love,*

you have chosen to demonstrate that you are in union with God.

So the choice seems simple—and it is. Do you know that energy that comes now and then in which you feel like it's a real struggle to remember Love? Hold this thought: The difficulty is never anything but your unwillingness to choose the Voice for Love. Resistance and difficulty is nothing more than a symptom that you've chosen, quite willingly, to hear a different voice. I know that's befuddling because the mind wants to say,

> *Well, I—but I'm doing so well, but then this situation arose and if this person hadn't done this, then I would still have chosen Love. If they would just get it straight, I could be straight.*

That's what keeps the world spinning! You thought it was Love—it's denial! Somebody has to do it differently. And you are that one. You are the one. It has not been given of me of my Father to be in this time frame as you are. I do not have what appears to be a body. And yet I have gone nowhere. I said once that I am with you always and I meant it literally. I am not absent to you at any time and I can be no further away than the width or distance of a thought, a simple choice. But it *is* given unto *you* to abide in a world that yet believes in separation and therefore sees the body as reality and time as the great authority. *You* are the ones that with every breath you breathe—you are the ones unto whom the power has been given to demonstrate the Real World. You! No special preparation, you don't have to stand on your head for half an hour every morning, you need only be willing to choose *not to tolerate error in your own mind—never*! No such thing as an idle thought! Each thought generates a world. Choose only the thought of Love and you become all that I ever was. You become the Word made Flesh, you become the Bearer of Light. Beloved friends, Grace is our only shared reality—Grace, and that alone.

You are not separate one from another, and you are not separate from me. Would you choose then, choose to allow this hour and this evening to be the point at which you decide to learn the curriculum? Right here and right now in your own beingness to say,

> *Okay, what the heck, I know I've got a few perceptions that seem to be blocking me from peace. I've held onto them for a long time; they haven't gotten me there yet. What have I got to lose? Maybe I should just set them aside.*

And allow—allow correction to come to the mind, to trust the safety of the Heart's vulnerability, to become filled with humility:

> *Of myself I do nothing. I don't know what a single thing is, but thank God my Father does! I don't even know what this situation*

> *is for, so I'm just going to be here as the Presence of Love, trust and allow it to unfold, knowing that there is one Teacher that has been given unto the world, the one that I have called the Comforter, who knows how to take everything that unfolds and weave it into the tapestry that awakens the Holy Son of God.*

Look lovingly upon every experience you have, for there is a purpose to it for you as well as for others. And every experience is the opportunity, the blessing to remember to choose Love, just like you did when you were sitting across from your friend in the pizza diner: "Oh, wait a minute! I brought you out here under false pretenses. I thought I *needed* something from you so I could hide from this conflict. But now that you're here I just want to love you!" And in that choice the conflict dissolves. And that moment, *that moment is the Atonement*! It's the moment that corrects the conflict that was set up in the beginning of time in which you seem to have been cast from the garden.

Can you begin to feel what I am seeking to share with you, then? That you do not experience ordinary moments!—there are no such things as ordinary moments, unless you forget they're extraordinary. That's what makes them ordinary: forgetting. Every moment, my God, is such a blessing! *The one before you brings you your salvation* if you would but love instead of judge them. Haaah. If that doesn't bring Light to the world, what can? To see that it doesn't mean what the world thinks it means. It's a dance and an illusion. It's a tapestry woven by One who would but bring the Peace of God back to your heart. You don't go to school to get a career so you can have a job! The soul is choosing to attract situations so that it can learn where it has failed to extend Love and to live from unlimitedness. That's all!

Just as you created your thought of separation, you as a soul are creating your pathway home. Nothing can arise by accident. And if you seem stuck right now for a while, it just means you're taking a break, a summer vacation. It's not that you *have* to take a break, it's that you're *choosing* to take a break.

Within you lies so much power! In the twinkling of an eye, the Holy Son of God could radically transform this world into the Kingdom of Heaven on Earth, but that can't occur until you allow that transition to occur within *you*, because, you see, the world, it's like a (what do you call those races where everybody thinks that if they can run thirty-five miles that it's a great feat of strength or something, so thousands of them gather in their senior cities straining to get to their...) marathon! Well, the world *does* seem like a marathon. All the crushing masses of humanity, straining at the starting line, waiting for somebody to pull the trigger to release all of this Divine Creative Energy! How long have *you* been waiting for someone to pull the trigger and tell you it's okay to get on with living an unlimited and joyous life?

> *Well I will as soon as everybody else does! What will they think of me if I give up pain and suffering and judgment and choose laughter and dance and play and joy? Will they think I'm crazy if I tell them, "Look! Hunger is old now, nobody on this planet needs to be hungry any more!"*

And they'll look at you and say, "Well it's always been that way, what are you talking, nonsense?"

Hm, no you're talking with great sense. Don't wait any longer. Look lovingly upon your own life. Look at your circumstances as something you've attracted to yourself and therefore it presents a blessing. Embrace it, honor it and then ask within and be really honest: Is this truly the life that the Son of God would choose to live if the Son of God was thoroughly awake? Hm! Interesting question! For you see it might be, and it might not be. It requires your willingness to surrender your perceptions of yourself and world. And if in your circumstances you can go inside and say,

> *I am at peace. I am where my Father is asking me to be. I don't complain about it; I don't make judgments; I'm just at peace. And there is a lightness to my step and there's a joy in my eyes no matter what the bank account says. I know I live in unlimitedness and if I only have a dollar today that's perfectly okay, because if I need ten*

thousand tomorrow, they'll be there!

And if you get in touch and inwardly you finally admit,

> *Who am I trying to fool? Who am I trying to be? Am I trying to pretend like I'm more spiritual than somebody else because I'm broke? Hm! Am I trying to believe or to express to someone that my suffering somehow is building me up? Do I look into the face of my brother and say, "Yeah, I'm really content," and then go home at night and inwardly feel something gnawing at me?*

Can you become so honest and just admit that you're living a lie? Can you say to yourself,

> *No, I'm not happy. There's something in me that wants to be lived and I'm pushing it down.*

Fear it no longer, for what you are pushing down is the Radiance of Christ that comes to enlighten and heal the world and to establish the Kingdom of Heaven upon it.

Is *any* of this making sense to you?

[Audience agreement]

Of course it is. I cannot say that I come as a grand teacher, I cannot come and say that I have much to give you that is going to make your life work marvelously, because, you see, I know that I cannot give you anything that you do not already possess. I admit it wholly, up front. I come only as your brother and your friend, to reflect to you the truth that you *know* in the depth of your being—in the depth of your being where the Real World resides and where the world can never possibly touch, and there is only safety to be found in being willing to let the power of the Mind of Christ to be lived through you, to no longer tolerate the errors of the thinking of the world and to demonstrate to your brothers and sisters through Love that there's always another way, always another choice, and that *nothing*— *nothing*—limits you, save the thoughts that you would choose to hold onto.

I said earlier that I do not have a body, but *you* do! And I know how to join with you. You don't have to know how, you only need to be willing. And because I love you, because I know that we walk to God together, I *will* come to you and I *will* walk with you, and I say this unto you not from a place above you but from a deep compassion and a love for you, whom my Father has created out of Love.

There is not a moment when, in your experience as you *un*learn the perceptions of the world and reclaim the perceptions of Truth, there is not a moment in which you might feel that your strength is lacking, there is not a moment that I will refrain from giving you mine. *All you have to do is ask!* And I will give you my strength until yours is as certain as mine—and my strength is *perfectly* certain because, like you, I lived once in this world and I chose to teach only Love. I chose the outrageous idea that death is not real, and to believe that no circumstances could separate me from my decision to choose Love. And I found that what my Father had taught me was true: Death is not real; this world is illusion. And the world dropped away from me as gently as does a dream dissolve from your mind when your eyes open in the morning and you remember where you really are. The world tried to get rid of me and in its insane attempt it simply allowed me the freedom to join with anybody I want!

[Laughter]

Hm! And *you*, I'm asking you in your own hearts to be willing to become the hands, the feet, the eyes, the expression and the Heart of Christ. Because, you see, the world believes in the body and if I come and whisper in one's ear as they walk down the street, they say it's just their imagination, "Oh, I've just had this sudden thought of Jeshua – pah, he wouldn't talk to me!" And on they go!

And I'm still standing, going, "It *is* me! What do I have to do?"

[Laughter]

"No it can't be, it's my imagination. First of all I'm a sinful creature, therefore he would never come to me anyway. Secondly, voices heard that aren't associated with the body, they must be somebody's, uh, insanity..."

I need you as much as the world has ever tried to tell you that you need *me*. Many of you have rebelled against that,

> *Oh God, they're telling me I have to worship this Jeshua fellow. Yuck!*

It has never felt quite right to many of you, thank God!

[Laughter]

But I need you, because my one purpose and my one task is to embrace the whole of the Sonship with the Love that my Father has given unto me. Because my Father embraced me and brought me into that remembrance, my only purpose and function is to give that remembrance to anyone who would receive it. And I can't do that without you—*without you*.

And in the most ordinary of moments, you can choose to remember the extraordinariness of the blessing of that eternal moment. You have the power, even if the one in front of you doesn't know what's going on, to take a deep breath and go,

> *Ah, only Christ is here,*

and to radiate Light and Love, to choose forgiveness, so they begin to look at you and they go, "I don't quite understand, you don't seem to be concerned about the things we're concerned with... Oh no, and yet somehow you're always there, you're always the same, and sometimes through you all this wisdom pours forth."

And then you go,

> *"Whoa, what did I say?'*

And they say,

> "God, you know what you said last night? It was the most incredible thing. Thank you, thank you!"

And you scratch your head and you go, "What? Did we talk last night?"

[Laughter]

"Yes, on the phone for just a moment and you were getting ready to go somewhere and suddenly you said something that seemed off the wall, and then you said, 'Well I have to go, bye.'"

You go, "I said that?"

You've just been willing to let the Holy Spirit reach your brother through you. And that occurs because you have opened the place for miracles to be extended through you by acknowledging,

> *I and my Father are One, and I relinquish my perceptions of what the world is, and I will go gently through my day, remembering the Grace that has set me free. And I will look upon my brother, not believing I know what they need—there is One who knows.*

That's how the mind begins to be opened so that what you channel is no longer the thoughts of the world—and by the way, everything in this world is channeled, everything *inspired* either by the voice of fear or the Voice for Love. Every moment of every day you are choosing what frequency to channel, what quality of thought to channel, what dimension of feelingness to channel—every second, it never changes.

Hmm.

In relinquishing your own ideas and acknowledging that you cannot save yourself, the Light of Truth begins to descend and to be re-awakened in you, and you will quite literally find that miracles become the stepping stones upon which your life is lived, upon which you step. And you will come and go as the wind, not knowing where it comes from or where it's going, but somehow you're in the right place at the right time, and everything's okay.

Miracles. Miracles occur naturally to minds that teach only Love. So you see, it gets to the point where if miracles aren't happening you won't even dare to get out of bed...

[Laughter]

because you know something is amiss in your own mind:

> *Where am I doubting, where am I fearful, where am I failing to extend Love? My God, I didn't laugh yesterday. It's been two weeks since I danced! Aah, now I know where to begin!*

... to bring lightness and laughter and the sense of play and safety back into the mind, and then the flow can continue.

Hmm. I know you're holding the thought, "Is he looking at me?"

[Laughter]

Yes.

[Laughter]

But not with this body. For you see, I do not come into this body, I do not take my beloved brother and kick him out. All that happens is that an ancient resonance is allowed to be made manifest and there is a blending at the level of mind—and mind far transcends the body; remember I said the body arises within the field of mind, it's really an illusion, just an apparition—and at the level of mind, I merely blend my energy with this particular mindset filled with concepts, filled with ideas, made up out of experiences much like your own, and I simply activate it in a different way. I bring a different level of integration and understanding, that's all. And if I can blend with this mind, rest assured, I can blend with *any* mind. And I can blend with yours. And no I am not going to acknowledge that you are the one I'm speaking to, not in this way, I'm going to ask that you acknowledge it in the depth of your own being, for when I turned this body in this way, a thought came, a thought of knowingness,

> *He's aware of me. Gulp.*

[Laughter]

The time for gulping has passed. I am aware of you because I know how beautiful you are. I see your light and your radiance and your purity and there is no guilt upon you. You have not failed me and you have failed no one, and the Radiance and the Power and the Light and the Truth with which you were created and are sustained *is in you now in its purity.* Be you therefore wholly joyous for in *this* hour a miracle does occur. And you will see the fruits of it unfolding in your life. Precious friend, you came doubting your own worthiness and as an ancient friend, I say unto you, your worthiness is established by God and the world has never taken it from you. I love you. Hmm. Hmm. There!

So how are all of you doing?

[Laughter]

Participant: Excellent.

My beloved brother has asked me many times: "Jeshua, what are you going to talk about?"

And I've always given him one answer: "My friend, your task is only to be available." Because, you see, *I* never know what's going to be said. I come and abide with you just as you abide with each other as friends. You get together and you sit around in your living room, nothing to do and nowhere to go—you just hang out. I come and abide with you and I read what is in your heart, and what is spoken is not deliberately chosen by me but it flows forth through my mind, then through the mind field of this my beloved brother. You seem to hear it as words spoken and picked up by your physical ears, but what is spoken is being generated from the Source of Oneness in which we abide—One Mind, together; that is what creates *all* experience, *all of it*.

Does that make sense to you? The gathering together of minds that choose to resonate at a certain frequency, that's what generates experience. If there were a tall skyscraper, an apartment building, and all of you got together on a Saturday and said, "Let's hang out on the bottom floor!" Isn't it true that you would look out the window and you would see certain things? And then the next Saturday you would say, "Let's go up to the fifteenth floor and hang out!" And you open the curtains and wouldn't the view be different? That's all that happens in your experience. You choose to come together with minds and the interplay of that energy generates what you call your experience of that moment. And wherever two or more are gathered in my name, there I am in the midst of them. When any two come together and choose to go to the penthouse, the view is unlimited. The table is spread, the finest linens, the finest china, and you sit down to a feast prepared by the Father for the Son whom He loves above all things and Who welcomes home the prodigal son no longer, but the one who has *chosen* to return.

There has been, by and large, an agreement by all of you, a desire just to hang out together in a frequency of Peace, of Love, to have echoed back to the mind the Truth the mind already knows. So by and large, we've gotten together in the penthouse, and in your daily experience, you have the power to bring the energy of the penthouse into your situations. Now, of course, that means that tomorrow morning when you get up and go to your job or wherever you go, you're having a very high elevated feeling and you go to work and everybody's doing what they call the 'bitching' or whatever it is they do…

[Laughter]

… and the complaining and all of the rest. A disappointment comes to the mind:

Oh, I thought I could change all this!

Don't give in to it. That's the trick, you see. Just because somebody else is being miserable doesn't mean *you* have to accommodate them by *joining* them. It doesn't mean you look on them and say, "Well you've created it, get out of it!"

[Laughter]

It means that you look upon them and go,

Aah, I'm seeing dimensions of ego, I'm seeing choices for separation, but I know that's not the Truth.

You look upon them lovingly and if they need your arm put around them, you do so, or you feed them with the love that they're capable of receiving, but the whole time, you remember what the Truth is. You hold the frequency of the penthouse. And the more often you do that, the easier it gets. And one day, you walk into that circle of friends or co-workers who are trying to drag you down into their state of being, and you realize something has changed:

It's not affecting me. I feel totally calm and at peace.

And no matter what they say, you just smile and go, "Oh come on, you know there's another way. Would you choose it with me?"

"No, I refuse!"

[Laughter]

"Okay! There will be another opportunity. As for me, I choose to wait only on the Lord, which simply means to wait, to abide in, Christ Consciousness. I choose only peace. Now let's get on with our day."

Grace As Reality

And you will wait for them to choose with you if it takes ten thousand lifetimes, a millenium, it doesn't matter, you're hanging out in eternity! Hm. It's very, very important. When the whole world is seeking to drag itself down, the world needs just one to make a different choice, and you can be that one in every moment. Isn't that true? Hm! Indeed.

So there you have it. Grace as Reality comes when you consciously choose to accept what is the case:

> *This illusion isn't true, these feelings of lack are not true, this need to make judgments isn't true—that's all the voice of the ego; it's an illusion. My Father's Grace pervades my being. I choose to be wholly joyous and at peace, and each time I seem to forget I'll just choose to remember, and thereby the world is restored and healed.*

Grace as Reality is the *only* Reality—and please listen to this, and we'll be done here in a moment—Grace as Reality is the *only* Reality that is available to anyone at any time. What is real cannot be threatened and exists eternally. What is unreal exists not. And if the mind holds a thought that it does, it is only because you've allowed the mind to choose illusions over Truth, that's all. Grace *is* your Reality and it means that you can go gently in this world. There is indeed a way of living in which there are no laments of the past, no anxiety over the future. A sense of the eternal comes to fill your days, so that even as you wash your dish, there's *something* that is eternal that is felt and known, and a peace descends gently upon you. There is a way of being in the world without strife and without suffering, and the way to that is *to embrace honestly every illusion that you insist on carrying and see that it is untrue*. Every judgment, every thought that would seem to limit the Holy Son of God, is unreal. And just beyond the drama of the world is the Peace of the Kingdom of Heaven, waiting only for you to grant it welcome by making the choice to be a finder and not a seeker:

> *I and my Father are One. I might as well admit it and love it!*

Grace. I offer this unto you. In any situation from this hour in which you are tempted to think with the thoughts of the world and you notice that it doesn't feel very good, remember that simple word: Grace. Gently let it come to the mind and it will be your willingness to send me a telegram, it will be your willingness to open up the place of the heart—and I will not fail to come to you. And as you gently abide with it, certain things that have been said in this evening are going to come to you as if you are hearing them for the first time and you will swear that didn't get said then! And a feeling will come, a certain little resonance, much like that which has touched many of you in this hour, for remember I'm not in this body—for all *you* know, I'm right behind you.

[Laughter]

And with that thought, a different vibration, a different frequency will again begin to come to you. Some of you will have times when, as you begin that, all of a sudden it will be like the pot's really been stirred, and the mind will be going, "I know it didn't work, I know it doesn't work, these bad feelings really are here, I know it, I know it, I know it!" That's just the same thought of denial! But,

> *Oh! Grace… Grace… Grace…*

until the voice of the ego begins to realize, "Wait a minute you've always listened to me before, I guess it's not going to work this time." And the voice of the ego withdraws from your Holy Mind and Peace is restored.

So please be willing not to look beyond the simplicity of what was just offered. It will work, and work beautifully. It will lead you upon revelation and revelation and revelation—and revelation is really nothing more than the unwinding, the unlearning of concepts and perceptions that have imprisoned the mind and kept you away from the peace that you seek. Hmm.

For a moment now, just turn and look at someone next to you. Just turn enough so that the eyes can meet. Now it doesn't matter if you believe this is true or not, just do it anyway. Each of you, one unto the other, take just a moment—and you can decide who gets to go first—look at your brother or your sister, your eternal friend who has journeyed with you throughout all of time and space and has shared every world with you in one form or another...

[Laughter]

... and say to them that "I promise to live my life *for you* as one who has found and acknowledges the Truth, so that no matter if we ever see each other again, wherever I am, I promise to keep my promise." So in your own words, go right ahead.

[Audience members share this promise with each other]

So how does that feel?

[Comments and laughter from the audience]

What seems sane to the world is wholly insane to the Mind of Christ and all beliefs of the world are diametrically opposed to the Truth of the Kingdom, so how then to use a bit of a measurement for knowing which voice you're listening to?

If you're not standing out as just a little crazy, you have conformed yourself to the world. Hmm. I taught certain friends many things in secret, something that wasn't meant to be broadcast to minds that really weren't interested in learning anyway, but the essence of what I taught my closest friends was the simplicity of the great power of choosing laughter, dancing, play and singing in each and every day until that frequency permeates every decision you make and every experience you're having. For you see, it is lightness that *enlightens* the mind and lightness carries the mind out of density, out of seriousness. So if you're feeling a bit heavy and a bit down, ask yourself, "Did I laugh, did I sing, did I dance, did I play this day?" If not, and it's eleven o'clock and you're laying in bed and you're dog tired and you're feeling depressed... Get up!

[Laughter]

And if you're with your spouse and you suddenly jump out of bed and you begin to dance around the bedroom, they'll say, "What are you doing, dear?"

"I'm remembering!"

[Laughter]

Indeed.

Is it not time to release seriousness from what you call spirituality? Is it not time to transcend religiousness and to know that Spirit dwells within you as the voice and the whisper of God's Love that brings you into being?

> *Do I exist? I sure do! It must mean that God still loves me and that God's Love is in me. Haaah!*

So . . . I extend unto you my thanks for your willingness, because you see, think that just on this little evening you've opted to come to this place, perhaps out of curiosity, perhaps because they haven't changed the movies downtown yet, whatever the reason is on the outside, that's not what matters. You are always compelled by what the soul is choosing to attract to itself as experience. I thank you because—please don't minimize this—in this evening, you chose as a soul, no matter what the mind was saying, you chose as a soul to come together and set aside all of the millions of other things you could have been doing in the world, and you came to simply abide, as much with one another as with me.

And when you leave here... No matter what the mind is doing, you are always going to know, *you are always going to know* that the one who walked this plane as a man is like unto yourself. The one the world has tried to get rid of, first through crucifixion and then by making him into a grand savior so far removed and above every other human being, that is untouchable and unreachable anyway, so why try? All attempts to continue the illusion. You are going to know that what I said then is true: "*I am with you always, even unto the end of this age.*" And when you fully understand who I am and have become—that is, in shifting identification from a man in space and time to identification with the Mind of Christ—when you come to that place in yourself, you are going to laugh like you've never laughed before, for you will understand then that, for God's sake, I couldn't *be* anywhere *else* but where you are, *because we are One, always.* I am you, and that lifetime is wholly yours. Separation does not exist; *it does not exist.*

Am I the Christ? Oh yes, along with you and *never apart from you*. And I love you. Not as the world gives give I unto you, and not as the world gives can you give unto one another, and that is the glory of Grace. Peace therefore be unto you. Those of you that would like to leave, you're feeling quite nice now, whatever it is, or you just want to get home to the late movie, whatever it is, go always with my blessings. If you choose in this hour to say, "No I'm not ready to learn the curriculum," it's fine with me. I can wait! I've waited a long time and because I live in that which is eternal, rest assured, I *will* outwait you!

[Laughter]

And not one thing you say and not one thing you do will ever, even for an instant, turn me from you. My Love for you is as unshakable as our Father's Love is for each of us, and in loving you in that way I know the Love of the Father for me. And when I said, "Go you therefore and teach all nations," I was *not* talking about walking around with a Bible under your arm! To teach is to teach only Love. And to go therefore and to teach all nations means to go to everyone you see and to realize that right there, you can be the one who brings the gentleness of Peace and the warmth of Love to *that situation, that moment*. Teach well. Teach well by being what you would desire to learn; and by teaching it you *do* become it; and as you give you have received, in all ways and always.

Peace therefore be unto the only begotten of God, being neither male nor female but Light, and Light alone: the Light that lights all worlds and brings Creation back to God.

Peace be unto you always, for the things of Heaven are indeed united with the things of Earth, and the Peace of God is extended as far as from the East to the West, held lovingly in the arms of Christ—your arms.

Amen.

HEAVEN ON EARTH
August 1994

Now, we begin.

And, indeed, once again, greetings unto you, beloved and holy friends. In truth, all that occurs within your dimension is not unknown or unavailable to us. For where we abide (and there are many of us), we abide in a state of consciousness in which the transmutation of energies through your third-dimensional realm are entirely observable by us. Yes, this does mean that there is not at any time a true state of privacy—if by privacy you mean secrecy and avoidance of relationship. This means that, as you call to yourself your physical earth plane experience, in *each and every moment*, whether you choose to acknowledge it or not, you are in relationship with the whole of Creation. And the quality of that relationship is what mirrors back to you the state of consciousness that you are choosing to abide within.

It is, therefore, always wise to look clearly and honestly at the nature of your moment- to-moment experience. What are you truly aware of *now*? What thoughts are you permitting to flow through the mind? What feelings are those thoughts generating within the field of energy that you call the body?

Why is this important? To come to where I am requires a complete transcendence of the physical domain or experience—not an escape *from*, for transcendence does not rest on escape. Transcendence can *only* rest on *embracing*. For how can you transcend what you refuse to acknowledge as a part of your experience? Therefore, the heart and mind that is willing to utilize each and every moment of its experience in whatever domain or dimension it finds itself existing within, is that heart and that mind that will indeed come to where I am: to the finality of what you might call evolution, in which *all* seeking has ended, in which the *need* for experience is over, where there is not one question, and not one doubt.

Imagine, if you will, such a state in which you abide in such perfect wakefulness that the mind does not even entertain the *thought* of desiring a physical form through which to funnel a limited sphere of experience. A state of being in which, by simply turning the attention of your consciousness, you can abide anywhere you wish in a moment's notice: actually, even quicker than that. That, just by turning your consciousness, you can abide in any time frame within the physical dimension: to observe it, to interact with it, to bring your wisdom to it. To turn your consciousness to a dimension and a time frame seemingly far removed from where *you* are upon the earth, and all in the twinkling of an eye.

These things are your potential. They were placed within you in the moment of your creation. And if you would well receive it, you have *already experienced* the state in which I am, and there is a part of you that has never left that state. What then has occurred? For look well upon what your experience is in *this moment*. Where do you find yourself sitting or standing? What is the climate of your environment: is it noisy,

is it chaotic? Have you lit a few candles and burned your incense, have you played some of your favorite music so you can begin to evoke a physiological change in the body that you will then call a state of peace?—as if peace were dependent upon the body. To each and every one of you, wherever you are in *this moment*: stop. Observe the things around you, and the things within you. For there is a very direct correlation between the two. For what you see around you expresses a quality of energy, a form of experience, that emanates from the quality of thought that you have been willing to entertain and to *allow* to enter into the field of your energy, into your domain. And from this choice, you look out upon a world that you have chosen to create.

I have chosen to look out upon you and to recognize that you are my brothers and my sisters. I have chosen to learn to look out and see *only* the Light of Christ within you. That Light—that shines radiantly beyond all limitations—it is that Light that I speak to, that Light that I come to, that Light that I join with, not only in this manner of communication but through your dreams and in the space between the thoughts you would choose to think.

If this is so, it must mean that what you are seeking is already within you. And that perhaps the pathway of transcendence rests not on *efforting* or *striving*, but on *wondering*. Perhaps it rests upon looking at all that you see and accepting the fact that you have no idea what it is, how it has arisen, where it has come from, what it could possibly mean, or where it's going. Perhaps the pathway of awakening requires that—after all seeking and all attempts to learn magical formulas to draw enlightenment *to* you—perhaps it truly rests on the recognition of a state of humility in which you finally acknowledge that you have moved nowhere and made no progress. Oh, yes, you've called to yourself many experiences, high and low, and yet none of *them* has sufficed to help you transcend your common or ordinary or consistent state of being. No matter how good the love-making is, no matter how good the food, no matter how delicious the states of consciousness in meditation, still you find yourself coming back to states of being painfully familiar.

What, then, is the key? It rests in only this: to begin at the end. To first acknowledge,

> *In reality, I have never changed. In reality, I am as God has created me to be. In reality, I have already tasted all experience and there is nothing new under the Heaven of my consciousness. I am perfect and whole now.*

From that choice it then follows that you can begin to accept that, regardless of what you think you *see* and what you think you're *experiencing*, there is a depth of wisdom within you that can bring enlightenment from the higher self, if you will, from the soul, down to the levels of the personality, all the way into the cellular structure of the body—if that be your true desire.

The true pathway home, then, my precious, precious friends, rests on the willingness to withdraw the value that you have placed on all of the perceptions *you* have created. To be willing to stand with empty hands. To look upon an object, a person, an event, a feeling, and to begin with the thought,

> *I am whole and perfect, and I am bringing the light of my infinite consciousness to shine upon this mysterious phenomena that has*

arisen in front of me.

Or 'within' me if you call the body within you: it, too, is on the outside in some sense. And to acknowledge that you are beholding Mystery, and that you cannot rely on your own ideas to understand anything. *That* is the beginning of wisdom.

For if you cannot rely upon yourself, what are you going to do? You could try committing suicide, but all that does is dispose of a certain body; *you* remain. You can try to distract yourself with the ordinary phenomena of cultures. That doesn't work, either. In the end, you must *submit* yourself to something which is, in truth, the grandest mystery of all: the presence of the Holy Spirit. You must surrender your self—all of your ideas about what you think is true—and ask that something you can't even see (and, at least in the beginning, you can't even hear), to ask some mysterious *something* to teach you the truth of Reality. It feels very much like dying. And, in truth, it is the only true death—the giving up and surrendering of your justifications for anger, your rationalizations for judgment, your *certainty* that what you *know* is true.

The acceptance that what you have called 'knowledge' is highly suspect, indeed. For, if you believe you are a body in space and time, and if you look out and see a limited world, you are therefore using a limited consciousness to decide that *you* know what the whole of Creation is. And the part can never comprehend the whole.

Yet, paradoxically, there is within you that which is already the wholeness itself, the Mind of Christ, and that which rests within you is a perfect wisdom, a perfect peace, a perfect knowingness, is ready to speak to you (so to speak), to speak to your consciousness so that you actually and literally have an *awareness of being the wholeness of creation.* Even though the body still seems to be right as it is, even though the objects seem to be around you, imagine seeing through them as though they were transparent and beholding all distant realms, and all past and all future, in the twinkling of an eye. And allowing that state to be the normal state in which you operate, even while the body seems to last for yet a little while. All this is possible, and more, when you first use the *power of choice* given unto you to dedicate each and every moment of your awareness—notice I said your awareness, not your experience. Dedicating each moment of your *awareness* to the process of surrendering everything that you thought you knew and needed to hold onto, to allow a mysterious *something* to bring the grace of enlightenment to you.

Beloved friends, you who seem to find yourself in this third-dimensional realm, this physical realm of limitation and duality and conflict, and birth and death—and surprises? Hm! Rest assured you have truly never surprised yourself at any time. There has never been a moment's experienced that has come to you that you have not *deliberately* ordered and received. Nothing comes by accident.

And, of course, you are quite free to choose how to perceive what comes to you. And if you allow that mysterious *something* to teach you anew, what once horrified you can now bring a smile to your face; what once seemed insurmountable can seem like the smallest of stepping stones beneath your toes. All power under Heaven and Earth is given unto you to create *as you are created* in each moment, from and within perfect unlimitedness. And now here's the real secret: you are literally and exactly doing this all the time. You never lose the power of the infinite being that you are; you cannot lose what God has created, or God herself is limited. You, as you are right now, with every breath you breathe, with every thought you think, with every action you perform (even if you have no body), you are literally and always using the infinite power of *your wisdom* to create. That is the only thing you've ever been doing.

And you have therefore created heavens and numerous hells. And in those hells you have created an infinite number of shades or hues or vibrations. You can just as easily create as many heavens blessed with shimmering, beautiful light that the earth has not seen for quite some time. In each moment of your day, *nothing outside of you* causes your feelings and your perceptions. Does this mean that, if you experience another soul, another human being, that they themselves do not carry certain frequencies of energy that you can detect? Of course not. But the detecting of energy from the field of another mind does not *cause* you to perceive them in any way at all. You will therefore perceive them as you *choose* to perceive them, regardless of their name, regardless of their action. You are the one who is free to see that your power to choose your perceptions is a power that overwhelms and transmutes anything and everything that your world can direct at you.

I hope that this is beginning to sink in, because it is an extremely important message. I want you to truly spend some time each day in the simplest of actions. You might simply be closing your fist and opening it again. You might feel your feet upon the earth as you walk forward in a direction of your choosing (and all of your directions are of your choosing). Whatever you choose to bring your attention to, notice with perfect wonder and awe that *you* are *literally* choosing to create the experience you're having. Because this is true, Heaven on Earth is actually no further from your experience than the width of the thoughts you are willing to think. *Heaven on Earth is no further from you than the width of the thoughts you are willing to think.* Heaven on Earth is not apart from where you are.

Would you, therefore, be willing to join with me in daring to think the thought of a planet healed and a humanity enlightened? Are you willing to allow yourself—not to run around with placards in your hand and placing billboards around what you call your highways (we would perceive them as low-ways... hmm)—would you be willing to allow yourself to rest in each of your days and simply feel the *reality* of Heaven on Earth, and *know* that this has already come to pass? And in the field of time, it seems to be taking time for that to occur. But, after all, that's what time is about: process. In reality, if you hold the thought, *it is done*. And, in truth, you can acknowledge it. For what the Son of God decrees *is*—no matter the state of mind in which you decree it—what you *say in that moment*, whether you speak it out loud, whether you merely think the thought, you have literally created that reality. [Snaps fingers] That fast, in the twinkling of an eye.

This seems like madness to your world because your world *is* madness. It is the complete reversal of Christed Consciousness. The world represents the complete *opposite* of Heaven. It is upside down and inside out. So that when I say unto you: when you think the thought of Heaven and Earth, you have decreed it and it is so, now, and you're totally free to experience unlimited radiance, perfect peace, perfect joy, right where you are—now! The world will say: that is nonsense. And this is the theme of this hour's discussion, for you to understand that right there is the point that you *must begin* to make a new choice, to learn to think with the Mind of Christ rather than against it. By choosing to think with it, you become it, and when you become it, you realize a discovery: a discovery of what has always been and is never changed. You are, indeed, and you forever remain, as you were created to be. You are the creator of all worlds. And never, ever, ever, ever are you losing, or in a state of loss of, your power to create precisely as God birthed you. That is how powerful you are, right where you are.

And there are some of you, even now that listen to these words, and you think

> *Well, that might be true for somebody else who's a little more powerful, but you see, my situation is such-and-such. I only have five dollars in my wallet!*

Look at the five dollars with *wonder*. Where on earth did it come from? It came into your being and into your wallet because you decided to put it there. And you can just as easily put a million of your golden coins there, if that is what you want to experience. Nothing but your own thought expands you or limits you. No one can create *for you*. No one can bring you the answers you seek—you *are* the answer you seek. You have merely trained yourself to believe that you are less than you are. You have trained yourself to believe that right now in this moment, as you reach to scratch your cheek with your finger, or you hear the sound of a barking dog outside your window, or you see the flash of sunlight as it begins to disappear beyond the mountains to the west—and for some of you, by the way, if you happen to look out and see the streak of light as it begins to rise in your eastern sky, for some of you will listen to this early in the morning—if you believe that you're just some ordinary person trying to figure it all out, *stop where you are*. Look at what you see and truly see it. You do not know what a single thing is. It is Mystery, and yet you have brought it into form, even if it's nothing more than the table in front of you.

How could it be that you're experiencing a physical body in some city within your twentieth century America? How could these things be? What has brought them to be? You have—the infinite power of creation, sitting right where you are, choosing to look like an ordinary human being. The same creativity that moves the sun and the moon and stars, the same creativity that brought forth what your scientists would call from the 'big bang', all forms of creation. The big bang, by the way, was nothing more than an aha! in your Holy Mind as you dreamed up a new thought that had never been thought of before: something called physical matter, a condensation of light.

If you can begin to truly understand, as you place your hand around your cup of tea or your coffee, as these things are called, when you brush your teeth, when you watch how the chest rises as you inhale—if you can truly look upon these things with awe and with innocence, you can behold the mystery of Life itself. And you can come to see that *you* are constantly, moment to moment to moment, manifesting world after world after world after world. You are choosing where to be and how to be. *You* are the one sent forth from the Holy Mind of God to be the agent of the forever extending Creation.

I want to say, also—and this will seem very radical to many of you yet still—you are perfectly, completely free to create whatever you will. You are perfectly free in this moment to go and sell all that you have and to take up your cross and follow me. Some would say that means to become a rather bizarre radical. Hmm. I felt insane the first time I dared to think the thought, "I and my Father are One," just to try it on. It created a tingling sensation from the crown of the head down through the body. It was a sensation I had not yet experienced, but I liked it. And I decided to ask myself this question: What would happen if I were to entertain that thought until it excluded every other thought that seemed to swirl within the mind? What would occur?

For you see, many of you are wondering: Why cannot I seem to manifest what I want to manifest? It is because you entertain conflicting thoughts. And where there is conflict, there is stagnation. Be you therefore of single intent, bring the consciousness to a single point in which the thought you would truly desire to manifest is the only thought you imbue with reality. When you have mastered the ability to discipline the mind, you will discover that you can create an entire universe with one thought. You will discover that you can literally create a golden coin in the palm of your hand, merely by holding the thought of it. And if this is true, and I assure you that it is, you will be the bearer of miracles. And lo and behold, you might dare to think the thought of Heaven on Earth and put all of your focused intention on that one thought until it is your only reality and nothing else matters, nothing else holds value, nothing else can exist for you. And if the rest of the world thinks you're crazy, so what? That, too, is just a thought. You can bring Heaven to Earth in the twinkling of an eye. And it will come to pass that Heaven on Earth *will* be the case, and when it is established, it will seem to have occurred effortlessly in the twinkling of an eye.

Why? Because enough of you will have chosen to energize that thought, and only that thought. You will live that thought, you will drink that thought, you will dream that thought, you will extend that thought, you will feel and live that thought to the exclusion of anything that could contradict it, or be in dissonance with it; and then you will be the *embodiment* of Heaven on Earth. And the time will come, in time, when suddenly the whole of humanity gets it, in the twinkling of an eye. And in that very moment, that which is called the pollution of your waters and airs will vanish as if it had never been. That which is called strife between races will vanish as if it had never been. Anything you can imagine representing conflict will vanish from the face of the Earth. And why? Because the Holy Son of God, manifested as the family of mankind, will have moved sufficiently into a momentum that creates the stabilization of one and only one thought: Heaven on Earth. That fast, without blinking an eye, without lifting an hand. That is what you're struggling toward as a collective consciousness.

You are beginning to discover, from your scientists, that you can literally create what is called virtual reality. Well, guess what? That's what you've been doing all along anyway. Manifesting on this physical third dimension virtual reality, which means pretty close to the real thing. Hmm. Think about that. For as long as mankind has been on your earth—and there have been many generations and many civilizations, great civilizations that have risen and fallen and been washed away, that your scientists and archaeologists know nothing of and can't even believe could have ever been; cultures so far beyond the one you now live in that yours becomes archaic and primitive—and, yet, all of them are an aspect of virtual reality. Heaven on Earth will be the final happy dream that can be made manifest in the physical dimension, reflecting to all consciousnesses the truth of consciousness itself. Heaven on Earth will last but for the twinkling of an eye. And then even this physical dimension will be as a thought that had never been dreamt of, as the Holy Son of God returns to take up his rightful place at the right hand of God—which just means right-mindedness, creating only what is unlimited and without conflict, only that which mirrors and reflects the vast grandness of His radiance.

And now here's the paradox: *You* can't wait for that to happen, because you are the one through whom it occurs, and yet *you* can't bring it about. You can only allow that mysterious something to accomplish it for you and through you. I once said that it is important to become again as a little child. And now we come to a clear and deeper and more presently meaningful interpretation of that teaching.

For a little child surrenders the need to be the maker and the doer. The child just holds the thought. It wakes up in the morning and says, "Ha, I'm hungry, I wish to be fed." And, voila, the mother appears at the door and says, "Oh, my little child, are you hungry? Shall I feed you?" And the child says, "Well, of course, why do you think I called you here?" Hm. Creation. The child *submits* to something beyond itself to bring about the manifestation of its thought.

Does that makes sense to you? Can you become the innocent child who first dares to dream the unbelievable dream, the dream of Heaven on Earth. It seems so outrageous to mankind. Are you willing to dare to let into your consciousnesses light seeping through a crack in the wall, the fortress you have built against the Kingdom of Heaven, the thought,

I and my Father are One. I am Christ incarnate. How about that!

Right here, wearing my Nikes and my Levis and my (what do you call this with the...) New York Yankees baseball hat upon your head. *You* are the incarnation of Christ pretending to be human so as to be in relationship with a lot of sleeping minds. Dare you, therefore, to think the outrageous and improbable? Dare you to contemplate, and to allow with wonder, that there is a mysterious something that can bring forth your highest creative thoughts when those thoughts are in alignment with the way God thinks. And God thinks only in terms of effortlessness, joy, unlimitedness, expansion—and Love. Love. *Love!*

Do you know what has frustrated your attempt to be the maker and creator of your world? Fear. And fear is the opposite of Love. *Love* is the essential energy of the mind of God. Yet how many times have you prayed for a new job or a new career, a new relationship, or a new washer and dryer, because you *fear* not having these things? Because you *fear* survival, which is already to hold an insane thought: what could you survive? You are Life eternal, and it will never be taken from you. You try to hold your reality together through your attempts to be the maker and the doer because you *fear* letting go of them. And yet, in truth, it is nothing more than the fear of the child letting go of an invisible monster under the bed. But where you choose to create from loving thoughts, the universe, that unseen something I call the Holy Spirit, can begin to blend with the energy of your consciousness and begin to bring forth manifestations that reflect the vibrational quality of Love. And Love is that which *heals*. Love is that which *forgives*. Love is that which creates the *space* for a mind and heart to choose again. For you see, that is the energy in which God sustains you with every breath, creating the space for His creation to create anew.

Love. What would it mean for you to go through each of your days and ask yourself honestly,

> *Is this action I am performing, is this thought I'm thinking, is this grounded in my desire to extend and teach only Love?*

Many of you will become quite frightened to discover that ninety-eight percent of what you do is not founded in love at all, but in fear. Therefore, if that is the case, learn to embrace fear itself. Ask of it:

> *Where do you come from? What am I truly afraid of? Can I feel that feeling? Can I embrace that thought? Can I embrace the whole idea, the perception, that is causing me to choose actions out of a desire to survive, out of a desire to control another, out of a desire to prove to myself that I am unworthy of unlimitedness?*

Love. To think only from the foundation of Love is to return to your rightful place, in which Creation flows through you as the vehicle of manifestation. Yet what flows through you is no longer yours. You are the enjoyer, the witness of grand Mystery. You are free. You are awake. You are at peace. You are home. You are Christ.

Imagine a life in which all of your creations were wholly loving. That is the same as Heaven on Earth.

So you see, there's never been a single thing that has *caused* you to be fearful. Fear itself can only arise as a chosen creation from the infinite and all-powerful Mind that you are. If you could look behind your mind in any instant when events or whatever it is seems to unfold, and you begin to feel fearful, you begin to react out of that fear, if you could take one step behind the stage curtain, you would discover yourself saying,

> *From the depth of the Christ I am, I choose now to create a fearful world and the experience of fear and all that comes with it—and I step into that creation now!*

And there you have it. The experience you're having that seems to be causing your conflict. Hm. That does rather take away excuses. And it takes away blame. For even your most fearful creations can be embraced with perfect innocence. And why? Listen carefully: All that you see in the realm of beginnings and endings is an illusion. It is a momentary, a temporary, call it a modification of the creative energy that flows through you. You've just sculpted it for a moment. But think on this: Has there ever been anything you have attempted to create from a non-loving space?

So, the theme of this sharing with you will come to have its point, as it will begin to be a building block upon which we will build Heaven on Earth within *your* consciousness. For if you are listening to these words now, created out of a free and unconditioned blending of two minds—two minds that are willing to love one another so wholly that nothing can serve as a barrier to their joining and to their creations—as we build upon this foundation, your life is going to change, as it must. For if you are listening to these words, there is already a part of *you* that has heard the call to awaken and to bring Heaven to Earth. To dare to join with the most insane thought that has ever penetrated the myopic and narrow field of consciousness called humanity. What you could almost say is nothing more than the attempt to resist unlimitedness.

Into egoic consciousness there crept a tiny, mad idea.

> *What would it be like to have Heaven on Earth? That's insane. I can't think that thought.*

The next day:

> *What would it be like if all the waters were running purely and all the children were well fed and loved?*

All of you, each and every one of you now listening to these words—each and every one of you is a being, a soul, an entity, call it what you will, a focus of unlimited creative potential, a spark of Divine Light. You are one that has already allowed such thoughts to begin to seep into your consciousness. And the first thing it does is it begins to create a polarization within you, because as Light begins to descend into the mind, and then also down into the personality and body, it's much like turning on a light switch, and the first thing you see is all of the things within your consciousness that are *unlike* the thought of Heaven on Earth. That are unlike the thought of being the presence of Christ. That are unlike the thought of "I and my Father are One."

And sometimes it seems to be not a pretty sight. And, yet, it is a very necessary process for you *want* to learn to shed light with wonder and awe and innocence upon all of your miscreations. To wonder about how such a thing could ever arise: a thought of judgment, a thought of fear, a thought of lack, a thought of limitation. Let that mysterious something shine the Light of Truth upon everything within your field of being that is unlike the simplicity of Love. For the shining of that Light upon it already begins to dissolve it from your consciousness.

This is why I once said that it is not necessary to seek for Love. It is only necessary to seek for all of the ways in which you have blocked Love from being your only reality. *That* is your purpose, that is the gift of time, to ask:

> *How in this moment am I using the infinite power of my beingness to create something which is less than Love, something less than what I truly want?*

This tape, then, is the first in a series that will be shared with you through this vehicle, through this joining, in which many of us, what you would call teachers, friends, masters, will come to teach you how consciousness works and how to begin to re-discipline the focus of your mind so it becomes like a laser, unwilling to see anything less than Love.

We want then to suggest also that those of you who are listening to these words take the time to re-listen to them on several occasions. Do this in a very relaxed state of mind, not trying to grasp each and every word, but allowing certain phrases and words to strike you. And the ones that strike you, write them down. And then begin a process of writing those words and phrases consistently in each of your days for at least fifteen or twenty minutes, in a state of aimlessness and innocence. Write the phrases and the words that have *struck* you, for it is that which strikes the *emotional* body that begins to create the space for something new to be birthed through you. Rest assured, you are not alone. You've never had any privacy. We see it all—and it's okay.

With that, we are going to take pause for just a few moments, for there will be some questions that will be asked by those present. Many of you will be a bit startled to realize that they're the very questions that are on your mind. Be at peace then, and now we will pause to wonder what the question is.

[Break]

We were just speaking then, as we return, that when a question comes into your consciousness, it comes for a reason. Because questions—listen carefully—questions are what form the basis and indeed sculpt the answer that you will discover. Therefore, if you want the greatest of answers, ask the greatest of questions. If you want clarity to come to you, be clear in the questions you are asking of yourself and of the universe.

A question, once it arises, is an impulse of energy that has come into your consciousness, and it is designed to help you expand from a contracted state. A question, once that impulse enters into the consciousness, into the mind, that question never leaves until you allow the answer to be realized and integrated into your being. And in that very moment, the old 'you' has died, and you will never return to it. Therefore, why not ask questions such as,

> *How can I be the presence of Christ?*
>
> *Is it possible for me to manifest miracles?*
>
> *Can I choose peace in any circumstance?*

Rest assured that by asking such questions you literally begin to redirect how you create your experience *so that* you discover the answer. Therefore, if you desire to bring Heaven to Earth, rather than looking upon the world as you think it is and saying,

> *Oh, my God, what a big task I have,*

why not simply ask,

> *Hmm… How is it that Heaven can come to Earth through* me *in this moment?*

The answer will not be hidden.

And so, with that, have you questions?

Participant: Yes, Jeshua, thank you.

It's the first time in feeling the sense of wonder that you're inviting me and us into, that I'm approaching—I usually experience goals and desires as kind of burdensome, but it's the first time I'm feeling a certain goal that I really like is something that I can approach in the spirit of fun. And I don't even really know what my question is, but I know that's what I want to talk to you about.

Now, listen well to what you've just said, and contemplate what was said a moment ago to you. There was a reason for it.

If you would indeed draw to yourself the clarity of a certain answer, *make sure that you ask a clear question.* Therefore, allow yourself, beloved friend, to just relax for a moment. It does not come from the mind, it comes *into* the mind from a relaxed state of being, a relaxed emotional body. Merely begin within yourself to say,

> *What question would clearly attract to me the answer that I seek to discover?*

So we will pause, while you allow the question to be birthed. *[Pause]*

You almost had it.

Participant: How can I discern Love's questions from fear's questions?

It is actually very simple. Love's questions literally create within the physical body a sense of joy. It may be subtle. A sense of excitement, a sense of wonder, a sense of well-being, a sense of expansion. You can learn to discern the quality of this feeling in the cellular structure of the body itself. Fear's questions create exactly the opposite: a loss of aliveness, a sense of foreboding, a contraction, a coldness, a darkness. A very good practice, then, for you as well as for many (and luckily your question can serve more than just yourself)...

As you sit in your meditation and allow questions to come, as you begin to become disciplined in your awareness that you're watching what's going on in the mind from moment to moment, when questions come up in your mind, pause and look at it, and ask yourself,

> *Is this a question from Love or from fear?*

And then ask yourself,

> *What do I notice in my beingness that is associated with the arising of the question? Is it a feeling of fun and wonder, a bit of an excitement, a sense of expansion? Or is it a contraction, a coldness, a foreboding, a dissonance instead of a resonance?*

Does that make sense for you?

Participant: Yes, it does.

It would be very good for you to practice with that. For you see, everything is a matter of vibration. Thought is a frequency of energy. God's thoughts are the highest form of energy—Love unimpeded, meeting no obstacles. Love is a state in which fear cannot be present.

Therefore, look well and learn now to *feel* the quality of energy that you are abiding in, as different questions arise in your mind. You will come to see very, very clearly that the qualities of energy revolving around and emanating from questions being birthed through and in the vibration of Love are completely and totally different from the feeling and vibratory quality of the questions arising in and around the energy of fear. In fact, they are as far from one another as the East from the West, and have literally no similarities. One specific quality that comes from questions of Love is a feeling of relaxation, so there is not a sense of urgency and impatience. Hmm. Just a thought to think about, to *wonder* about.

Beloved friend, because you have chosen to take the time to allow the clear formulation of the question, now that 'unseen something' can begin to direct a much clearer answer to you. And the clarity of the answer is what moves you from who you are toward what you wish to be. And, of course, what you're wishing to be is who you really are.

Participant: Yes

Indeed.

Participant: Thank you, Jeshua.

Do you know why this work occurs? Because I was willing to ask a clear question of myself when I was a man who walked upon this plane and saw the incredible limitations of physical form, and dared to think new thoughts. How could I possibly find a way to communicate with all minds in all dimensions of creation? What would I have to become? How would I need to change in order to experience unlimited communication? The answer was the process of crucifixion, resurrection, ascension, Christed Consciousness. So the answer taught me, because it became my experience—all based on the desire of finding an answer to a clearly asked question.

Where there are no questions, you already have your answer. And how many in your world never ask new questions, and then wonder why nothing changes?

Participant: The question is how to develop a greater clarity and discernment around wearing one's own emotional body and energy and staying clear with that and not, so to speak, take on the cloak or clothes of another's emotional body and wearing theirs?

Beloved friend, imagine that you are sitting in a grand orchestra and there are many violins and many flutes and many oboes and many clarinets, and what have you, that comprise this orchestra. And the show has not yet started and so everyone is tuning up their instruments. And as you sit there (you are a flute player) you place the mouthpiece in the instrument, and as you raise it to your lips you're a little nervous because, after all, this is a new show for you, you're the rookie on the block, so to speak. And you seem distracted by the sound of the oboe, the sound of the clarinet, the beating of the drum, the little squeal of the strings of the violin. For a moment you are distracted. Which sound is *my* sound? How can I hear my own sound if all these other things are making noise around me?

The virtuoso, so to speak, the master of the instrument, learns to put their attention on what they *want* rather than on what they fear is *preventing* what they want. And what you want to do is hear the sound of your own flute. And so you bring your instrument to your lip, and you begin to blow across it, until you find just the right angle so you can begin to emit the note.

> *Oh, that's the one I like. Oop, now I'm being distracted by the oboe again. Rather than thinking, how can I separate myself from the oboe, focus only on what do I want to hear? My own flute.*

Practice blowing the note again. By turning the attention to what you want, by releasing the oboe players and the violinists and all of the rest from being blamed for distracting you. Focus on what you want. What is the frequency you want to feel in your body, what are the thoughts *you* want to think? Put your attention on generating the momentum of blowing the note that you want to hear in yourself. And as you build that momentum, it begins to sound like the note struck from a crystal glass: shining radiantly, sounding radiantly through empty space, where nothing obstructs it. So that even that the oboe player and the violinists are doing their thing, you are so absorbed, you focus all of your attention and all of your desire on not worrying about what *they're* doing, or how their sounds may be affecting you—but when you feel the effect or distraction of the oboe, you turn again to creating the sound of what *you want*. Whether it means breathing deeply, whether it means smiling lovingly, whether it means thinking a thought that "It is done and I acknowledge it." You learn to turn the attention of your mind in the direction of what *you* want to feel and to experience, to call into *your* reality. That is what builds the strength.

And, you see, that is what brings the answer to the question. For, as you begin to stabilize—by focusing on what you *want*—you become familiar with the frequency of the note that you are creating as the flute player. And the more familiar you become with that note, the clearer it becomes what is *not* that note.

And in just the same way, whenever you think you're feeling energies and you're not sure whether it's yours or somebody else's, turn the attention of the mind from that thought—that's a useless question. Bring it back to the focus of:

> *Who cares what I'm feeling now or what I think might be going on. What do I want? Oh, I want my body to be relaxed. I want to look lovingly upon the world that I see. I want to walk as a Christed being in feminine form. I want to be happy. Well, what would that feel like in this moment? Ah.*

Begin to use the power of creation, that you're always using, to create differently—by bringing the attention from worrying about the oboe player to focus on the radiant jewel that you can bring into being by blowing your own note. Strengthen that. Become it.

If you were to go to a gymnasium to exercise a muscle, and you go to lift the weight, you would not allow yourself to look around and wonder who's lifting what weight, and why can't I lift that weight over there, and all of those other things. You would know that you're only there to focus on what *you* are doing. How are *you* moving your muscles? How are *you* lifting that weight? What does it *feel* like within you? For you know that if you distract yourself, you might hurt yourself. Is that not true?

Participant: Uh-huh.

Each time you choose to let yourself be distracted by what others are doing, by dissipating your attention away from the note *you* want to learn to play, and that comes by asking the question:

> *What would it be like to be perfectly at peace in this moment?*
>
> *What would it be like to be Christ incarnate?*
>
> *What would it be like to be with no fear?*
>
> *What would it be like to be free of my past histories?*

By focusing on your note, you discover that the only time you ever harmed yourself is when you put your attention on trying to figure out what was somebody else's, and what are they doing? The more you focus your attention here on blowing the perfect note through your flute, all of this around you will begin to fall away. It is called, I believe, vigilance and discipline.

[Laughter]

Let me give you a picture.

Imagine being a Jew, the son of Jewish parents, middle class to lower middle class, as you might call it, in a cultural time frame of great upheaval: great fear and doubt and struggle and conflict. Imagine standing in a circle, what you might call a plaza, I suppose, in an ancient city called Jerusalem. And seeing the bedlam all around you, and suddenly realizing that none of it matters. The only thing that matters is *what do I want*? I could have made the choice and said I want to be a successful merchant, or a successful money changer, like everybody else. But, instead, I decided to go for the gusto and ask the impossible thought, the improbable thought, the heresy, the heretical thought: What would it be like to be Christ incarnate in the midst of this place? I turned my attention to focusing on asking what I truly wanted. And that has made all the difference.

Would you be willing, then, to begin to discipline the mind, to bring it back to asking yourself that question:

> *What is it I truly want? What would it be like right now, to become so outrageous in the midst of what I think is an insane situation, to choose to be unlimited and perfect peace?*

Any such thought like that will do, as long as it's highly unlimited.

Participant: Okay.

Does that help you in that regard?

Participant: Uh-huh, very much.

So then we'll be seeing if you decide to play the flute well. Beloved friend, you might as well, you've already explored the vagaries of the clarinet and the oboe and the trombone.

Participant: Don't forget the drums!

And the drums.

Participant: Jeshua, what is like to live the Christ vibration in 3-D?

It's a lot of fun. It is the wonder of wonders. It is so sublime and so grand that no words can contain it. It is to be in the world but not of the world. It is to be so filled with wisdom and compassion and love and power and capability, and at the same time to know that you are literally nothing. Of myself, I do nothing. And many sought to make me their god. And, yet, I was telling them, don't look at me. I'm not the maker and the doer. I am the witness of grand mystery that I now allow to flow through me. And each so-called miracle was a miracle unto me. It brought a freshness in each moment, to step with a foot upon the warm earth at mid day, and to be in total awe that that experience could arise, that by placing one foot in front of the other, I could end up at a well having a conversation with a woman that changed her life, that the holy spirit could speak through me to wonder how I even arrived at the well in the first place. It wasn't my intention. It was only my intention to be in a state of awe and wonder and allowing.

To be Christ in the third dimension is a very unique experience. It lasts only the twinkling of an eye, but that's how long the body lasts. But while it lasts, I can tell you this, nothing you can imagine or ever create, nothing any mind has ever pondered can match the sublime fullness and fulfillment that comes as the result of asking the question you have asked. For each question must be answered. And the answer is always the experience of the fulfillment of the question. Continue, then, to ask that question.

Participant: There's one that goes with it for me, and that is, if being the Christ vibration in 3-D is as sublime as you just described, then being co-creating Christ in 3-D must be a blast. And I wonder if that's ever happened in the 3-D history that we've known of before?

The answer is no. It has never occurred upon this plane. There have been many grand civilizations, but each, no matter how far removed and even beyond the one you know, as we stated earlier, by comparison yours is extremely primitive in relation to some that have existed. But in each one of them, the thought was held that some could be Christ, but not everyone. They just held that perception that there had to be this hierarchy. Does that make sense to you?

Participant: Yes.

Therefore, the thought that is penetrating or descending is the thought of a world in which all body minds manifest the fullness of the Christed consciousness. Second coming, indeed. No, it has never occurred, but it will.

Participant: So that's one of the real opportunities we have in Shanti Christo.

It is not just one of the opportunities, it is the only opportunity. Everything serves that, or can serve it. Everything grows out of whether or not there will be minds willing to ask that question with you and be committed to receiving, which means to become, the answer. For my two cents, if I had cents, I would say there could be no grander adventure than the field of time. Does that help you in regard to the question?

Participant: Yes, thanks.

Oh. Then the answer is already being received.

Participant: What an adventure. I feel like I'm waking up in the conversation we're having.

Ah. Wonder of wonders. Hmm.

Participant: The question has arisen about the Shanti Christo membership, and the comment was that it was 'exclusive' to have tapes only go to members. And the question is—what is the question? For those not able to manifest the means to become a member right now, whether the Shanti Christo play in that role to open up and extend tapes to those? What's your view on that?

Not able to manifest the means?! Beloved friend, well have you asked the question for it states a universality in human consciousness to deny the simple truth of all that we've said in this hour: *There is never a time that any soul is limited*; it *chooses* to manifest and experience exactly what it's experiencing.

No one has a dollar bill in their pocket unless they have chosen that experience. There is absolutely no one who is without power to manifest the means of manifestation if they are willing to take responsibility for their miscreations. And they smile and say,

Well, if I created that, I can start anew.

Exclusivity is the most interesting word in your language. Listen well. When one views something as being exclusive, *they* have literally chosen to place themselves on the outside of what they see as being exclusive. It is not the thing in itself, whether it be an organization, a group, a relationship. That is not what causes exclusivity. Perception creates experience—always, always, always. And if anyone would view anything and judge it as being exclusive, then there is an opportunity for them to stop and see how they literally created the feeling of being excluded. Does that make sense for you?

Free will choice is never taken away. I have never excluded anyone from me, and yet many, many, many have judged my work, both at the time I walked upon this earth, as being highly exclusive. Why did you only selected those disciples? Why are there more women than men? I didn't choose them. They chose themselves. The same is true now. Does that help you in that regard?

Participant: Uh-huh, yes.

Now. You have an interesting phenomenon in your culture where there are many clubs that are created. Men have clubs and exclude women. Women have clubs and exclude men. Whites have clubs and exclude blacks. Blacks have clubs and exclude whites, and reds, and everything else on the planet. Yet I say this unto you: all that matters is what do you truly want. If you look upon anything occurring in your society and see it as some form of exclusivity, stop and look and check your own energy. *You* are feeling excluded from something, and that is why you have called to yourself the experience that reflects the quality of exclusivity. There is something *you* are excluding yourself from in your own consciousness. It may not be that club: that is a symbol of the energy that is going on within your beingness. Therefore, if one says, well, this is exclusive, the wise student pauses, reminds themself that what they experience, they have created. And if they are seeing exclusivity, they need to begin to ask the clear question: what am *I* excluding from myself? How am *I* shutting up energies of exclusion? Does that make sense to you?

Participant: Yes.

So are there any more questions? *[Pause]*

So to each and every one of you that has heard these words, remember that it is a stepping stone. Begin to look at each and every one of your days and all of your experiences, as you being the *literal* and *only* creator of your experience. And it can be anything that you want. God doesn't care. You see, God is content to create *you*. What you do with the power that She has given unto you is your business. But part of God's creation is to extend complete freedom to his creations. It doesn't matter to God because He knows that you're going to come home, when you choose to. And your throne awaits you: the throne of mastery over *your* creations.

We begin then, now, to weave a blending that will create a vibration and frequency through this 'family'. Hmm. A family which is limited because we're excluding others! [Laughs] It is an open invitation. And any are free to join in the dance, if they have heard truthfully the desire to awaken within themselves.

In closing, then, in this hour, my peace do I give unto you—and not as the world gives, give I unto you. Why would I want to give as the world gives? Surely that is the height of insanity. For the world gives only to take away. The world gives only that you might recognize the world and its greatness. But I give as my Father once gave to me— freely, unconditionally, as the overflow of love.

Therefore, peace be unto you always, creators of heavens and hells, who are free at any time to choose anew. And because I am without time, I can wait forever for you to choose with me.

Amen.

IGNORANCE IS BLISS
September 1994

Ignorance is Bliss

Now, we begin.

And once again, greetings unto you beloved and *precious* friends.

Is it not true that wherever you look, whether within you or around you, there is but the Face of Mystery shining back at you? For from the very first, have you ever truly known what a single thing is or what it is for? Yet the thoughts within your mind, your perceptions of things, both within and around you, would lead you to believe that you do indeed *know* what a thing is and what it is for.

You would look upon an object such as a chair and *you* decide what that object is and what it is for. You would look upon the rain that falls from the clouds and *you* would decide what that thing is and what it is for. Indeed, you would look upon your brother and sister and — perceiving something about them or relating their presence to some past history you have had with them — you would decide who and what they are *and what they are for*. And when you decide what a thing or a person is *for*, you then become justified in using that thing or person according to *your perception*. You would look upon a chair and decide: because it is a chair it must be for sitting and I will therefore sit upon it. You would look upon the rain as it falls and, deciding that it is called 'rain', immediately the mind decides what rain is, where it has come from, and what it is for. You therefore act accordingly.

And yet, even this is not quite consistent. For a farmer would look upon the rain and see it much differently than what you call an athlete playing upon a field on a Saturday afternoon, or a family preparing to go upon a picnic. Therefore, what is it that decides *for you* what a thing is and what it is for? Consciousness, the nature of the mind, is very slippery indeed, and it requires great vigilance to learn to see —to comprehend, to transcend, to grasp — how consciousness, the nature of mind, is operating through you, through the body, through the body's senses, *in relationship to all created things*.

But we'll take a slight shortcut. For the things that you look upon when you decide what a thing is and what it is for, you have *projected* your value system upon these things. Something is already operating in the depth of your consciousness that stimulates an impulse which requires you to shape your experience of what you see and what you believe these things are for to fit what you most value in the moment.

Always, then, what you *truly* experience is not the thing in itself, not what it may or may not be for within itself — you experience only the boundaries of your own mind. Nothing more. And nothing less.

There are many who look upon the rain as it falls and see not just that which nurtures the soil which will grow the plant, or they see not that which is interrupting their Sunday excursion to the park, they do not necessarily see that this will change the texture of the grasses and the soil so that the athlete might have to slip and fall upon his rear-end occasionally — but rather they look not with the physical eyes and they look with a mind that is not attached to any specific need of their own, and they have learned to ask the Mystery of Creation: What is this thing? And what is it for? And they have come to see that rain itself, to use an example, is *symbolic* of Consciousness and Creation itself. They look upon even a chair or a person or a blade of grass, and they look past the perceptions they have *learned*, to inquire directly what this thing is and what it is for.

And resting in the purity of Mind, resting in the neutrality of Mind, a different process occurs. For there is no impulse arising from within their own separative consciousness, their own individual mind, their own egoic state of being — believing they need something and therefore the world becomes that which fulfills what they need — they therefore project no value upon what they see, but they await a value to be given from some source deeper than the mind associated with personal history and with the body itself. And from that deep neutrality of Mind something indeed *is* revealed. And yet what is revealed is not of the world, for what is revealed is a *Radiance*, the reflection of a grand Mystery, a *symbol* of the laws of consciousness itself in its universal rather than its personal nature.

The rain becomes that which brings sustenance to creation. The rain becomes a symbol of how gently and easily the grace of a Perfect Love descends and is given to any who would but receive it. The rain becomes a symbol of that which is purely innocent, yet gives itself to be perceived and experienced as the receiving mind would choose.

Likewise, a person is not looked upon according to his or her history, is not looked upon according to whether or not the body is pretty enough to be taken to bed for sex. The body is not looked upon as being large enough or strong enough to bowl over several smaller bodies and then you will give them a contract with big golden coins. A person is not looked upon as something which is (what is your word?) utilitarian — that is, able to perform a certain function, able to fulfill some need for yourself. And therefore what begins to shine forth through that person, your brother or sister, is not their individuality — that is, not their foibles, not their personality structure — but Light, but the presence of the mystery of Consciousness itself which arises as a gentle wave from the ocean of Mind that is without beginning and without end.

Why is this important? Because as you go through your day you believe you are directly experiencing *what is*, and you are absolutely certain that what is is *outside of you* — the person, the chair, the rain, any perceived thing is outside of you. You have not yet truly learned to understand, to comprehend deep in the cellular structure itself. For the body is a knowing mechanism. It is the way in which you attract energy to yourself. It is that through which you project the energy of your mind. It's the meeting place of inner and outer, just as the skin is the meeting ground of what is within and what is without.

You believe that what you are perceiving and therefore knowing is something outside of you that is etched in stone: it is defined, it is complete, and you know it. And yet again, I say unto you, *not in any moment whatsoever* do you ever see or perceive *anything* except that which you project *upon it* until, through the use of vigilance and mastery of the Keys of the Kingdom of Desire, Intention, Allowance, and Surrender, until the mind is retrained to rest at peace, wanting nothing, needing nothing, knowing not what a single thing is or is for — only then does the mind become capable of receiving a higher knowing, a higher intuition. Only then does the body begin to restructure itself so that its deeper, more latent possibilities arise — called third sight for one, to begin to perceive an object through the senses of the body, to *feel* a color, to hear an object that the ears cannot hear. The body itself is an incredible mechanism for joining with and experiencing all of creation.

But what blocks you from being able to hear a color is what you are choosing to project upon creation by deciding that you already know what a thing is and what it is for. Hmm. That is my pet and my pet is to give me companionship, it is to please me; and if therefore the pet acts in a way that is not pleasing, anger arises and the world is a mess. This one is my employee and my employee is a utilitarian device to assist me in doing what I think I must do to create money to survive, as much of it as I can. And therefore when the employee says, "I'm going through some sort of spiritual crisis and I won't be able to be in on Wednesday morning," immediately frustration arises because what the employer values is the production of the useless items of your culture (by and large) and therefore there is something wrong with the employee and perhaps we should replace *this thing* that does not seem to understand what it is and what it is for.

How many times in each of your days do you believe that that which you perceive around you is not fulfilling its function? Which means, of course, that it's not quite fitting in to what *you* have projected upon it.

How often in each of your relationships are you *so certain* that the other has forgotten their place, and is therefore disrupting your world? And yet how often have you truly learned to *forgive yourself* for what you have believed your brother or sister is and what they're for?

How many times have you relinquished your own ideas of what Creation is and what it is for, to rest into that place of neutrality where one's own ignorance is accepted and embraced and loved and trusted — that place in which there is a suspension of the projection of your own valuation?

How often in any given day do you rest in the peace that forever passes all understanding and ask of something unseen:

> *What is this for? What is the meaning and purpose of this moment? What would you have me see shining through the chair ... the rain ... my brother and my sister?*

For I say unto you, the eye of the needle is found at the source of your own consciousness. The way to a spiritual life is not found outside of you, but within you, deep within the core of everything you have built up around the simplicity of an innocent mystery called Creation.

The way to peace, the way to a miraculous life, lies not in insisting that the world conform to what you have believed it is for and what you have believed about yourself — but rather, in relinquishing all of the ideas you have learned, in relinquishing even the belief that you *exist*, in relinquishing the belief that you must continue into the next moment as a physical being, to look upon the most primary perceptions you carry as a consciousness that is having a third-dimension, or physical, experience, to relinquish *all of them* upon the altar of your heart and to own wholly your *complete* ignorance. For only a mind thus emptied of itself can be taught anew.

The way to peace in life, the way to mastery, the way to union with all of Creation — indeed the way to a perfect and completed Christedness — lies not in trying to make or do, but in mastering the art of relinquishing, the art of resting in the humility and innocence of a divine unknowing.

> *Father, that which is the Source and Creator of all, that which pervades all things, mystery shining forth from mystery, I know not what a single thing is or what it is for. I thought I did yesterday, and even in the last moment, but now I choose to relinquish all things*

> *and rest in that Perfect Peace whereby, perhaps, I will be shown how to perceive and therefore to experience anew.*

Herein is the path of *power*.

Power in your world means to manipulate, to control, to get what you want. But I say this unto you: Are you sure that you *know* what you want? Or what you want, is this not resting on what you *believe* you must *have*? And what you must have, is this not a belief in perception that rests on your *prior determination* about what the world is and what you are? If you do not know yourself, how can you know what you need and what you want?

Therefore, beloved friends, we would begin to ask of you to be determined to utilize your experience of each moment as an opportunity to bring vigilance to the mind by *choosing* to acknowledge *your complete state of ignorance* in each and every moment. For he who says that he "knows" probably knows not. And he that says "I know that I know not" probably knows.

Contemplate that phraseology, for within it is much wisdom. The first is the expression of the consciousness of the world. For all you need do is sit upon a park bench and watch your world drive by and walk by, and everybody knows what they're doing, where they're going, why — and of course it's important. But only that one that knows he knows not rests for a moment upon the park bench and says,

> *Father, what would this day be? Teach me. Show me. I know nothing.*

For the one who knows nothing rests in humility and then is free to marvel at that which he or she is guided to do and that which is *revealed* to their consciousness.

For only when the mind is released from projecting can it become an empty vessel in which it can receive the radiance of a mystery shining forth from the Mind of God through each and all created things.

The way of awakening, then, is the way of acknowledgement of one's *perfect ignorance*. The way of peace requires the relinquishing of *all* of one's ideas. For only then can the mind be taught anew.

So, let's begin with something quite simple. Just where do you think you are right now? Think about it for a moment and be honest with yourself. When you sat down and placed this tape within your little machine, were you not already operating from a place of consciousness that said:

> *I know exactly what I'm doing. I'm in my house. I'm in my car. The weather is such-andsuch. I only have so much time and oh my goodness, shouldn't the government be doing this and shouldn't that be happening? What about that athletic event? What a dummy to fall on his butt because it was raining, and now the game is lost, and therefore I'm depressed.*

All of these things are going through your mind. You put the tape in and you've already decided you're going to hear something that either will uplift you or make you think. Perhaps you've already decided that you're going to be hearing me communicating through this, my beloved brother — rest assured, in the future you will have some surprises. You have already decided what *is* before you begin it.

You have already decided how to approach the experience: by turning on your thinking analytical mind so that you heard the words in the sentences and therefore believe that you will come to understanding.

But I say unto you, there are some among you who have learned how to move into ignorance and innocence. And when these words are spoken, you do not so much hear them as see pictures. You feel them rather than think about them. You receive insight from the silence between the words. You feel a transmission of energy that you could not ever explain to anyone because it has nothing at all to do logically with the formation of little sounds you call words to which you have already ascribed meaning. Although you seem to be listening to a tape, you are already in a quality of consciousness that transcends the normal process of listening and analyzing and drawing conclusions.

It has been said that the meek will inherit the earth. What does that word truly mean, then? The meek are those who have learned the futility of their learning.

The meek are those who know and accept that there is only Mystery arising. The meek are those who know they are not what they thought they were. The meek are those who wait in each moment for revelation to occur. The meek are those who smile at the futility and insanity of acting in the world *as if* they knew what a thing is and what it's for. They wait on divine consciousness. They wait on the purity that emanates from the Source of Being that can shine through them and reveal to them, moment to moment, what the purpose of any moment is.

Any master, any true master, is one of the meek. For mastery does not rest on the accumulation of knowledge. Mastery rests in divine ignorance, in which true knowledge shines forth — the knowledge that would radiate through your mind from the mind of God, the knowledge that would enlighten even the sensory mechanisms of the body so they receive what is being transmitted from all created objects in ways that transcend ordinary knowing and seeing and hearing.

So look around you, right where you are. You think you know what time it is and therefore perhaps you think you're supposed to still be in bed. You know what time it is and so perhaps you are supposed to be hurrying out the door to get to some kind of a job that you *think* is going to provide you with what you *want*, because what you *want* is linked to what you *think you need*, and what you *need* is linked to your *belief* that you must survive into the next moment in a certain way of lifestyle. Or perhaps you believe that if you did not have that job that the whole universe would collapse around you and not support you whatsoever and therefore, of course, reality *is* that you must be on your way out the door to get to your specific job, even if that job is not your heart's desire. Do you see how it all works?

Somewhere in the depth of your mind you have taken on perceptions about what things are and what they are for, including your body, your mind, your thoughts, your feelings. And from these, deeply embedded, deeply habituated, you have decided what you *need* to fit what you *believe* to be true. And from what you *need* you project impulses of what you *want*. And what you want determines how you will see every object and every person and every drop of rain and every wisp of cloud and every chair around you. But again I say unto you, meekness truly begins with the complete recognition that *you don't know* what you truly want, unless you have come to a place where there is silent voice calling within that says to you,

> *I want God. I want Peace. I want to come Home.*

Earlier I asked you if you knew where you were, and I say this unto you: If you believe you're sitting in a chair, if you believe you know what time it is, if you believe you know what this day is to mean for you, you do not know where you are. *You literally do not know where you are.*

Would it not be wise if you're going to act in any given day, to at least begin to contemplate the simplicity of the question:

> *Is it not wise to first know where I am, before I decide what I will do?*

The human mind believes it knows where it is, and yet where it is is within the complex of insane notions and fearful perceptions it has made in error to replace the simplicity of the reality of being in the Mind of God — unlimited forever, totally supported and provided for in each moment.

If you knew where you were, truly, if all of humanity knew where it was, the world as you know it would *stop dead in its tracks* and soon cease to be. That which is called Wall Street wouldn't even open in the mornings. No one would go to the great halls of government. Many of you would never step foot in what you call an automobile again.

Do you know what would occur? First, there would be a delight in waking to watch the first rays of light shine forth from the sun, mystery of mysteries, and to begin to touch the gentleness of the earth. Your delight of the morning would be to discern the subtle qualities of how light changes the coloration of the world around you. And you would tune in and *feel* the vibratory quality of how nature around you begins to wake up with each coming day. You would hear the sound of a leaf coming to life in the morning, not through the ears, but through the very skin of your body. You would delight in allowing your awareness to touch and caress and embrace each created thing in that moment. Perhaps you would be moved to plant seeds within the soil, or perhaps to harvest what you have previously planted. You might be called to join with your neighbors in singing and dancing, or in quiet prayer. You would be so amazed at what is unfolding around you, within you, that your mind would not be able to analyze, compare, contrast and judge. You would be too blown away by the incredible, powerful mystery that Creation is and you would know beyond all doubt that this day you will be provided *all* that you need and that your daily bread will come to you. 'Daily bread' is not just what you stuff down the mouth of the body. It is emotional nurturance. It is play. It is laughter. It is fulfillment. There are many levels of daily bread. And yet it falls upon your shoulders like the drops of a soft spring rain without ceasing, manna from Heaven. You would be so immersed in the contemplation of the Mystery of God, who is but Love, that never would a fearful thought arise, never would a judgmental thought arise, never, never would you actually believe that you know what a thing is and what it is for. You would delight in allowing these things to be revealed to you.

And so I ask you to compare that definition, that picture, with how humanity lives, and then ask yourself:

Does humanity know where it is? Do I know, as a part of humanity, where I am? Am I willing in this moment to completely relinquish all ideas I have ever had about what anything is and what it's for and therefore what its meaning is, what its usefulness is?

Can I choose to rest in the place of neutrality and to allow something beyond myself to teach me anew?

So, if you are standing, I want you to sit, and if you're sitting, remain where you are — now that that phrase has new meaning. Truly *feel* the fabric of the object you are sitting upon. *Feel it!* Open up the cells of the body and allow the vibrational quality of where you are sitting to penetrate into your beingness. Let the skin be an organism for hearing and not just for feeling. Can you hear the note being sung by the thing upon which you are sitting? All things contain consciousness, or life.

For all of creation is but Life itself, and therefore there is wisdom and intelligence radiating through each and every created form. Feel the quality of vibration. Does a color come into your mind? Not the color of the fabric, necessarily, but the color of the vibration represented by this object. Is it a color that you like? Does it feel good where you are? Rest assured if it does not, get rid of that object and give it to someone else in need, and procure for yourself that which creates the vibration that brings you a pleasure beyond the ego.

Begin to bring into your life those things, whether a chair, whether a flower, whether a pen, the color of paper that you use, let all things begin to reflect and exude toward *you* that which reminds you of the infinite creativity, the infinite loveliness, the infinite quality of vibration of peace and beauty and mystery — the quality of God's Presence. If you now have clothing upon your body, feel it for just a moment. Feel the fabric of the clothing on your body. Who told you you needed to wear that? Who told you you needed that color or that style? Does it truly resonate with you? Does it feel natural? Does it come from the earth or has man made up his own fabric that you now place upon the body. For I say unto you, that which has not come forth from nature, left untampered, blocks certain frequencies that are emitted from the natural world, from your Mother Earth.

Therefore it is always wise to use the most natural of fabrics upon the body.

Does it express beauty and wholeness to you or is it something that you "made do" with because it saved you golden coins? And if you buy something to save you golden coins, are you not telling yourself that you live in a universe of lack and you have no power within yourself to bring abundance into your life? And if you have no power to bring abundance into your life, are you not saying that your Creator has created you limited and unworthy of Creation? *Everything you see around you in this moment is a reflection and a symbol of what you have believed is true about Creation and about yourself.*

Well I didn't mean to become quite so forceful, but it is time for the truth to penetrate consciousness, for soon the earth will no longer tolerate any vibration of consciousness that does not radiate and resonate with light and beauty and freedom and innocence and play and unlimitedness. Therefore, if you would change the world, change your mind. And if you would change your mind, relinquish all of your own ideas.

For those of you in relationship, or those of you that can create a relationship, even if you must run an ad and say that you pay ten dollars of your golden coins per day for someone to be a temporary friend — in other words, if you can find another to be in a relationship with — a very valuable exercise is just this:

Sit with someone. Look into each other's eyes. Place the hands upon whatever you're sitting on, possibly the floor or chair, whatever, look into each other's eyes; and each of you admit to the other the truth about yourself. What will first happen is that you will begin to say,

> *Well, my name is so-and-so and I live in such-and-such a place*

and I had these parents, and oh my God, and I have these skills…

None of that is the truth of who you are. The truth of who you are is that you don't know who you are, you don't know what you're for. You are in a state of *complete divine ignorance*. And you can prove it to yourself in this way. Look upon the person sitting across from you for at least two or three minutes and then tell them the thought that is occurring in their mind in this moment. You'll find that 99.9999999 percent of time you are totally wrong. Ask them to do some gesture, to change the body language, and then tell them what they are trying to express.

You will discover again that they can fool you any time they want. Do you know what a thing is and what it's for? Do you really know what's occurring in any given moment? My reply to you is that you do not, as long as you are relying on your own thoughts and ideas.

After doing this exercise with each other for a few moments, then practice resting in the neutrality of your own ignorance.

Father, I know not what a thing is or what it is for.

Then ask the other person to hold a certain thought within their mind. It could be a picture of a pink elephant. It could be anything. And as you rest in your ignorance, giving up all hope of knowing what is, what it's for, what needs to be communicated, you might just find that you begin to realize that some idea is being predominant in your mind. It could be outlandish. It could be a pink elephant. And then simply say to your friend,

I think you're holding the thought of a pink elephant, or that your body language is conveying a certain thought.

Through this practice you will refine your ability to receive knowledge in a new way. And as you refine that you will find yourself in a state of what is called Cosmic Consciousness, or Christed Consciousness, where you have so mastered the relinquishing of your own ideas that what is *truly* real and what holds purpose in the moment is revealed into your consciousness moment by moment by moment, even it concerns someone who's on the other side of the planet. And then when you ask within,

> *What should I do with this?*

the Holy Spirit tells you, and you will know when to speak and when not to speak, when to act and when not to act. Resting into the quiet of your own unknowing allows Life to reveal itself through you and to you. But what is revealed will not be perceived as your own and you will understand that you can taken no credit for what unfolds through you. And you will say as I once said,

> *Why do you call me good even when miracles are done through me? There is none good but God. I am but a channel of the Mystery of Life. I am empty. There is no one at home.*

And when there is no one, there is everyone.
And when there is nothing, there is everything.
And when you are empty, you shall be filled.
And when you are at peace, you will know the meaning of power
And when you want nothing, you will have all things.
And when you need nothing, you will know the meaning of freedom.

Beloved friends, contemplate well what is shared this day, for it is time to truly bring vigilance to the mind. Recognize that as you go through your day everything you *think you perceive* is a reflection of where you have *allowed* your consciousness to reside, either in the attitudes and beliefs that you have learned in the world, which will show you only what is insanely unreal, or in the quiet neutrality and peace of your divine and perfect ignorance.

We will spend much time together, moving more deeply into this understanding and into that which helps facilitate your return to ignorance. For consider this: The meek are the masters of creation and yet they seem to know nothing at all. And each and every moment of their existence is given over to the practice of the Keys of the Kingdom, desiring only perfect union with God, setting the intention of relinquishing all ideas of their own, practicing the key of allowing, resting into neutrality so that life might reveal itself to them and through them.

And finally, surrendering every trace of belief that there's something inside your body called 'yourself' that is uniquely yours and that you must take care of and it must get what it wants: the hungry little ghost called the ego. Surrender means to awaken to the reality that there has never been anyone where you are, except the presence of Christ. When you know yourself, you will know that you are all things. You'll know that you are empty and that no one's home, that there is only Life living itself. You will have learned that it is not by striving but by relinquishing that the Kingdom is revealed. And you will discover that you've always been at home.

Contemplate well these things, then, and by all means bring lightness and humor to it. Laugh at yourself. Laugh at the self you thought you were. Whenever you believe you need something to be a certain way, slap your thigh — that would be a good use of it at any rate — and laugh, and tell yourself,

> *My God, I actually thought I needed something to happen in a certain way. Hah! The joke is on me.*

And then the wisdom of how things are unfolding can reveal itself to you. And when you know that there is wisdom flowing through the creation of each moment, you just might make the decision to once again *trust* Life. And Life is but Love radiating forth from the Mind of God. And that is where you are sitting right now.

Peace then be unto you, beloved and precious friends.

Amen.

CHOOSE TO SEE
October 1994

Now, we begin.

And indeed, once again, greetings unto *you*, beloved and holy and only-begotten Child of God. Listen well to this greeting. Greetings unto *you*, *beloved* and *holy* and *only-begotten* Child of God. This is, in Truth, the truth of who you are. This is in Reality all that you can be.

For before the time when the first stars were set in the heavens, already did you abide as your Father has created you to be. No, not as the mind would show you 'yourself'. There was not such a thing as what you know as a body. There was not such a thing as a thought of temporality. There was not the trace of the thought of birth, and therefore, no concept or experience of what you would call death. In that ancient beginning, before time is, already were you created *whole* and *complete*, the perfect loving extension of the Mind of God. And God is but Love. This being true, it is true *always*. There is not a moment in time in which this truth is interrupted. There is not a moment in any of your experience in which the real world ceases to be.

How, then, can it be that you find yourself seemingly constricted into the space and volume of a physical body? It is very dense and often quite hard. How is that you look out through physical eyes *so certain* that what they show you is real? And certainly you can prove it to yourself. Just try to walk through a wall and you will convince yourself that that wall is completely real, that the body is who you are, that's the way it is, and it cannot change. Taking that conception into the mind, taking that perception *to be what is true*, you teach yourself to deny the gentle Voice given unto God to His holy and only creation—you—and placed lovingly *within* you, from before the beginning of time.

That Voice is with you still and always. But it requires, if you would hear it, a willingness to surrender every perception you've ever believed about yourself or about the world—and that very act feels like total insanity.

What will happen to me if I give up my belief that that wall is real?

> *What will happen to me if I give up all the perceptions that I know are etched in stone and I must act from them in order to survive in this world that I certainly didn't make? After all, I came into it as an accident born of my parents' passion. I simply found myself here, and this is the way that I am.*

It does seem absurd to give up such deeply-rooted perceptions and beliefs *and experiences* that you believe have helped you to survive, in order to entertain what seems to be sheer insanity.

I have said often and through many channels that the world that you perceive is diametrically opposed to the real world. It is the exact opposite. Therefore, if you would know the real world, the first step that is required is to retrain the mind to be willing to *accept* that all things you believe you see are *only* temporary reflections, or illusions—that the physical eyes have never shown you the real world, that your ideas and perceptions based on the data that comes through the senses of the body, these ideas have *always* been diametrically opposed to the truth of the real world.

If there is, then, a call born within you, if there is that spark within you—which means simply that the Voice for God has finally crept in a little bit and you've begun to hear—if there's something in you that calls you to know the *real world*, if there is something in you which calls you to know the Peace of God, if there is something in you that is even just a little willing to surrender whatever needs to be surrendered to know that reality of God's Peace and that Perfect Love which already you are, then you must make a decision. And the decision is this:

> *If I have used time and experienced time to gather evidence that what I have taught myself to believe is true, then perhaps I need now to use time to* relinquish *what I have believed to be true.*

The decision is the choice to be fully committed to allowing the experiences of time, beginning right where you are in your daily life, to be reinterpreted for you by a Voice that is in you but is not quite yours. At least not yet. The day will come when you will be one with that Voice. The day *will come* when you will know the truth that

I and my Father are One.

The day will come when, though the physical eyes still seem to be operating, you look lovingly upon the world that has been made in error, this physical dimension, this constriction that you perceive within your mind—for you will be looking at it through an *inner eye*, an aspect of your beingness, your consciousness, that does have certain physical correlates, yes, and you will activate that eye and you will open that eye and you will look upon all things *through* that eye. And the sensory data that comes into you will be as though filtered or transmuted so that what you judge of what you see comes not from the beliefs and ideas that you have mis-created, but those perceptions cleansed and purified by the Light and the Wisdom that will shine through that inner eye.

Once when I sat with my friends that you have heard are called disciples, I said unto them: When the eye becomes single, then you will enter the Kingdom. What does such an odd statement mean? First it speaks on many levels to a truth that can only be understood through the concept of levels. "When the eye becomes single" means that you have learned to relinquish your fixation of having the attention of your mind linked *to your physical senses alone* and therefore to all of the concepts and perceptions you have built *upon* sensory data coming in through the body—and you have moved that attention to become centered and settled in the *inner eye,* so that the Light of Consciousness that shines upon your experience *reveals* the reflection of the *real* world *through* all that you see and experience.

The second level is this: You find yourself in conflict, you find yourself in a world of duality. There is not a single thing—there's always this and that; up and down; light and dark; good and bad; right and wrong; best value, worst value; best choice, worst choice. Everywhere you go throughout the day you are confronted with the need to make a choice. This or that. Quite frankly it is simply the choice between Love and fear. But in your world that duality prevails, and that is why the world in which you find yourself is *not* the real world. For the real world is single and whole and *only* Love abides there.

Now, to move then into the "single eye" requires that you solve the dilemma of living in duality. How do you do that? For everywhere you find yourself, there you are in the physical world as long as the body lasts—and the body will last as long as *you*, as a conscious being, continue to make the choice for it. By retraining the mind to choose only Love, by retraining the mind to surrender every perception you've ever held about anything or anyone—in this way the day will come when there will not be a *choice* for a physical body, but you will find yourself much indeed with a body yet.

Now, how do you do that? How do you dry the skin while you're swimming in the stream? How do you still the noise while you are abiding in a deafening concert of music? By learning to retrain the mind. There is no other way.

We spoke to you earlier that you do not know what a single thing is or what it is for, and *that* is very good beginning to the process of retraining the mind. The goal, then, is to reach a place of consciousness *prior to* every decision, in which you *remember* the truth of who you are and that you are not yet living in the real world—that what you are seeing before you as a choice that you think you have to make is an illusion based on your past experience.

When you train your consciousness to abide in a clarity of singularity that exists just prior to every choice that confronts you, then and there you can learn to hear the voice of the Holy One who will choose for you, with your permission, until *your* consciousness has learned that that one's choices, the Holy Spirit's, are always one hundred percent accurate and serve the highest in you. You then assimilate or take on, you allow yourself to re-abide in the consciousness of the Holy Spirit itself, and you *become that Voice*. It is no longer outside of you, no longer hard to hear, for you have surrendered everything that kept your identification linked to something other than that Voice. Then, in truth, there *are no more choices*, although you seem to abide yet within the world, living from the singularity of the eye that sees clearly the reflection of the real world through the illusory world that you have laid over the top of it. From that place, although you live seemingly yet within the body, you will know directly the *experience of living without choice*. The dilemma of duality is solved, for there is no longer fear within your mind—nothing to hold onto, nothing to seek, nothing to gain and, most importantly, nothing to lose. For the fear of loss is what keeps you forever entrenched in the conflict of duality, and the 'single eye' remains unknown.

Retraining the mind, then, is the greatest use of time that you have before you. None of the directions in which you think you are going will ever take you to Heaven if those directions have grown out of the way you've learned to make choices. Let me give you an example:

> *I am a body. I must survive. The world is out there and I know it can be rather cruel. I better stay with the job I've got because survival is the greatest value to me. Therefore I will choose (one believes freely) to remain where the heart is not at peace.*

That is not a choice. Not a choice at all. It is an effect of fear and a lack of right knowledge.

Freedom from all circumstance, freedom from conflict and fear, does not come when the body seems to die. For if conflict or the end of conflict does not come into your consciousness before the body dies, rest assured you will find yourself simply and yet again in and as a body perceiving a world in which conflict and duality reign.

There is no choice, then, but to awaken. And to awaken means that you *relinquish* everything you thought you knew and allow an inner Voice to *retrain the use of your mind* until you recognize the real world and abide in that Peace that forever passes all understanding.

Many in the world will not recognize you when this has been completed; for you see, no one can recognize a mind that has awakened unless at least some degree of awakening has occurred within *them* as well. And that's okay. For while the body lasts you are free to teach only Love. But not from the perception of believing that *you* know what that means. Only Love knows what it means; and only

Love knows what needs to be extended in each moment. Therefore, while you seem to live yet in the world, from that singularity that is established through the retraining of the mind and the relinquishing of fear, from that place you will find that before each breath you are constantly and simply asking:

What is this moment for? What would You have done through it?

And you will come to hear the voice of the Holy One so clearly and so distinctly, that you will totally relinquish any doubt, any fear, any anxiety. And from that moment you will indeed enter the Kingdom, for the eye will have been made "single". You

will go then as the wind, knowing not where you came from or where you're going. There will then only be the eternal present in which you know beyond all shadow of doubt that you are infinitely free and radiant forever and there is only the Love of God present wherever you happen to find yourself. Love will be present when fear is gone.

Therefore, in retraining the mind, begin by recognizing that you do not know what *this* moment is for, whatever this moment is, as it arises. Acknowledge that there is one that you can trust—the Holy Spirit, the teacher and guide given equally unto all until all have returned to the real world.

Learn to trust what you cannot see. Learn to hear what seems not to be spoken out loud. Learn to feel that which does not come *through* the senses, but emerges from *within* them and enlightens them. Learn to look truthfully upon the places where fear has made your home, and as you look upon that place, look lovingly, for you have learned to fear looking upon your fear. And why? Because you believe you *are* that fear expressing as some pattern in your so-called personality. Because you are identified with it, your deepest fear is that if you allow Light to be shined upon it, it will dissolve —and you with it. That is why I said earlier the deepest fear is the fear of loss of a self that never was.

Choose to See

By retraining your mind through the humility of recognizing that you don't know what a single thing is for, that your only choice that you would make is to know and remember and live in the Peace of God, the mind will come to be restructured, to be cleansed and purified—and you will look out upon a world transfigured, and you will see shining through it the reflection of the real world. You will know that you are fear-less, for there is no longer a self that requires your constant protection against the great forces that seem to stand against it. For there can be no great force standing against the True Self, that which shines radiantly with you, throughout you, and throughout all of creation. And that Self is the real world.

You are that One, shimmering brightly, far greater than ten thousand suns. And when you look upon the vastness of your sky, realize that it merely reflects a speck of the Light in which it itself has emerged—and that Light is you. All worlds, all dimensions, all planes of existence arise from within *your* Holy Mind. You are the great vastness that contains Creation even now. And even now, in Reality, you abide and live and exist only in the real world. And the only distance between you in the real world and the you that you think you are in the unreal world is the width of a thought that you would insist on thinking.

Learn, then, to retrain the mind to relinquish that thought whenever it appears. And you will know, though it takes many forms, for you will always feel constricted, you will feel separate from your brothers and sisters, you will feel that the love of this earth of yours is distant from you and that the Peace of God is nowhere to be found. That is a sign that you have chosen to identify and to insist upon a thought that can only birth unreality. Stop trying to defend it. Stop trying to cherish it, because you think you made it and therefore you must keep it. Simply let it go. A thousand times each day let it go. And choose a new thought, a thought of simplicity:

I know not what a single thing is; Holy Spirit, teach me anew.

And allow time to become not that through which you seek your own ends, but rather that through which you allow complete correction to come to the holiness of your Perfect and Radiant Mind.

> *But, but, I have all of these problems. Jeshua, what am I supposed to do with all of these problems?*

Relinquish them. They are illusions. Everything that you think you see as a problem to be solved is the *effect* of first having chosen an insane thought. Simply choose again, as often as you need, until peace returns.

I promise you this: If you become *wholly committed* to awakening from the dream you have dreamed since the stars first began to appear in the heavens, and even before that, if your one desire is to be only what God created . . . then lay at the altar of your heart with every breath, everything you *think* you know, everything you *think* you need, and look lovingly upon every place that fear has made a home in your mind, and allow correction to come. It will come. Regardless of how you experience it, it *will* come.

And the day and the moment will arise when all of your pain and fear and suffering will have vanished like a wind that pushes the foam of the wave away, revealing the clarity of the ocean beneath you. You will literally feel throughout your being that there never was a dream. Some memories will remain with you and you will know that somewhere you must've dreamed a dream or had a thought of wondering what it would be like to be other than the way God created you, but it will be such a faint echo that it will leave no trace upon you. In your heart you will smile gently, regardless of the circumstances in which you find yourself. There will be peace from the crown of the head to the tips of the toes, so to speak, and that peace will walk before you wherever you go. It will enter a room before you enter it with a body, and those who are becoming sensitive will wonder who has come into their place. And some will even say, "Behold, I believe Christ has come for dinner." And you will be that one, for that is who you are—Christ eternal.

Enter with me then now into that place of peace. Those of you that yet believe you are but a body, then begin there. Begin by allowing the body to relax and know that that's not something you can *try* to do: you need only allow it. And as the body relaxes, let your attention recede from the things that you believe are around you.

Give up your need to keep an eye on the world. Give up your need to believe that there is something to accomplish and somewhere to go. Let it sink into the depth of your own being. Not looking to see what's there, but surrendering. Let the breath flow through the body as though something else were breathing it for you. Relax even the activity of the brain, as though it were just another muscle that you could allow to relax. And as you rest and surrender into that inexplicable place of being—the mystery of *your* existence far beyond what the body could ever touch and know, far beyond what the human emotions are capable of containing, far beyond every thought and every belief and every experience you've ever known—there rests the shimmering brilliance of the Light of your Self. Abide in that. Surrender into that. Know only that.

And there, in that place, the great depth of your own mind and being, this day, make a new choice.

> *Father, I know not what I have done, I know not how I have dreamed the dream of separation from You, but I relinquish it. I acknowledge that I do not know what a single thing is or what it's for. I know not the moment of my own creation, and therefore I surrender into the radiance and purity of your Peace and your Love. I open my self to receive only You. This alone I am asked to do of You, and this alone I choose. Grant me that wisdom and that strength and that passion by which I might learn to use time constructively as a sacrament of surrender of all that has been unlike Love within me. You are the Way, the Truth, and the Light. And I return to the sacred place of our union. I remain as You have created me to be.*

So, remember then that you will awaken to your own call. You are doing so even now. What you experience along the way is completely and freely chosen. Not one bit of it has been necessary, yet not one trace of it extinguishes or limits the radiance of who you are. It's all in the simplicity of a moment's choice. Let time, then, become your precious friend until time is needed no longer and is given over to the Holy Spirit. You might then yet find yourself in time again and yet again, but you will not experience it as the world has taught you to. You will see it only as a temporary dance in which you are enjoined freely as a way through which the Love of God can gently descend and touch the unreal world, lighting it again with Reality and bringing the unreal to the real, bringing Heaven to Earth.

You are that one in whom our Father remains eternally well pleased. You are that one unto—what has been given unto you, all power under Heaven and Earth, right now in the palm of your hand. For the power of Heaven and Earth, which is a duality, is the power of *choice*, the power of *consciousness*, the *power* to be committed to own all that you see as self-created, the *power* to relinquish it to that one Voice within you that knows alone how to transmute and translate every thought you have ever held to that which reflects perfectly the radiance of the love that joins you with your Creator. In Truth, the way *is* easy and without effort—if only the choice is made.

Herein we come to the close of this moment's message, again as a stepping stone linked to what has been shared previously. Use it well, use it wisely, and contemplate it often, for it will remind you of the path upon which you walk. For in Truth, if you hear these words now, you *have already chosen* to reclaim the real world within you.

So, we will give pause for a few moments here. And then if you would be willing to give me some of your time, we will entertain and be entertained by certain questions that have emerged within the minds of your brothers and sisters. And many of you will know that these are likewise your questions.

Be then at peace, beloved friends, and know that I am simply here in the real world, waiting for you to recognize that that, too, is where *you* are; and that you no longer entertain a desire to be anywhere else.

Amen.

Participant: How does Jeshua explain his acts of Crucifixion and Resurrection in relationship to us, and what is the symbolism that he intended?

Indeed unto you, beloved brother, this is a question that has been asked of me many times and I would confess that there was a time when I asked these questions of myself!

First, precious friend, when you speak of the Crucifixion and the Resurrection, you are referring first to an activity that *did in fact occur in time*. Let no one make a mistake about that. Rest assured that as a man, like any other man, as a human being like any other human being, I walked my path to remembrance of my union with God. I learned along that path that ultimately I could give nothing to anyone without first receiving it for myself. I became what you might call Divinely selfish: that is, I utilized the body, the mind, the emotions and every experience and every opportunity to teach myself to choose only *with* the Holy Spirit. And the Holy Spirit taught me that death is unreal—period.

How then could I know that? How then could I bring it into the depth and core of my being? By allowing certain environmental pressures, you might think of them— political pressures going on in the time-frame in which I lived—to become not my enemies but my servants. I made a decision in the depth of my prayer and meditation to allow myself to enter into a drama, into an arena that took place in Jerusalem. I allowed myself to be given over into the hands of those that would become my persecutors. I allowed myself the experience of being helplessly imprisoned by those who were governed by fear and not by Love. But rest assured, *I* was governed by Love and not fear, although it did arise one final time, when I separated myself from my friends, and they separated themselves from me by falling asleep. And in the middle of the night I indeed cried out my last cry of anguish,

> *Father, take this from me. I think I've made a slight mistake here... Nevertheless, not my will but Thine.*

Now, with that last surrender, I walked through my final ring of fear and allowed events to unfold as those that were in charge of those events wanted them to unfold. I used even those moments to look lovingly upon my persecutors, to use time constructively, to see beyond the superficialities, to see the loveliness and the Christ within them and quite frankly, as I did that—even as I was stripped and whipped and beaten, as the body seemed to grow weaker and weaker, as they placed a crown of thorns upon my head; and yes, I felt the pangs of pain at a physical level, what you would call pain, without *fear* of that pain— still I focused all of my attention on seeing the face of Christ in my persecutors. And as I did that, it illuminated or refined for me, it took me to the end of my journey. In retraining my own consciousness to see only God's creation, I became one with that Power, one with that Truth without fluctuation or variance. As the events of what you would call the Crucifixion unfolded, rest assured, all anyone was watching was what their *physical eyes were showing them*. Because the masses believed the body is real, because they were identified with it, they actually believed that *I* was dying, that *I* was suffering, that *I* was being taken from them. But this pain and this anguish can come only from the delusion of believing that what is unreal is real.

Now, in time there was in fact what is called a Resurrection. There have been many, many stories about this; it's not quite as fanciful as some would make it out to be. It means simply that because my consciousness, through this final lesson to myself, had become thoroughly settled or centered in the recognition only of the real world, there came a point when the body, or the dust of the ground, merely lying there upon what you would call a sheet, upon a small platform within a certain cavern or cave (given unto me, by the way, by my uncle Joseph of Arimathea; I just wanted to get that in for you)—now there was a time, then, when there was simply no need for even that dead physical form to abide. It began to dissolve, quicken its—what do you call this?—decomposition, if you will, and literally returned to what you would call a molecular or atomic state, a place of almost pure energy and certainly not to be seen by the physical eyes, but trust me it was still there. Specks of dust, you might call it, but much, much smaller.

Now, when certain friends of mine came to the tomb and found that it was empty, they marveled. Why? Because deeply embedded in their beingness was the *belief* that the *body is real* and that consciousness is secondary. Rest assured, it's just the opposite. Now, I chose to reactivate or recreate the form of the body for very specific purposes. If you wish to communicate with someone and they do not understand that a telephone is available, you must go to their house, take them by the shoulder and speak into their ear. If even your best friends have not yet quite learned to believe that they can communicate with any mind at any time, I therefore had need of recreating the telephone of the body, to demonstrate: Look! I *am* alive, death *is* unreal, I've learned the final lesson! Touch me, hear me, feel me just as you did before the Crucifixion—and yet rest assured, I will again leave you because if I do not, the Comforter, the Holy Spirit cannot come to guide you into Truth. But the day will come when you will finally relinquish your need to believe in the world the physical eyes show you. I will come yet again to speak to you from the real world and assist you in moving into that place within yourself. I know not yet the day and the hour, but I will come when *you choose it*. Beloved brother, because you hear these words now, you have chosen, and I have come.

So, that's the historical essence of the Crucifixion and the Resurrection. What did it mean? I have already shared that with you. It was *my path of learning*. I chose it, it was not forced upon me. For my Father's will is the same as for you: that I simply abide awake in Him. It was my simple and particular path for learning that. Rest assured, this should cause celebration, for it is not necessary for you to be nailed to a cross! And why?

I have said many times that everything in your world is a *symbol*. Ask what the symbol is and it will reveal the truth, it will guide you to the real world. Therefore as you look upon the Crucifixion and the Resurrection, understand that it symbolizes the willingness to allow a death within your consciousness of what you choose to be identified with. If you choose identification with love and unlimitedness and freedom and perfect peace—with the real world—then the events that unfold, even as you experience them, lose their power to enchant you with delusion.

Contemplate that deeply. When you've retrained the mind to teach and choose only Love, and to look lovingly and perhaps laughingly upon the events that pass through you, even the body's arising and passing away, the day will come when you can enter into any experience in perfect peace. And when you enter any experience in *peace*, you will transcend it. When you enter an experience in *fear*, you lock yourself into it. That is called the creation of hell and the need for rebirth. Any experience that you wholeheartedly choose to enter from a place of perfect peace is transcended.

Let then there be the Crucifixion of all of your false ideas of yourself. Be willing to take the leap off the cliff, to entertain what seems to be absurd and insane and outrageous and arrogant, according to the world. Dare to claim that you are as God created you to be and nothing in this world holds a candle to your radiance. And long after the world seeks to destroy you—and it's always trying to do that—and long after the body has been laid down by whatever means you may choose, you will remain and you will laugh at the thought of loss and death.

This is the Resurrection then, the resurrection within your *consciousness* of the *truth that sets you free*. See in my earthly experience only a symbol of what can occur within you, as you choose to give your thoughts, to give your perceptions, to give your fears, to give your petty wants and needs over to your persecutors—for you'll believe that the angels who have come to dismantle your illusions *are* your persecutors, because death feels like persecution. Give yourself over to it. Let the mind be corrected. Let the heart open and be healed. Let crucifixion be finished that resurrection might be experienced. And when that Resurrection called awakening has occurred, you will ascend to the Father, for He will take the final step for you and you will abide in the real world.

Thank you for asking the question.

Participant: How do I know when I have surrendered myself to the Holy Spirit?

Indeed, beloved friend, you will know that you have surrendered yourself to the Holy Spirit because you will hear a loud bell go off, there'll be much confetti tossed by those in buildings above you! Hmm. Hmm. And someone will rush up to you with a microphone and say, "You are the winner!"

[Laughter]

And you can stand upon the stage and say,

> *I'd like to thank my mother and my father.*

Hm. Beloved friend, I approach your question with *levity*, for levity is something that you fear. You allow the seriousness of the intellect to interfere with the *feeling* of receiving the Love of God, like a gentle peace descending upon the cells of your being. So, there's always a point to my seeming madness.

Now, there are indeed signs that you will come to recognize. At first they're slippery because you're used to recognizing something else and calling *it* the real world. You will know that you have surrendered to the Holy Spirit, first in a brief moment here and then another moment there, but you'll begin to feel and sense a certain quality. That quality is peace, no anxiety felt throughout the cellular structures of the body, no longing, no sense of loss and no dread, just the simplicity of witnessing and allowing what unfolds as your experience in any given moment—and it is totally acceptable to you, no matter what is occurring. That seems like madness to the world, for the world says, "Well you're on the right track when you know what's happening is taking you where you know you need to be, where success is coming to you, where comfort and safety in the world is coming to you."

> *Ah, then I must be on the right track!*

No. You're on the right track when you know that from the crown of the head to the tips of the toes, you are at peace with yourself and the world around you. And as you look out upon the world in that circumstance, you see no one to blame, no one to fear, you see only innocence. It is a *palpable feeling* because, you see, you believe you're a body and that's how you judge things. Therefore as you learn to feel peace through your physical beingness, as you notice that the throat relaxes when you speak, there's no anxiety or hurrying up of your words where someone could be ranting and raving and you just allow them to do so, while *you* are undisturbed. Rest assured, part of your mind has relinquished you to the guidance of the Holy Spirit. Holy, because it's whole and not fragmented. Spirit, because it is the real world, not the unreal world that you have made.

You will know, beloved brother, when you have surrendered *wholly* to the Holy Spirit, when the thought of wanting to surrender no longer arises, when the recognition dawns that there's no longer an energy of seeking within you, when no longer do you experience fear arising in your being, when you notice its absence and realize it's not been there for a very long time. You will know that you have become One, through your surrender to the Voice for God.

Participant: What role does Jeshua want me to play in the bringing of Heaven to Earth?

I want you to sell the tickets! [Laughter] Hmm. Might as well create some profit for yourself here! Hmm.

Again, beloved brother, *levity*—for as you ask the question, it comes from a certain pattern of heaviness that there is something you must look to *outside* of yourself, that you must subordinate yourself to something you *should* do. That is a pattern of the world's thinking,

> *Well, I have to go off to work today. Well, I should get out of bed. After all, it's what's expected.*

The world mind is constantly looking outside of itself, for an employer, for a boss, for God, for a priest, for a lover, for a child, for whatever. Some in their drunken stupor would look for a lightpost to give them direction of what they should and shouldn't do. Hmm!

And yet I say unto you, beloved friend, listen well: you *need do nothing* save to choose to open and receive the Love of God, to allow the mind to be corrected so that wherever you are, you know you are

Home, you are at peace, you and your Father are One. Then, as the Holy Spirit weaves the tapestry of the Atonement, since you will probably find that your body is still existing, there may be some requests made. They will be simple and you are always free to accept them or reject them. What really matters is that you choose to become the Peace of God and allow that peace to pervade your being. That is what influences the vibrational frequencies of other minds, even if you never lift a physical finger. Compare not your path or your life with others, merely teach only Love. And seek first the Kingdom before all things of the world by reminding yourself daily:

> *I and my Father are One! I need do nothing and I remain as I am created to be! This world is harmless and already it is being translated into reality. And the Holy Spirit doesn't even need me to accomplish it!*

Therefore be happy in each day, trust what the heart says to you each day, allow yourself to touch joy each day—and be at peace. And for you especially, tell yourself a joke or two!

Participant: Is Christ different from Joshua or Jeshua?

This is a very worthwhile question. As you know, an entire religion has been built up on the exclusive identification of Christ with *me*—that is me as the historical Jeshua ben Joseph, or Joshua if you prefer. Use any name you wish, it doesn't matter to me.

Now, Christ is God's creation. Jeshua is a name given to a particular manifestation of humanity called a man in physical form, a name that separates him for utilitarian purposes from other men with different names, and women too. Christ is pervasive and eternal. Christ is the depth of your own beingness. Imagine it to be like an infinite ocean from which have arisen all waves that you call individual persons, whether male or female. Jeshua, or Joshua or Jesus, that name signifies one of those waves.

Christ signifies that which pervades equally the depth and reality of all minds and hearts. It is really more an energy, a quality of beingness.

It is the literal reflection or extension of the presence of the unlimited Love of God. Christ is God's Son, being neither male nor female, it means merely the offspring of, that which wells up out of. Jeshua or Joshua or Jesus became one with Christ, identified no longer as a man but *as Christ*. That passageway is the same one that everyone walks, since it is merely the return to right-mindedness. If you see yourself only as the wave upon the infinite ocean, that's a start; but eventually the goal is to shift your sense of identity, so that my words *become* yours:

> *I and my Father are One. Not of myself do I do these things, but my Father does them through me. In other words, there is nobody here but my Father.*

Christ and Jeshua are different at one level. They become one and the same as the mind or the individual that I *was* surrendered the illusory perception of myself as separate from God and became identified with *only* the Mind of Christ. Then, there is only Christ and the man has disappeared, except as a temporary symbol, an anchor, a roadmap, a direction that you can follow until you pass me by and become that ocean yourself. And when you no longer need me in any way, shape or form, then we will be together without interruption for all of eternity. Hm. That should give you something to chew on.

Participant: Please say more about non-physical reality.

More about non-physical reality.

[Laughter]

Have I accomplished the task? [chuckles]

Beloved friend and sister, what on earth ever gave you the thought— literally what on earth ever gave you the thought—that physicality was real? If you ask me to speak of non-physical realities, you're already assuming that your physical experience is quite real. How do you know that? Because somebody's taught you it? Because you bang into a wall and therefore convince yourself that it must be real?

Does this not also occur in dreams? When someone plunges a knife into your heart in your dream, do not you feel the dread and terror of death, of being attacked? Until suddenly you open your eyes and it may take you a while to shake it out of your cells but you realize: that was just a dream. Sure seemed real to me!

In the very same way, physicality seems real—until you begin to allow correction to come to your mind, to think the insane thought that maybe you are Christ incarnate. As the real world comes to be re-established through your awareness and consciousness, even while the body seems to abide and exist, you will sense it to be very limited. Just as you may enjoy the experiences of your dream state, but when you awaken you often feel that they were limited, there was something arising from inside of you. As you awaken to the real world, you begin to perceive and feel the body and physicality as something that is smaller than you that has arisen from within your vastness, in other words that you are much more than the body can contain.

It is therefore very appropriate not to think that you live within the body but that *the body lives within you*, it arises from within you, you contain it as a temporary teaching and learning device. Love it, embrace it, have a great time with it, but don't identify yourself with it. Don't limit your understanding of yourself to what transpires between the crown of the head and the tips of the toes and when you extend your arm out, don't you think for a moment that you stop at the end of your finger! You are pure energy, pure light, and your radiance shines through *many* dimensions and you are linked to them all continually.

Non-physical 'realities'—there are many of them, if you wish to look at it that way, and in fact the greater aspect of your beingness is non-physical. Your physical experience is like a drop in the ocean. Let that sink in. It is like a dot on a page and the whole while the vastness of your being is moving merrily along, experiencing dimension after dimension. And often this will creep into your awareness in your dreams or in your meditations: it will slip through the cracks and you'll have what's called an ecstatic experience. You'll feel like you opened, when in fact you simply allowed the openness to seep into the smallness of your physical experience.

How then to struggle to attain experience in non-physical realms? By not struggling, by beginning by acknowledging that you are pure Spirit, that all worlds have arisen from within one Holy Mind, the only creation of God. You are that vast ocean and you have merely focused all of your attention on the physical experience you are creating. You can do that joyfully or you can look at it as some kind of a dread disease. It's your choice. Nevertheless, to experience non-physical realities, merely loosen your fixation of attention on the body-mind and its experiences and problems and all of the rest, and allow yourself to entertain thoughts of your grandeur and greatness. Rest into—through allowing—rest into the feeling of infinity. The mind, or your place of awareness, will begin to open bit by bit and more, more and more until you can no longer squeeze your attention into the space and volume of a body.

This doesn't mean you're going to step on it like a bug and get rid of it! It means you'll just embrace it as another aspect of yourself, like the ocean embraces each and every wave, allows it its experience but doesn't cling to it and doesn't try to make it last; doesn't try to make a wave become rigid as though if it failed to do so, nobody will ever see the ocean. It allows the wave to rise, and then it passes away. The ocean delights in it, but the ocean itself is never identified with any particular wave.

That will do for now, because in what has been shared, as it is contemplated, beloved friend, you will find that correction is coming to certain ideas you have taken upon yourself about what non-physical realities must be and be like, and what must occur for you to experience them.

And again, 'tis a good question to have asked.

Participant: No more questions.

We will end then by saying: That's what you think! [Laughter] There will indeed be many questions and we will begin a process then in which some of this time is allotted to addressing the questions which come from this family.

Therefore in closing, know simply this: there can be no such thing as closure to the extension of Love. Be you all therefore that which you are *this one day*, don't worry about tomorrow, there is no such thing. This day, walk upon your earth while making a choice to delight in perceiving yourself as awake and alive and at peace, roaming through a countryside called the physical dimension for a very brief time. Enjoy it, look lovingly upon it and bless it with the blessings that can come only from the Mind of Christ within you.

Peace then be unto you always.

Amen.

MASTERING COMMUNICATION
November 1994

Now we begin.

You have asked in this hour for me to abide with you, to join with you yet again as your brother and as your friend, and perhaps as one still seen as one who has gone ahead a little bit. Yet I say unto you, always our minds are joined, always our hearts beat as one, always our very life is the life of the Love extended from the Mind of God that is the extension of Creation itself—and forever and always, the Son is One. And yet within Creation it can appear that I have gone ahead a little ways, while you believe you yet linger, getting a final taste of shadows long since outgrown.

And yet we are a conspiracy. That is, we *breathe together* to bring light to every shadow and every illusion. *We breathe together* to bring forth the perfect remembrance of God. And God is but Love. And if we are to breathe together, if we are to embrace Creation and allow through us a transformation of Creation to occur so that all things are returned to the light of God's Love, it becomes necessary to look at what Creation is doing.

> *Where am I in this moment?*

Do you abide in a world in which it is not necessary to speak words? Do you abide in a dimension in which it is not necessary to strive to communicate from one mind to another? Do you live in a world in which it is clear that there is no divisiveness between minds? Of course not. Therefore, if you would breathe with me, if you would desire truly to bring forth the Love of God and to transform the shadows, the illusions, the obstacles to the presence of Love, understand then that you are asked to assume responsibility for *what* you would choose to communicate and for *how* you would choose to do so.

Communication is a simple term. It simply means to create that experience in which two minds come into union so that one idea, one vibration, informs both minds and is valued equally by them. All of you have had the experience of genuine communication. For when communication succeeds, the mind is transcended, the heart opens, and there is a joining at the level of the Soul within the depth of the Mind that far transcends anything which can be uttered by words or even symbolized by words. So the goal of communication is always the same—to link two minds together at such a depth of union that separation is transcended and the Love of God remembered as the only reality. Communication: to establish communion.

I have shared with you before that there are four keys to the kingdom: Desire, Intention, Allowance, Surrender. Therefore, what you desire in any moment is of utmost importance, for from your desire you will begin to *move* Creation, move the energy of mind in a certain direction that will have a certain flavor, a certain vibration. If you desire to breathe with me, let your desire be singular of purpose.

> *Father, how might I extend my treasure this day? And my treasure is the gift of union with You that you have given to me before the foundation of all worlds. And I long that my brothers and sisters awaken to the remembrance of that union that lives within their own hearts and their own minds. Let my life in this world while it lasts be given only to the extension of the Good, the Holy, and the Beautiful.*

And if that is your desire, set it in stone, if you will, with your intention. An intention is simply a clear decision in the mind that the wholeness of your being will be committed to and dedicated to the fulfillment of your desire. In the realm of intention comes one simple question:

> *How can I communicate in this moment the depth of my intended desire to bless the world with the love of God?*

You will always communicate what you most desire and intend to communicate. You are infallible at this in each moment, and you never blunder. Therefore, where communication seems to be *unclear*, you may rest assured that there has been an *unclear* intention and desire, perhaps even a *denial* of the desire to join in loving union with another: that is, to be the presence of Christ who blesses the world. This is why if you would truly master communication you *must seek first the Kingdom* that all these things might be added unto you.

What does that mean? The path of awakening requires discipline—and well do I know that many of you think that discipline is a heavy burden. It is not. Separation is a heavy burden. To be disciplined simply means to be 'a disciple of'. And of what? Of Love. To recognize that Love is the greatest good, that Wisdom your greatest power, that Union is your greatest truth; that you are as God created you to be, and why would you ever again want to waste a moment trying to be something you're not?

So discipline means to turn away from the illusion, the temptation of giving up your Christedness, and assuming the mantle of responsibility.

> *I will be a disciple of the truth and I will rest at its altar even prior to every breath. I will cultivate within myself the skill necessary to turn every decision over to the Comforter, the Holy Spirit. I will discipline my mind. I will learn to be a master of the kingdom given unto me...*

which is simply your own mind, your own field of awareness...

> *And I will dedicate the fields in my kingdom to that which can bring forth great fruit, and offer it to my Creator.*

What would your life be like if prior to every thought you remembered your primary desire and thereby remembered your purpose for incarnation? What would your life be like if you were so fully disciplined within your own mind that only loving thoughts were spoken with your words? If you remembered your Creator so thoroughly that before any situation, before anything is uttered or done, you ask within quietly:

> *Father, what would you have me do that love might be extended and offered?*

Communication, then, requires *discipline*, and discipline grows from committed intention and a clarification of your deepest *desire*. You will always experience exactly what you're desiring.

Muddled communication? *Look within.* Is there a fear of genuine intimacy? Is there a reluctance towards forgiveness? Is there a blockage in the emotional body?

Here is a simple prayer that you can utilize each of your days, until it becomes second nature for you. When you rise in the morning, before you speak a single word or take a single action, go within the heart. Lay upon the altar of the Heart all that you think you've learned up to this point and remember that *you need do nothing*, remember that you *know nothing*, and then ask:

> *Father, this day I find myself in this world. What would you have me communicate this day with my actions, with my words, and with my very thoughts?*

Then rest in silence and see what presents itself to the screen of your awareness. Trust that prayer. Learn to use it often until it's second nature—so that in any moment, at any time, that is as the soil from which each moment is springing.

> *Father, what would you have me communicate in this day or in this moment?*

You see, the essence of genuine communication is the remembrance that you belong to *no one* but God. The essence of communication will flow more effortlessly when you behold the other as belonging *only* to God, not to the ego, not to illusion, not to you, not to another. They too are Gods, and therefore your Creator wishes only to communicate *through you* to his own. And nothing can have greater value than the communication of that which heals, that which enfolds and embraces, that which forgives, that which loves. For what you communicate one unto another, rest assured you immediately receive for yourself.

And here's the nub of the issue. If you want God, if you want to breathe one breath with your Creator, become so selfish in the domain of your own mind that all you communicate are your loving thoughts, that all you do is bless the world. For in this way you *are* blessed, and as you *give* Christ, you *remember* Christ, until Christ never fades from your awareness. And then, indeed, you are free.

Communication requires, then, in any given moment of relationship that someone assume responsibility for remembering that neither party knows anything. Now often we would see that in your relationships one would like to enter that state but is quite sure the other one doesn't want to, and so then needs to defend themselves and steps into ego consciousness—and off you go, spinning like your planet, getting nowhere. The purpose of communication is to teach only love. Therefore, wait on no one. Don't wait to see if your mate or friend wants to enter that place. Assume responsibility for doing it *for yourself* so that you can offer it freely to another. Rest assured that if you resent the fact that they haven't entered into it with you, you didn't offer it freely. Become selfish enough that you will not settle for communicating anything less than that which your Creator would extend through you, so that by doing so *you receive it yourself.*

Communication is life. Communication *is* relationship. It has nothing to do with the juxtaposition of bodies in space and time, since that is not what you are. *Communication is relationship.* Relationship is the means of your salvation.

Therefore, if I might paraphrase a phrase from your Bible: Count it all joy when those around you persecute you or attack you, for remember that in that moment you are given the power to teach only Love, to remember your desire to stay firm in your intention and thereby receive the gifts of being the one who blesses this world. Hmm. That rather makes sense, doesn't it?

> *Oh, that's right. What is it that I want to communicate? What is it I am most desirous of learning more thoroughly? . . . That only Love is real. I want it for myself, so deeply, so thoroughly, that nothing can enter into the field of awareness I call myself save the presence of God.*

Can you care enough about that, that you couldn't care less what anybody else on the planet wants? You become so selfish that you see that each moment of time is an incredible opportunity to remember the Truth by extending it. To remember that there is no such thing as 'time off'. Since each thought creates an experience, a domain, a world, that fills your awareness, what would you drink into your field of awareness? Pain and suffering; or joy and freedom, peace and the presence of Christ?

When I walked your planet as a man, I had need of learning exactly what I am seeking to communicate with you. And if there has been any power that has touched you in the few words that I've used so far, it is *only* because I have *cultivated* the clarity of my desire and *made concrete* my intention. And through the use of time as a man and through the use of communication since I left your planet with every mind that would open its heart to me, I have perfected the purity of one desire: *to teach only Love.*

The power of your communication, then, flows from the depth of your commitment and your discipline and the willingness to learn how to use the tools available to you, whether it be a pen and a piece of paper, whether it be a drawing or a painting, whether it be a hug or a handshake, whether it be a smile or a kiss upon the cheek. Can you use every gesture, every tool available in your world, to teach only Love, to discover what it means to lay your hand on the shoulder of a friend *out of* union with God, having asked first:

> *Father, what would you have me communicate? How can this hand be a vessel or a vehicle that extends the blessing of the Comforter?*

To learn how to speak in complete sentences. To learn how to take a thought and struggle with whatever you need to struggle with until you have crystallized it in the best words that you can find. Can you care enough about yourself to perfect and master the forms through which you can communicate while in this world? And can you ever come to an end to that? Of course not, since perfection is unlimited. Creation merely extends itself more and more and more and more, revealing the Good, the Holy, and the Beautiful. And all of you know what it's like to sit down and listen to someone who's just learning to play a violin. Hm! And you know what it's like to listen to a master. Something in what the master has accomplished can touch your heart more deeply, more purely, like a sword that cuts to the core reveals its gifts.

Would you be willing to become committed to One whose communication is so pure, so crystal clear, that when you communicate Love to another, *they get it?* They get it so profoundly that lifetimes of suffering is resolved in an instant, that merely by looking in your eyes they remember God. For that is the commitment of anyone who birthed Christ in their own awareness.

Oh yes, communication is very important. For what you communicate and how you choose to do so speaks to the world of what you most desire and what your deepest intention is *for yourself.* Therefore, in each word, in each gesture, in each activity you choose to participate in, you are speaking your message to the world—you are telling the world what your judgment of God is. Pure and simple.

Become, therefore, very, very selfish. Find your glory within yourself. Desire to communicate to this world the presence of God. Embrace the moments of time that you might use them constructively, that you might taste the perfect freedom of walking this plane as Christ incarnate— and never settle for less.

Now in the process of mastering communication there is an extremely important and very serious element—innocent play. Innocent play.

> *Well, I've decided to communicate Christ to the world. Hm, I have a feeling I have spent many lifetimes trying to do the opposite, but the past is passed away. Thank God for that. And today, I choose anew. Huh, how do I communicate Christ in this moment?*
>
> *Ah, I'll ask the Comforter. I'll give up my own thinking and simply ask what would be the best way to communicate Christ in this moment. If you really want to have fun, tell the one in front of you, "You know, I've decided to communicate Christ in this moment. Now just take a deep breath and give me some time, because I am learning by doing."*

Rest assured, that if you would begin each communication in that way, you will immediately disarm the one in front of you and you will have asked them to offer *you* the space of innocence. It makes it easier for them and easier for you. Then communicate whatever you will, and then ask them,

> "Well, how did I do? Did you feel it? I really love you. That's my intention here. How did it come across?"

In other words, bring innocent playfulness to your communication. See yourself as a child who is on their way to remembrance of mastery. Have fun on your planet. Drop the seriousness. Drop the veils, the personas and the egos in which the world has taught you that you need to look like you're already an expert. What do you have the commercial 'Never let them see you sweat'. Why not let them see you sweat:

> "Look, I'm just here trying to embody Christ. That's all I'm committed to. I love you. You're innocent. Now just take a breath, give me a moment, and we'll see how I do."

Then touch them, and kiss them. Then if it is words that need to come, speak the words. If it is a feeling that needs to be shared, share the feeling from the place of your perfect innocence and the fact that you are a student in the University of God Consciousness. So much seriousness comes into your communications one with another. And seriousness is the opposite of the Kingdom.

Last of all, in this short communication, always begin by acknowledging your oneness, your union with the one to whom you would communicate, whether person, whether plant, whether mineral. Hm? When you go to water a flower, begin by acknowledging your oneness. Therefore, see the sacredness of the moment and give it over to the Comforter, who alone can guide it into bearing much good fruit. And yes, I know very much that in your world there are still a few minds on your planet that prefer conflict over peace, dissonance rather than resonance. Does it matter? If you wait for another mind to want what you want, you will never achieve what you want. *Be*, therefore, what you most desire, and you are Christ, you are the Light that lights the world, you are the field of Love that attracts others to release their illusions, to release their suffering, to let go of their seriousness, to let go of all attempts to defend their rightness. You become the field that attracts the seeker of Reality to itself, *because you have accepted it first for yourself.*

Many of you that will hear these words know that I have said that a teacher of God has one responsibility: to accept the atonement for him- or herself. If you are reluctant to master the forms of your communication, have you truthfully accepted the atonement? For the acceptance of the atonement pops the mind open and you realize that your brother or sister is yourself, and you can only have what you give away. That is why communication is sacred. That is why it has always been taught: Observe the thoughts in your mind and think before you speak. For each spoken word is as a pebble dropped in a pond; it creates a ripple and a vibration that returns to you immediately. Think only loving thoughts. Speak only with the wisdom of Christ. Celebrate and honor the one before you, asking only:

Father, what would you have me communicate?

And in this way, the pebbles that you drop in the pond of human consciousness become as diamonds shimmering in the light of God's Love, radiating Light in all directions, bringing joy and abundance and wealth to those that behold your presence.

Become the Love that you seek. Master communication. For the day will come when you no longer need the body, or space and time, as a teaching or learning device for you; and yet communication will continue unbroken according to the degree of your mastery. That mastery will carry you to where I am; to a place in which separation is impossible; to a place in which by simply turning your attention you are one with the soul of anyone who's present for you. In the twinkling of an eye you will travel through a multitude of dimensions and everywhere you go you will be the presence of Light and you will touch the farthest reaches of Creation—which, by the way, goes on and keeps expanding—and you will bless it with the Love of God, and you will know such bliss and such unlimitedness that you will wonder why you ever resisted taking responsibility for communication. And you will thank God that you became so selfish as to want to *truly* teach only Love.

For now, we will let that be enough on communication. Rest assured that if you will meditate on each word chosen—slowly, deliberately, carefully, innocently—the very vibration communicated in this short sharing will already do much to bring about a correction of vibration in the depth of your own mind—that your own communication almost magically, effortlessly, will begin to improve, will flow from a deeper depth and therefore be far more satisfying in your own heart.

A teacher of God is a master of communication. Communication is the bridge that brings you home to your brother or your sister. And in the perfection of communication, the Kingdom is remembered and restored.

So with that, blessings unto you, all those of you that will hear these words: Master your communication. Well do I know that whatever it is that I have accomplished, and even am still accomplishing, greater things than these can you bring forth. I am just a beginner in the Mind of my Father.

So. Hmm. Do you think that that will be sufficient?

Beloved sister?

Participant: I think it's wonderful. Thank you.

What would you wish to communicate in this moment?

Participant: I love you.

Now. Take a moment and go into the mind and simply ask:

> *Father what you have me communicate in this moment?*

and when you're ready, say it again.

Participant: I love.

Mmmm... Now the rest of you here, did you feel the difference?

[Audience agreement]

A greater depth, a greater expanse, a greater *power?* . . . a greater *joining?* Did you feel it?

Participant: Yes.

Indeed. So just maybe that little prayer works. And did you notice how you changed it from "you" to *"I love"*?

Participant: Yes.

Indeed. That is the truth of who you are. Hmm. Thank you for providing an excellent example for those who will read these things.

Participant: Jeshua I'd like for you to address two sentences that I keep hearing in my mind as we go through this, directly out of your Course in Miracles. The first sentence is: "Never tell your brother that he is what you would not want to be". And the second one is: "Words are but symbols of symbols and therefore twice removed from reality." Would you elaborate on those two?

Certainly. Words are indeed symbols of symbols, since they represent an idea; and when a word is spoken it again gives the message that this is the idea that you are valuing. Hm?

Now that is why I asked you when we began: Do you live in a world where words are not necessary? Since you abide *here*, it must be the Father's Will that you be the one who finds way to communicate Love *here*. And the wise teacher speaks the language of the student. Therefore, words are necessary in this dimension as a way of pointing beyond themselves to the symbols they represent and even beyond the ideas to the direct experience of the revelation of Love's presence. Now when you communicate to a brother or a sister in a way that indicates to them that you believe they are less than Christ, because of the power of thought and words you have immediately placed *yourself* in a position less than Christ. So that sentence refers to the divine selfishness that we have spoke of in this hour.

Do you want to be less than Christ? If not, then communicate in such a way that honours the truth of your brother or sister regardless of the degree of insanity they may temporarily be choosing. Honour that place first. We do not mean by that that you overlook the behaviour of insanity but that you *see through it* and offer first the truth.

Does that make sense for you?

Participant: Yes.

Does it help in regard to those two sentences that 'somebody' must have stuck in there by accident?

Participant: It's nice to know you have a sense of humour.

Beloved friend, the further you go into God the more you have to just laugh.

THE MEANING OF ASCENSION
November 1994

This transcript is from one of the only live video recordings of a Jeshua channeling. The video is available through www.wayofmastery.com

The Meaning of Ascension

Now we begin.

Indeed, greetings unto you beloved and holy children of Light Divine. Indeed, greetings unto you, beloved and holy and *only* Son of God! Indeed, greetings unto you, precious brothers and sisters.

And indeed, I come forth from that place which is of perfect Peace, and of perfect Love, and of perfect Light, and therefore I come forth unto you in this hour from the place in which *you abide* eternally. Forever the Son of God *is One* and the appearances of this world cannot shake that and cannot take your Truth and your Reality from you. Therefore, understand well that I come forth always in joy to abide with you, to walk with you, to celebrate with you the one Truth, the one Reality that is before time is and shall remain when the purpose of time is completed. Hmmm...

Who, then, am I? I am but what you are, and therefore I come forth from the place *in you* which is of a perfect remembrance: a remembrance of a Reality given and not created, given and sustained in Love—for in Truth, the Holy Son of God, being neither male nor female, is but the offspring of God; and God is but Love. And therefore, since before time is, *you* are the offspring of Light Divine. And if that is what you are, and I assure you that it is, it means that forever you *remain* that Light and that Truth and that Love.

I have said many times that you are your Father's *only* creation. What then is this world that you would see through the eyes of the body, that you would see through the perceptions that you have constructed out of experiences that you have had—and those experiences stretch back indeed to the very beginning of time, for there has never been a time that you have not been. Therefore, indeed, you've already tasted all worlds and all times. And there is nothing outside of you that you have not already tasted. Hmmm...

What, then, is this world? In Reality it is a world made in error, it is a world that has been made, sprung forth if you will, from but one thought, and that thought is:

> *I am separate from God. Therefore I shall create unlike Him and I shall be the maker of my own world and my creations shall not mirror the eternal changeless Beauty and Love that the Father is.*

And what more perfect place could there be to house that part of the mind that believes itself to be separate from God than in the appearance of a body? And you all know what that feels like to truly believe beyond all doubt that you abide within the structure—the space and volume—of a body. And therefore you look out through the physical eyes, and at times you believe you see a fearful world. At times you believe that you can be hurt, that things can be taken from you, that there can be gain and loss, and above all—through the perception born of what must be called an illusion— you begin to believe that the Peace of God can be taken from you, that the Reality of who you are can be threatened, and then there comes complexity upon complexity upon complexity as you strive to create your safety in the world of your perceptions.

And you have journeyed countless times through the fields of birth and death, creating bodies, if you will, struggling with them, doing the best you can, always feeling a bit of anxiety because you can't seem to quite control this thing and it always seems to end in death. Friends come and go, projects seem promising and then falter, and in the end, always, there seems to be waiting for you the experience of death. And the mind that would seek Peace, the mind that would choose to understand, to know, to transcend, begins its journey with *honesty*—to look truly at the feelings that are held within, to understand that there is this core of not feeling quite safe in this world, as though you were a stranger here. And yet your world would teach you to struggle to *make* yourself safe here, to *not* be a stranger here, to learn to control this world so that you can find the safety that you seek.

That process is what I have called the drama of the illusion of separation, and if you would well receive it, it has all come forth from but one thought held in the Holy Mind of the Son of God. And imagine, if you will, a grand Light without beginning and without end, vast beyond all imagination—and into that Light one thought emerges:

I am separate from my Father.

And with the perception born of the belief in that thought, that One Light explodes, becomes fragmented into an infinite number of points of light, all seemingly separate one from another and yet still made of Light.

With the perception of separation there is born fear, and with fear there is contraction, and contraction creates density. And the point of light that you become identified with as yours and yours alone, in being separate from all others, begins to take on the form of what we could call the ego: the small part of your True Mind that believes *it* is your master, that believes *it* is in control. And indeed, that small part of your mind is where fear resides, it is where contraction resides, it is where the experience of hurt and doubt and confusion resides, and you have become, indeed, unwittingly identified with that small part of the mind. And yet the whole while, in Reality, no fragmentation has ever occurred. For the Son of God, that grand and vast and perfect Light that is the perfect reflection of God's image, which is but Love, remains united as One. And in all the journeys of space and time (if you subscribe to the belief in reincarnation, which indeed holds value if it helps you to learn that life is eternal), through all journeys, lifetimes belong not just to you—for, if you would well receive it, *you* have lived the life of *every being*.

For though you would look through your eyes, the eyes of the body, and see other bodies and therefore draw the conclusion that there must be other minds, other souls, I tell you that in Truth, the Son of God remains One. And if that is true, and I assure you that it is, love your neighbor as yourself, because your neighbor *is* yourself. And when you look upon the face of your brother or sister, learn, indeed, to begin to look beyond the appearance of the body and see naught but the Face of Christ before you. For in your recognition of the one that stands before you, you must then acknowledge that it takes the Eyes of Christ to recognise the Face of Christ.

Can you then begin to imagine where time began? It began with *you*, it began in *your* Holy Mind—and if time began there, it resides there, *and the end of time is found nowhere but in you.*

Now, in these journeys there have been a multitude of experiences, some pleasant, some painful—and they have slowly created for you a construct, a prison if you will, through which you would view Creation. And the process of Awakening, the process of the Atonement, the process of Salvation, truly requires not a striving but an allowing, not a seeking but a finding. The process of the Atonement is the process whereby you remember the Truth of your Reality and celebrate with me the *only* fact that has ever truly been:

> *I and my Father are One! Now, here! Before, prior and through all times, I remain the Son of God.*

The process of the Atonement is the process of *remembrance*, of joining back together what had seemed fragmented. And what joins back together that which has been fragmented? Love. Love, a simple four-letter word in your language and a rather grand one. Indeed, only Love heals, only Love overcomes separation. Only Love restores the Son to the Kingdom of Heaven. Only *Love*—and why? Because Love is what you are. That is why it is so important to remember that every loving thought *is true*, and everything else is but a cry for help and for healing. Whether it is something that arises within you or within your brother or sister, rest assured that *every* such cry truly is coming forth within *you*. Are you therefore your brother's keeper? Indeed you are! Not out of moral sanction but because it's the truth: you *are* your brother.

And that is why salvation cannot be found *apart from* your neighbor. Gone is the time of disappearing into caves, hoping that by focusing your attention on your eyebrows that somehow you will achieve a great and enlightened state. This time is the time of endings. There is indeed a great quickening going on in the consciousness of mankind, an acceleration of the process of remembrance—because mankind *desires* it. And salvation comes in relationship. For you cannot return into the Kingdom by yourself. But as you extend yourself to your brother and sister and embrace them with the arms of the Love of Christ that dwells within you, you will bring them to yourself—and together, *we walk* to God.

I have come forth in this hour to ask you—to all that will hear these words—to ask you to join with me *now* in wasting not another moment, but in setting aside the roar and din of the world, in setting aside your fears and your doubts, to begin the practice of claiming the Truth of your only Reality:

> *I and my Father are One! And where I walk, my Father walks also and where I am there is naught but the presence of Love, for I have learned how not to tolerate error in myself, and because I choose to be the presence of Love, through me, Salvation is given unto this world.*

I have indeed come forth as your friend and as your brother, not as someone above you and certainly *never* as someone apart from you. I have come to ask *you* to join with me in being the Light that lights all worlds, in being that Love that restores the union of Father and Son. And in that union indeed there will be a healing that shall be witnessed upon this plane, this physical world—and why? Time itself never needed to be created, but it was; and because you've chosen to perceive yourself as separate from God, *in time* you then remember your union with God. And time is given unto you only that you will use it constructively.

And if you would dwell upon it for just a moment, if now in this moment you would abide with me and contemplate this simple question, surely the answer will not be hidden:

Can there be *any* use of time that holds greater value than the practice of remembering that *you* are the Holy Son of God, that you are safe and in perfect union with Him always?

Can there be any purpose to experience unless it be the practice of extending the Love of Christ—not to try to solve your problems, not to *seek* for the Kingdom, but to acknowledge that you have found it? For lo, indeed the Kingdom of Heaven *is* within *you*.

Does that mean that it's a something? It's a physical place that can be found within the body? No. It means that it is within the construct of yourself that you have become identified with, and as you choose to turn your attention from that construct to begin the practice of identifying with the Truth of your Reality, that Light within you begins to *outshine* first, your image of yourself, and then the image of your brother. And as that Light extends outward, it outshines your ideas of what the world is, what it is for, where it has come from, and where it is going.

Beloved and holy friends, think not that anything arises by accident. Your world would teach you that accidents abound, that there are "coincidences"—you just "happen" to run into a friend at a corner. Hardly! There are some of you that know perfectly well that just behind the appearances of things there is indeed a grand orchestration taking place, and I have called that Wisdom, that Mind, that One who is the orchestrator the Holy Spirit: the bridge that brings the Son dreaming the Dream of Separation back into Truth and Reality. And the bridge is set before you, and He makes straight your path.

And if your would receive it, every moment of your experience is a joyous blessing. For it will reveal unto you either the joy of union with God or it will reveal to you the small corners you are keeping for your illusion that need Light to be brought to them. Count, then, every experience as a blessing and give thanks for it, and your gratitude and your appreciation is what allows your Light to outshine the world you have made in error. If Light be your Home and if Light be your Truth, then surely Light will outshine all worlds of limitation.

The greatest of gifts that you can give to anyone is not to try to fix them, but to forgive them as your forgive yourself and choose to be only the presence of Light. And in that choice, because all minds are joined, you must necessarily be the one who uplifts your brother and your sister. Every time *you* choose to think a loving thought, every time *you* choose to look past circumstances and appearances to see the Face of Christ in your holy brother or sister, *you* are the Power and the Light and the Truth that uplifts and heals the whole of Creation. That is the *power* that is given unto you and has been with you since before time began.

And because nothing arises by accident, it is not by accident that those of you that are here find yourself here. Out of curiosity, perhaps, you have come—that is an appearance; behind it there is a place where all minds communicate. Some of you seem to be more aware of that than others. That doesn't matter, because in the end there will be perfect knowledge. I want you to understand that there will be no one who witnesses this (what you call) tape and hears these words who has not already been in communication with me, who I will not *guide* to hear these words. And, yes, that means that everything the human mind has ever created is used by the Love of God as the very stepping stones that must bring the whole of Creation back into remembrance of Perfect Union.

There is but the slightest of differences between you and me. And the difference is simply this: as a man I remembered my role in the Atonement, and *lived* it. And the only difference between us seems to be a difference of time, but not of quality of our Being—for we are equal. And there is but one curriculum to master and it is given unto you to have the freedom to decide *when* you will learn it. But the choice is not yours *whether or not* to learn it.

The time comes very quickly, and some of you know what I'm talking about, in which the curriculum will be mastered—will be learned—very, very quickly and more and more quickly as more and more learn it. And why? Because of miracles. Miracles indeed shorten the need for time itself. And *you* are miracle-workers. You are the presence of Light in this world—as everyone is—but while time yet seems to continue, it is given unto you to be the demonstration of one who has allowed correction to come to their mind, so that they see no longer a fearful world, so that see no longer separation between themselves and others, that they see only the presence of the Face of Christ. And indeed miracles—*miracles*—are given to you to be extended and expressed *through* you. And the Awakened Son of God looks upon every moment of every day, and if miracles aren't occurring he pauses and takes a deep breath and allows correction to come to his mind. He doesn't try to fix it; he gives it to the Holy Spirit. For the Awakened Son of God knows that every moment *is* miraculous, when that mind abides as the presence of Love.

I want to share with you in this hour that there is indeed a grand orchestration occurring. Where does it occur? In a mind outside of yours? Not at all! For if you would well receive it, from the moment of that first thought of separation, already the Father has healed that separation. And time is but the enactment of separation—and its healing. That means that you will witness, in time, a growth of miracles, an expansion of miracles, and there *will be* established once again the Kingdom of Heaven on Earth. Is that the end of the journey? Hardly! But it is the correction of an unhappy dream into a very happy one, in which no longer shall be seen judgment and fear and doubt and anger and distrust—indeed, brotherhood of Man. And when the Son is re-awakened in all minds, the Light of Christ will shine so brightly that even this world, having completed its purpose, shall be dissolved in Light and shall be seen no more.

It is not possible to speak of that hour and that day, only to say: Trust that it is quickly coming to pass. And who has proclaimed it? Who has decreed it? You have! You have: that deep part of your mind that has never left union with God, that deep part of your mind that *is* the Mind of Christ has already collaborated with *all* minds to bring about the healing and the Atonement. Do I come, then, to bring the Atonement to you? Hardly! I just come to dance with you, to laugh with you, to play with you, to celebrate—*to celebrate*—the rebirthing of the Kingdom of Heaven.

I have said before that God needs you as much as you need God. Can you truly come to understand that?—that that Light which seeks to be reborn and expressed even in the field of time, requires *your willingness* to be reborn. And precious friends, all power is given unto you. *All power under Heaven and Earth is given unto the Holy and Only Begotten and Sacred and Beautiful Child of God* to be restored, to be remembered, to be the Light that lights all worlds.

And the hour *is* come, and the time is upon us, the time to set aside all fears and all doubts, the time to *allow*—the time to allow yourselves to remember the melody of an ancient song that seems to have been forgotten. In Truth, though it seems to you that perhaps only a small part of the melody has stayed with you, in Reality the whole of it is within you, even now. A song and a melody that speaks of perfect Peace, a song and a melody that speaks of Power, and of Grace, and of Comfort, and Compassion, and a song that speaks of *Passion itself*: the passion to be the one through whom a new vision can be restored to the mind of Mankind. Oh... Indeed, I have well watched everyone in this room be touched by vision, a vision that seems to transcend what the small part of your mind can comprehend, and all of you know what it's like to set your dreams aside, to set aside vision because you have been fearful of not having the ability to bring it about.

But can you understand that the orchestration that is occurring requires that *you* be willing to *give birth to your visions*, the part of the vision given unto each and every one of you, as though the vision of the healing of the Son of God were shining like many great Rays of Light, touching *each* mind and *each* heart, and the Holy Spirit whispering to you in your dreams: "Please fulfill this tiny part, and it is enough." It is not unlike the part I was asked to fulfill—and in Reality, even the gentlest of smiles that you give to your brother or sister, in which you see the Face of Christ in them and therefore set up the field in which their healing can occur, that smile that you offer is *every bit* as powerful and as miraculous as anything that was ever manifested through me when I walked in your world. Please come to understand that *we are equals*.

Your love can *heal* this world. Your resistance can only *sustain* this world. And the question that must be asked is but this:

> *Will I choose, now, to be the one who is awake?*

> *Will I choose,* now, *setting aside all anxiety of the future, all fears*

> *and judgments of the past, will I choose,* now, *in my perfect freedom to be the one through whom the Light of God lights the world?*

And if you would know your Father's Will for you,

> *Where shall I go to bring about the Atonement?*

Open your eyes: where are you in *this* moment? And if you find yourself here in *this* room, then understand, here and now is the *only* place given unto us where we can celebrate the Truth of the Holy Son of God is one with God. And the one sitting next to you is the one to whom *you* can extend the Love that lights the world. And if it true in *this* moment, it is true in *every* moment, for you do not walk alone.

And what will carry you into a world of perfect Peace? Your willingness to extend that Peace, now, wherever you happen to be. To see no longer ordinary moments, to see no longer mundane experience, to see that everything that happens is sacred and holy and blessed because *you* are present within it—you, the Holy Child of God—that when you buy your groceries, you are not experiencing an ordinary moment unless you see through the eyes of the world. But if you would shift just a little bit and see through the eyes that God has given you, you would know that *you* are the savior of the world: you are the only one who can bring Love to that moment. You are the Light shining in darkness, you are the presence of a Light that outshines the world, and where you walk, Christ walks with you, because Christ dwells within you as the Truth of your only Reality—now.

So what then can be said about the meaning of Ascension? By its very nature, the word signifies a lifting up from, a transcendence of; it brings images and pictures of becoming lighter and lighter. And you all know what that is like, when you allow gaiety and joy to come into the very cells of the body and you don't feel as heavy any longer—when you give up seriousness, and put your hands on your hips and laugh at the ego. That is already an aspect of the process of Ascension. In Truth, there is *nowhere to go,* because in Truth you are

The Meaning of Ascension

that vast Light, that vast Mind in which all worlds arise. And even the body, that you think is yours, has come and arisen *within* that one perfect Light. And knowing neither beginning nor end, you certainly don't move from one place to another, but all movement and appearance of it seems to arise within you.

Ascension, then, *is* the Atonement. It does not involve great magical techniques in which you learn how to take this bag of dust and somehow transmute it into Light so *you* get to rise into the clouds while your brothers and sisters are stuck on the ground... Although in perfect Atonement there is perfect freedom, through which the Holy Spirit can create demonstrations as miracles that catch the attention of others and force them out of their rigidly held perceptions. My Resurrection was such a miracle, my appearance to many friends—*many friends*—was really nothing else but a tool to help pry open the mind to see beyond the appearance of birth and death. Never was it designed so that you would look upon me and think:

> *Boy, well he's a great master and I'm just some shmuck...*

Hm! It was designed *only* as a demonstration that could reveal to you the Truth that must be true *for you*, if it is true for me.

Can there, then, be what is called bodily Ascension? Of course! If all worlds can arise, what's an Ascension of the physical body? Why is it perceived as something so *grand*? The fact that you can look upon your brother or sister and actually believe that they are other than yourself, now that is incredible! The Ascension of a bag of dust is not a big deal.

And in this hour I've also come forth to bring some correction, for there are some perceptions that are getting a little bit out of hand. And there are many who would seek, actually believing that if only they can learn to make the body ascend, and *then* they will find peace and *then* they will find the Kingdom of Heaven. Without abiding in that Kingdom, no possibility for Ascension of the body can emerge. Therefore, indeed, understand: *you must be* the goal you seek, *now*. And in that Atonement all possibilities are reborn.

Will you then seek it? No. You will not seek bodily Ascension, because you will have been delivered from the erroneous perception that you are separate from God and must go *somewhere else* to get it. And then if the Holy Spirit says: "We need a little bit of a demonstration, would you mind?" You will say:

> *Not my will, but Thine be done.*

And if you're asked to just be a street sweeper, you will indeed say:

> *Not my will, but Thine.*

Why? Because the Holy Son of God can go nowhere and experience nothing that separates him from the Love of God.

The meaning of Ascension is found in *your* willingness *to be the presence of Peace*, to see with timelessness, to see with unconditional Love, to see through a perception that has been corrected—so that you know your safety does not rest within the body or within the world, but indeed it rests in the perfect Knowledge given unto you since before time is. You are home now, right now; you are One with God. There is not one thing you must fix, there is not one thing you must seek, save to allow correction to be reborn in the mind.

And what happens when correction comes? Some of you know perfectly well what happens. The past is gone, and all the pain of it. Though the memories may come, somehow it's been translated and no longer do you feel the burden upon the heart . . . but there is a spaciousness, an emptiness in which only Light abides, and no shadow do you keep a grip upon, for you've released them all to the Light of God and they have been healed and removed from you forever.

And what you do surprises even you! And when others look upon you and say: "Oh, you're so grand, what a marvellous thing you're doing on this planet, thank you so much," you look them in the eye and you say, perhaps in different words:

> *Of myself I do nothing, but my Father through me does all things! That's how simple it is. I gave up efforting, I gave up striving, I threw in the towel of trying to be the maker and the doer and I became the allower, I became the celebrator, I became the truster.*
>
> *And whenever my mind began to get into striving and effort, I remembered that my thoughts do not mean anything. And I remembered to choose Peace. And in that Peace a Light began to be remembered, and a song played more loudly, and that Light has outshone all of my dreams of separation, and of fear, and of doubt. And I abide in that Light—and holy friend, if I abide in it, so do you! Let us journey into it together: I will extend my hand to you, for however long it takes, until you see that the Light is in you also.*

That is the perception you will hold of yourself and of your brother. And if you would well receive it, it is given unto you now—*now*—to receive the only Truth that has ever existed, to be the one who proclaims,

> *I and my Father are One!*

For when those words become yours with every fiber of your being, the Atonement is completed on Earth as it has already been completed in Heaven. Remembrance has been restored.

To those of you who know of those who would seek to find ways to create an Ascension for the physical body, go and tell them that they have already completed it—and now is the time to release striving. It is Love that will heal this world. Love abides in its own Presence and in its own Certainty and in a Holy and ancient Knowledge. You cannot seek for Love, and you cannot find it. You can desire it, and your intention can become so pure that nothing else distracts you. But in the end Love can only *be allowed to be extended through you.* You cannot be the one who is the creator of Love, you can't puff yourself up with it *so* that you can give it away, there are no magical techniques that will build its power within you. It's already given to you freely. And miracles therefore must occur naturally to minds that teach only Love . . . That teach *only* Love . . . That teach only *Love*, because there's no dark corners of the mind left that you have sought to save for yourself.

I come in this hour to ask *you* to be that one—to be that one who from this hour forward will indeed teach *only* Love, will be the one who knows and lives the fact that all needs are already met, to be the one whose mind is corrected, to whom sanity is restored. For when you walk in this world for such a short time as the presence of only Peace you will affect everyone who enters your domain. They may not understand it. They may, indeed, think it's because of your body that they're attracted to you. They may think it's because of the wisdom that seems to pour forth from your mouth— although you won't remember what you said when you're done, because it's not you doing the talking. But they will feel the presence of Peace, and it must necessarily touch that place of Peace in *them*. And when that window opens, Light rushes in and their process of awakening can deepen, continue, or perhaps begin.

Please, please, understand that the Ascension has been completed, waiting only on your Remembrance—that you are not something separate that must be taken somewhere, or must experience some exalted state, so then you can say,

> *Ah, now I've got it.*

The exalted state of the rebirth of the Kingdom of Heaven on Earth waits on your *acceptance* of what is True *now*.

Can you imagine what it would be like if tomorrow—if tomorrow—you walked through this world and every time your brother or sister said, "Oh, God, life is such a bummer. Isn't it just terrible? What about that Presidential election?" . . . and you chose not to participate in that energy? Not that you pick up yourself and run from them, but that you transcend that limitation and shine forth only Love and Peace. You will know what to say because the world's words will be given unto you. Even as they were always given unto me. Know you that which is called the Sermon on the Mount? When those words poured forth, afterwards some of those friends—that the world has mistakenly called my disciples—came up to me and said, "O Lord, that was so beautiful, it was so incredible." And I looked at them and said, "What did I say? It wasn't planned. I am not the doer or the maker. Of myself I do nothing; the Father through me does all things." It was awfully difficult to get them to understand that, because the ego needs to set others on pedestals; because it fears recognizing that *the same power dwells within it.* You will be the one spouting forth Sermons on the Mount. And maybe sermons in parking lots. There may be sermons in grocery stores. Does it matter? One temple is as good as another.

I ask you, as your brother and as your friend, to begin to contemplate your willingness to join with me in the Atonement. Not by needing it, but from the foundation of your recognition that it is already completed within you. Some of you know what it means to be taught that you must honor me—as if I am separate from you. But I say unto you: He that does not honor the Son that dwells in fullness within their own heart, in no wise honors me—no matter how many prayers, no matter how much supplication is given unto to images of me made in the minds of mankind.

But when you, the Holy Son of God, honor the Christ that lives within you, indeed, let it be known that you have honored me as your brother, as your friend, and as your equal. And if that sounds like sacrilege to your world, then so be it. I can't help it. Because it is the Truth. I did not come to proclaim myself your savior. I came to proclaim the Salvation that has already occurred within you. I came to mirror to you the Truth of *your* being. And unto as many as would chose to see me *as* their equal, because I am in charge of the Atonement do I give forth the ability to pry open every last corner of the mind and heart, so that you are, indeed, restored in the image of the Son of God. And if that happens to involve healing of the body, so be it.

Unto *you*, there is extended in this hour the choice: *to choose with* me to be the presence of the Atonement. And in this, Ascension is already completed. And every time you choose joy, every time you choose gratitude, every time you choose unlimitedness, every time choose to allow vision to be your guide, you walk *with* me. And we walk together *in the Kingdom of Heaven*. Understand well, then, there is not one corner of your life that cannot be transformed, if there is a need for it, when *you* choose Love instead of fear. For Love begets healing; fear must necessarily deny it. And that Love is in you now.

When I said to a group of friends, "Go forth and teach all nations," all I said to them was, "Go forth and teach only Love." For by teaching it you must necessarily learn it. And as you witness the miracle of the extension of Love through you, and what it does in the life of your brother and sister, you must necessarily then *know* that the miracle has already occurred within *you*. And that is the process whereby your fearful dreams are translated into dreams of safety. And as you see that you *are* safe, you open more and more. And the power of miracles, the power of Light, can flow through you ever more freely. That is the importance for you of choosing to teach only Love: to feel a *passionate desire* to be the presence of Love; not to settle for anything else *ever again*. For your choice to settle for less than Love has given birth to all worlds that have mirrored the illusion of separation from God. And you know that you know those worlds well. You've tried every byway and every dead end.

Live with a *passion*; a passion to *be* the presence of Love. And if one says unto you, "Lo, the Kingdom is here," and another says, "No, it is there," stop and smile and say,

> *Precious friends, the Kingdom of Heaven is within me. As it is within you. Let us therefore rejoice and be glad in this day, for in this moment it is given unto us to be the Light of the world. And wherever two or more of us come together, Christ abides. And there can be no greater or more sacred place on earth than a place in which minds have joined in Love, having set aside an ancient hatred, born from fear, born from separation.*

Walk then in this world, and understand that everywhere you go—

everywhere—the minds of mankind are crying out for the opportunity to join in that sacred union, the Holy Instant that heals the illusions of separation. In your hands there is a pearl of great price. It is in *your* hand and everywhere you go you can extend that hand to everyone you see—no matter what they are doing, no matter what they say about you. None of that matters a bit. How can the opinion of an insane mind matter?

I have told many it's time to live a bit outrageously: a time to dance, a time to sing, a time to play. These things I did daily when I walked upon this earth, and I was only serious to the degree that the one in front of me could speak no other language but seriousness, until they learned the language of laughter and play and simplicity and ease. For my way *is* easy and my burden light. My cross is not heavy: it is made of Light. Therefore take up your cross and follow me. Come and join the dance. Come and join the dance in which you realise,

My God! I am an ascended master,

. . . right here in (what do you call the name of this village?) Berkeley. Right here an ascended master walks and it goes by your name. Does that sound arrogant? The only thing that has ever been arrogant is that *you* dared to believe is that you are something other than what God created you to be. Now *that* requires *great* arrogance! Hm!

Do you see the great paradox, then? For the Truth of the Kingdom is diametrically opposed to every perception the world has sought to teach you. It takes great humility to say,

I and my Father are One,

because you have to give up the world. You have to be the one courageous enough to speak the Truth. It is the height of arrogance to believe that you have ever sinned against God. It is the height of arrogance to believe that you are guilty, that you are not capable of fixing yourself, that somehow you're not even worthy of it:

> *Father, beat me and whip me for I have sinned.*

That one's been played out, and some of you have memories of what you would perceive as lifetimes in which you know what it means to flog the body. It wasn't a lot of fun! Are you willing to join with me in the outrageousness of a divine humility in which you simply set aside every conformity to the beliefs of the world and simply say to your friends,

> *I can't play the game any longer.*

And they'll look at you and say, "What do you mean?"

> *Well, I'm the Son of God. I've been trying to pretend I'm something else—but it's exhausting me! So I give it up. Father, live through me.*

And they will indeed look at you with a bit of an incredulous look and one of the eyebrows might go up. So what? In that moment, because of your willingness to be what *they* will perceive as arrogant and outrageous, a window has opened—*a window has opened.*

A window has opened because, for just a moment, you stopped their mind. Unknown to them, *you* have been the one who turned their attention from the roar and the din and the insanity of the illusory world to the real world. Now, will they get it? They might. They might call you crazy. They might leave your life, the life of the body. But you have a saying in your world that Nature abhors a vacuum, and if that is true for Nature, it is indeed true for God. *Never fear loss. For what is of true value can never be taken from you. It can only be added to you.*

As you teach Love, all that is truly valueless must necessarily drop from you: gently perhaps at times, at times seemingly not so gently—but understand that in those moments it's only resistance to letting go that creates the feeling of struggle. And suddenly the hour of your rebirth is upon you and you will look around for your past

The Meaning of Ascension

and find that it's no longer with you. You will look for your doubts and your confusions and you'll be startled because you won't be able to find them.

And suddenly you will know that the miracle has occurred: the Atonement has been completed. It has come as a thief in the night, and while you were sleeping it stole the cobwebs of all shadows long since outgrown. And you have awakened in the morning of a new day—and behold, your cupboards are bare of what you *thought* held value. And in its place is a feast set before the only begotten Son of God, a feast without beginning and without end, a feast to which your Father invites you to return as the guest of honour, and the Prodigal Son has indeed returned. And he sits down at his Father's table and lo, all he looks upon is good. And you'll raise the chalice to your lips and you will drink of a certain elixir called Love, called Salvation, called Awakening, Enlightenment—it goes by many words; it's really all the same—and then you will put the chalice back on the table and you will look your Father right in the eye, and together with Him you will laugh as you have never laughed before. And your laughter will be the song that is echoed out like a vibration through every molecule of Creation. Your laughter will shift the vibration of Creation, and Light will pour into every molecule until it becomes once again as Light itself.

That is the meaning of the true Ascension. It signifies the moment when the Holy Son of God has been restored completely. Will it come tomorrow? It might! Does it seem a long way off? Remember, such a perception is born in time, but miracles shorten the need for time. How then to create the miracles that shorten time? By acknowledging that the Atonement is complete within you *now*. Do you see how that all begins to make sense? Gone is the time for praying for saviors, gone is the time of looking to the future when the Son of God would return. *Now* is the time spoken of in many cultures and in many ways, and in all epics that have ever been—the Truth has always been spoken. *That time is at hand.*

I gave forth a promise that in that day I would indeed return. And though I sought to make it clear, there were many who did not understand. Let it be known that I *have* returned. I have returned not only to join with the mind of this my beloved brother, who finally threw in the towel because he couldn't figure it all out. Hm! I have come forth with an ancient friend that some of you know by the first name of Helen. I have come forth through what you would perceive as 2003 friends who are currently serving somewhere on this globe as what are called in your language "channels." And I serve with many others in many, many ways—for the promise I gave *has been kept*.

I have returned because I love you. In Truth, I never went anywhere. And I have worked without ceasing to whisper to you in your dreams, to gently guide you to the left when you thought you were going to the right. I have come to you because you have been given me of my Father. Even as there are already those who are—shall we say—assigned to *you* and will come to you when you allow, through your willingness, the recognition of the Atonement's completion to be remembered in you. There are many who are waiting for *you*, who will be sent to you in ways that you cannot begin to comprehend—and through *you*, the *very same* work will take place, even as this work has occurred through me. Do you begin to get the picture?

There's a network, if you will, being created, in which the Father Who has loved me gives unto me the power to give that Love to you. And in your receiving of it, it is given unto *you* the power to give it to another. And that giving *is* the miracle that heals the need for time. You do not walk alone, and you cannot take a step without me, for I promise you this: even as I said unto you then, I say it again: *I am with you always.* And I shall give you my strength until yours is certain.

Think it not a burden that you would call upon me, for you are worthy of all the Love that I could ever possibly extend, and that Love is but the Love of our Father. *You are worthy of that Love!* There is not a decision you must make alone, there is not a journey you must embark on, believing that you are alone. From the moment you know that you are awake in your mornings, before you lift your

The Meaning of Ascension

head from your pillow, I am with you! I cannot force myself upon you, but I come freely and easily to *anyone* who but opens the door *the tiniest of cracks,* who throws in the towel and says:

> *"Okay, come and teach me anew."*

Does that make me your savior? No. *It makes me your friend.* Please, go and tell the world I am only its friend. Please tell them it's time to take me down off the walls of their cathedrals. It's time to embrace me and dance with me as a *friend.* For in an ancient day, to call someone a friend meant that you were committed *for all of eternity* to seeing only the Face of Christ in your brother or sister. A commitment, indeed! You are my friends and I have never ceased seeing only the Light within you, waiting for you to acknowledge only that sight within yourself.

The Ascension is completed. It will be enacted in the field of time as a joyous celebration of what has already been completed. Rest assured that it is even now occurring. Though you don't see it, do you know that in each and every day more and more minds are suddenly awakening? What seemed to take journeys and the study with what you call the "gurus," lifetimes of magical techniques so that one mind could be illuminated, is now occurring *daily,* almost effortlessly. And every time a mind awakens, it quickens the awakening of the next mind. That is why some of you have been able to pick up a certain text that you would call *A Course in Miracles* and sometimes, just by *holding* it, you have felt perceptions in your mind healed. That quickening is accelerating. Some of you know what that feels like, and it's going to continue.

Every day in your world now, all around this planet, minds are awakening. And they will look for their own. There are many who are beginning to feel a call to what could be called community, a call to join with those of like mind and like heart. And even as I say that, there are many in this room nodding their internal heads: "Oh yes, I feel that!" Because the knowledge of how the Ascension, the Atonement, is going to be reflected, is already within you. And because it is dawning within you, you are giving forth your willingness to participate in a script long since written. That is what you're feeling. Not a desire to flee anything—but a *call*, a call that has gone out to every heart and every mind. And who has extended that call? You have. And therefore you can only awaken to your own call.

It is simply my honor to be asked again of my Father to be one who delivers your own telegram to you. Please sign for it, open it, and read it. And when you open it, you'll say,

> *My goodness, this is from myself! Dear me, the time is at hand: Awaken now! Before I've had my breakfast?*

Yes! Before *every* breath you breathe, before every thought you think, give thanks unto God because the Father has been a Power through which the Son has been restored to his rightful place, and *you* have taken up your place at the right hand of God.

What does that image mean? It means right-mindedness, and that's all. It has nothing to do with physical location at all. The right hand of God is right-mindedness, and even now you *are* restored. So yes, for a little while you've been plopped upon your throne, but you seem to be holding on to a different dream; and so you babble a little bit while your Father sits next to you going, "Mm-hm, yes, mm-hm, yes, mm-hm,"—waiting, waiting for you to stop long enough to see where you are *now.*

> *My goodness, I thought I was in the world.*

And He leans to you and says:

> *"Precious Son, you are in the Real world. The other one was a momentary dream. It has left no trace upon you at any time. And you are together with me, even as it was in the beginning, is now and forever shall be. We are but One—and I, the Father, see not where I end and you begin."*

Hmmm. So then what do you do with it all? You accept it. That is the meaning of surrender. I've said that there are four keys to the Kingdom: Desire, Intention, Allowance and Surrender.

Allowance requires some practice, and that practice replaces the practice of striving and efforting and doubting and fearing. Allowance requires trust and faith, acceptance. And as that is learned, you could say you slip into the sea of surrender; but of yourself, you do nothing.

Surrender is the same thing as the Father's final step for you in which perception is translated into knowledge. Surrender is indeed death; surrender is birth; surrender is the Atonement completed *in you.* And what comes after surrender? *It no longer matters.* Imagine living each day seemingly in time, as your brothers would perceive you, but knowing that you live in eternity, knowing that whatever transpires this day is just fine—because you're too busy being the presence of Love to worry about the small things of the world. To live in a state of a consciousness in which you have learned the *only* lesson that must be learned: that there is nothing outside of you. To look from a high mountain upon your great cities, upon your brothers and sisters, upon the very face of this most precious and beautiful planet of yours, to look upon your stars, to see the space between them, the emptiness, the blackness, to think about universes upon universes upon universes upon universes, and dimensions upon dimensions and dimensions and dimensions and dimensions of this dream, and to say:

> *There is nothing outside of me.*

Hm! And to *walk* in that knowledge. It's the meaning of incarnation. And what follows Ascension? Descension! The willingness to be *The Word made Flesh,* to incarnate the Truth. That is the final step. *That is the final step.* Not to seek Heaven apart from yourself or somewhere else, but to be the one who brings it *into time*, that time itself is translated into eternity.

Well, there you have it, that's what's happening on this planet. That is what has been happening since first the Son of God held the thought:

I am separate.

From that moment, everything has been translated into the means that restores the Son to his rightful place.

So how do you incarnate the Word of God? By having a very good time! By laughing, by singing, by dancing, by playing, by being the vibration of unlimited joy—because there's no longer a place in you to allow a trace of heaviness or seriousness. All of that's part of the world, you see; it's not part of you. And as you allow that frequency to be born within you, you will understand what it means to *live* the Atonement, not as a philosophical concept, not even as a belief, not even as an acknowledgment, but as a *lived reality*—and that reality, if you will, *must* be lived before this world becomes again nothing but Light.

And you could say, if I could borrow a saying that I find in the mind of my beloved brother: The joke's on *you!"* You are the ones who are here as The Word made Flesh. For a short time you thought you were something else!

And the essential point of this hour, and why I asked that this be created, is to strip from thousands of minds the perception that there is any other choice that can be made. To help minds see, is the only choice left: the choice of Love over fear. The choice of seeing that the Atonement is completed in them and *the meaning of Ascension is now being lived*, indeed. In this, for this hour, we have now come to a completion. And I extend unto each and every one of you my gratitude and my thanks.

I want to let you in on a little secret. Though these my ancient and precious friends strove and what you would call worked their little tails off, trying to let a whole lot of people know about this—hm! nothing is impossible—and you could say there was a bit of a delay mechanism put in because it was very important that only certain ones be here. You are those ones. And each in your own way has brought a certain anchor of energy—that's the simplest way to describe it—that actually is participating in a little bit of a miracle . . . because you are creating something that seems to be on a tape but, let it be known, unto everyone who views what you call your tape of what this evening's talk has been about, there is going to be felt—perhaps subtly, perhaps grandly—a bit of what could be called the transmission of energy.

And I want to let you know that at some deep level within each and every one of you, even those with the gadgets on their ears, you have chosen from the depth of that Mind of wholeness within you to participate in *this* aspect of the orchestration of the Atonement. Each and every one of you! Therefore, unto you I extend *my* Love and *my thanks*—for the Beauty and the Light and the Love and the Compassion that lives within *you*: Thank you, Holy Son of God.

For some of you, nothing's going to quite seem the same from this hour. *Give thanks for that.* And remember please: I *am* with you always.

Peace be unto the Son of God who chooses to bring the things of Heaven to wed them with the things of Earth, that the Light of the Kingdom might again be extended as far as from the East to the West. Herein is the meaning of the Cross: a Cross of Light in which the Child of Christ dwells with an open heart and arms outstretched, his feet on the Earth and his mind in Heaven, to demonstrate the reflection of perfect Love.

Peace be unto you, and for now,

Amen

THE DIVINE FEMININE
December 1994

Now, we may begin.

And indeed, it is with great joy and also with honor that I come forth in this hour to share with you, to abide with you, to remind you of all that is true within you. I come forth to abide with you on this very special occasion to speak of the heart of that which is so-called *the goddess*, to speak of the heart of that which is called *Christ*, to speak of the heart of that which is called *Divine Mother*, to speak of the heart of that which is called *Abba*, Father.

I come forth, then, in this auspicious hour as you abide together in a place that speaks of the heart through the gentleness of the waves, through the vibration that is felt on the breath of the wind, through the sweetness that pervades the air and the many beautiful flowers. I come forth to abide with you, as you have chosen to come together as seemingly a small group of women upon a tiny speck of dust hurtling itself through space, seemingly so separated from all of life.

And yet I say unto you: You have not come together by accident. You *have* come together because you have well recognized that there is a place within each and every one of you, a certain quality of vibration, a certain aspect of the soul itself that you share in common. Well does it transcend the physicality of the body that you would know as *woman*. And yet it is a vibration that is shared through all those who are currently choosing to *in*carnate—which simply means to bring into expressed form—to incarnate in the very particular and specific vibrations of the feminine body. And to embody the feminine body is indeed to participate in a certain strand or vibration of consciousness that has its own unique features.

Again, we speak here not of the body itself, for the body is merely the effect of a choice that the soul has made to *embody* a certain frequency of the soul. That frequency can be awakened, what you might called tapped into. It can be tapped into by those choosing the frequency or the strand of consciousness that brings forth the male body. But it is much more easily accessed, it is much more constant for those who have chosen in this incarnation to manifest as woman.

Why, then, is this important? For there is a dawning of a New Age in which a certain frequency begins to be again primary as it once was upon the earth plane itself. We're not speaking here of right or wrong, good or bad. We're not here to evoke your beliefs that you have been the victim of some trauma that is causing imbalance on the planet at all. For the world you see is the world of a dream. You, then, have chosen to participate within that dream. And you have chosen to come forth within your own particular culture, your own particular timeframe—in the form of 'woman'— to present yourself with the unique challenge of *overcoming an ancient perception* which currently pervades human consciousness—and that perception is merely that it is the masculine strand that holds the highest value, that must be placed in a role of primacy for decision-making, for running governments and businesses, even for running what is called the household.

And have you not come forth to discover that the power of the Divine Mother, the power of Aba, the power of the Christ, the power of the Goddess—these are just various names for the same thing—is indeed present in its fullness within the strand held deeply within the soul that expresses itself right down to the cells of the body in *the image of woman.*

Beloved friends, I have spoken before, and I will speak again, that for Christ to truly be birthed into the world, woman—the collectivity of women—will need to step forth and declare *their commitment* to again birthing forth the Divine Mother, the Christ . . . to embodying that frequency, and not standing back in the shadows, but stepping forward with boldness and with power to *reclaim* what appears to be lost, to manifest and demonstrate that which is indeed present in *all beings*, whether they be of male or female form.

The time is at hand. The thought that I've just shared with you has already been sent out upon the cosmic air waves, so to speak, to all who are currently embodied in feminine form. It is indeed time to begin to create a more noticeable expression of the joining together of womanhood that expresses, and that is devoted to, and holds sacred the frequency of the Divine Mother, the frequency of compassion, the frequencies of service that truly impacts the planet through the extension of love, through the capacity to *feel deeply*, through the willingness to trust the wisdom of the heart, to trust the wisdom of feeling over the supremacy of *mere* logic or rationality.

Therefore, beloved friends, look around at the seemingly small group gathered in a location that represents a reflection of a time when mankind, when humankind, lived in harmony with all of the earth, the water and the clouds and the creatures thereof, and did not sense any separation between self and other, between dolphin and woman, between cloud and man. When there was a recognition that play and that laughter and that the growing of flowers, the giving of gifts, the singing of songs and the making of music, held supremacy over the organization of armies, the creation of corporations through which the consciousness that has forgotten the feminine seeks to find *dominion* over the world and over the earth.

Look, then, around your seemingly small circle, for each of you has chosen as an infinite soul to choose *this* timeframe, to choose *this* incarnation to make a decision: to take on the embodiment of the feminine form and yet not to succumb to the vibrational pattern of what you call the patriarchy. Nothing negative here about it and you'll need to let that go through forgiveness. But simply to recognize that a neutral pair of energies has been imbalanced for a while and that a certain segment of the dream has played itself out. And that is all. No reason to make a judgment.

Is it not time, then, for each and every one of you to truly take *ownership of your womanhood* by taking *ownership of your divinity*? Is it not time to bring forth your power by creating a matrix through which women can be attracted to join with you in increasing numbers? All of them dedicated to, shall we say, no longer succumbing, no longer walking next to the patriarchal consciousness, whether it shows up in a male body or female body—but rather to begin to find ways to creatively express what you know to be true: Life is sacred; war has never brought peace; there is no need for *dominion* over the earth, but there is every need to live in *harmony* with the earth as though the human body and the blade of grass are one thing and *each* needs to be wholly respected. Is it not time to recognize that every child upon your planet cries out to be embraced by the Divine Mother, not the patriarchal mindset that would teach fear and the need for dominion? Is it not time, beloved friends, to *arise and truly incarnate* creatively, beautifully, playfully, powerfully that which the Divine Mother is?

Now, in truth, the Divine Mother and the Christed consciousness are one and the same, for only where wholeness has been decided for within the depth of your own heart and mind can you truly realize who Christ is and what the Divine Mother represents.

It *is* time, beloved friends, for *women* to begin to express awakened consciousness by assuming the position of *authority* upon the planet. Could that be done? Oh yes. Rest assured that if fifty million of your women went to your capitol and simply sat down and said,

I'm sorry. We will no longer allow any legislation that supports the instruments of war, you would quickly be joined by another fifty million. Many of them *would be male in form* who would say,

> Yes, it's about time.

The point we are seeking to make here is in this transition that *must* come upon the plane of the earth, it is through the form of womanhood that such a change will need to be made. And why? Simply because the patriarchy which has been in the ascendancy for so long is identified as being one and the same as the male form. Therefore even that male who has awakened the female and 'made the two within himself as one' is still viewed by the world as an expression of the patriarchy, and the feminine consciousness of the Christed mind is not necessarily noticed or listened to. Rest assured, then, if one of you would arise and truly begin to serve as a channel for me, it would get much more press, much more attention than the many channels who are in male form who perform this service for me.

Therefore, *look not outside yourself* for the power or the means to heal the things of time and space, to heal the things of your world. Look well into the mirror and ask yourself only this: Am I willing as a divine spirit to accept what I have set in motion and to no longer succumb to the perception that there is an energy outside of femininity that must still be placed on the seat of primacy?

Is it not time for womanhood to claim what they know to be true—there's never been anything real but love, nothing holds a higher value than compassion and nurturance for all of life—and to begin to speak loudly, to live powerfully, and to make an impact, to begin to ask other women to join *with* you?

Is it not time to stop jabbering over the back fence and rather to take time into your hands and to impact the world by being in perfect attunement to the Divine Mother which *you* have chosen to incarnate—and to be a physical representation thereof?

Indeed, beloved friends, while, yes, you have chosen to come and gather in this most beautiful location of yours to play together, to dance together, to cry together, to laugh together, to swim together with the creatures who know you and love you, rest assured you're also called by a thought that has been sent out as a thread of light to all of womanhood—that it is time to arise, to no longer believe that you can only arise if the patriarchy *allows* you to arise, that it is no longer necessary to wait to see if someone gives you *permission* to gather and become powerful. It is indeed time for womanhood to step to the forefront of the rebirthing of the New Age.

Rest assured, by doing so there will be many in male form who will very quickly also begin to complete that process of reintegrating the feminine into their own consciousness. There are many, many what you would call men on your planet who are still waiting for "Mom" to take charge. And what does that mean? Not their earthly mother, their Divine Mother whom they know their physical mother to be a symbol of.

Therefore, I come forth in this short message to ask you to take time together, to look at the obstacles, the fear, the pervasive places in your consciousness where yet you believe that a patriarchal consciousness is *still* your authority and is *still* the authority of the world. Look not to see who sits in the seats of your government. Remember the power is not out there unless *you* give it away.

What, then, can you do in *your* communities to be the one who arises and calls womanhood to yourself? How can you begin to form those groups that can begin to make impacts in your own communities in ways that have never been done before? . . . With language filled with power that will no longer tolerate a starving child upon your streets, that will no longer tolerate what you call the weapons of destruction in the hands of a teenager, that will no longer tolerate excuses for the waste of monies on the things of war that could be used to nurture and awaken a child. Is it not time to assume responsibility for your own decision to incarnate as woman, the embodiment of the Divine Mother? Will you then stretch your hearts open wide and find ways that you can nurture and embrace creation, even as the Divine Mother embraces you?

Beloved friends, though once I came in the form of a man, understand well that I did so simply because in that timeframe, without the proper what you call 'plumbing' of the body, I would never have been listened unto. And my simple gospel that there is only Love and only Love is real, that you are one with God, would never have been heard or remembered. And the name Jeshua in some feminine form would not have survived the thirty-three years of my life. And in fact, though I would have performed many miracles even in a feminine form, I would hardly have come to have been known outside my little village. That's just the truth of the timeframe. And yet the message I brought is the message of the Divine Mother. It is the message: *Only Love holds any value.* Only life is sacred; not power, not control, and certainly not fear.

Therefore, I come to ask you if *you* are now willing to begin to look more deeply, to playfully see what you can create together, what you can create in your communities to bring forth the gentleness of the Christed consciousness through feminine form so the world—who still believes that bodies are real—can look upon you and remember,

> *That's the way it is supposed to be upon this gentle and beautiful earth.*

Are you willing to give up the value you have placed upon patriarchal consciousness? Are *you* willing to be brazen enough to invite your sisters to join you in the highest vision possible throughout the domains of creation? Are *you* willing to do in *your* timeframe what I was willing to do in *mine*—to look into your consciousness and not allow any part of it to be shaped by ideas that pervade the air of the patriarchal culture in which you live.

Indeed, the time is at hand and the cry has gone out. Think not, then, it is by accident that you gather in a little house on one little corner of a small island. For that island represents the very fire and power of a strong feminine consciousness. Tap into that power. Drink it into yourselves. Create a ritual in which you open the frequencies of the soul to the Goddess of the island that has birthed the very island upon which you sit. Awaken that passion and that fire within your *own* beingness, and fear it not.

And then decide—look well within your heart and see if what I have told you is true. There is a part of you that remembers as a soul why you have taken birth in a feminine form. There is a part of you that knows that the time is at hand. Look well, then, and see for yourself if this truth is not etched in the depth of your heart and of your mind and of your soul and, verily, of the body itself. The body is but a communication device. Will you, then, declare the truth that is true always and be there for the embodiment of the Divine Mother from whom all things have come forth?

And—above all—rejoice with one another, play with one another, *love you one another*, even as the Mother has first loved you, as she has loved all of us.

And with that, beloved friends, though the message be short, rest assured, you could say there is much within the parameters of the beginning and the end. Know then that I dance with you. Know well that I swim with you. Know that I will be with you in your celebrations of this short time together. For wherever hearts have chosen to come together, to remember the truth, the celebrate the truth, the embody the truth, and to release all things unlike the truth, where any such gather in my name, I am with them. And my name is not Jeshua, as yours is not your surname. *My name is Love. And so is yours.*

Be you, therefore, at peace, beloved and holy sisters of the heart of Christ, the beloved of the Divine Mother.

Be you therefore at peace, and play well. Do what you call the pulling out of all of all the stops. And know that you are never alone and *all power under heaven and earth is with you, now.*

Go then in peace, and thank you for allowing one who once came in male form to participate in your circle. It is indeed an honor.

Amen..

Epilogue

In the classic American film, *The Wizard of Oz,* the main character, Dorothy, transported suddenly to a new world, spoke for the soul when she said to her small dog and faithful companion: "Toto, we're not in Kansas anymore!"

My experience, related in *The Jeshua Letters,* was much like Dorothy's. I still notice twinges of disbelief at times – it was as if I was swept up and deposited on a different planet! Of course, I *was* swept up, turned inside out, and deposited back on the very same planet, emerging as a radically different 'me' in the process.

The call of ceaseless surrender – no matter what – leaves no room for the mind to reasonably assess things, as it comes to release the one thing the small ego mind wants: control!

It seems as if it was yesterday when Jeshua gave me such a key statement of universal wisdom: "My brother, what would you control save that which you mistrust?" Every step on the path of healing, and every call to incarnate more of Christ Mind has required me to rest first in this Truth, learn to see the fear underneath my desire to control, and then surrender it and leap!

My mind still cannot fathom how all that has occurred in the last thirty-plus years was possible, unless, of course, it is true that God's Love does collapse the need for time…and that we are truly supported in our willingness to submit to the alchemy of the spiritual journey, so that we become conduits for what Jeshua calls in *The Aramaic Beatitudes,* 'God's new creations.'

We cannot experience these 'new creations' unless we surrender and become willing to engage our inner demons, learning more deeply how to become the Presence in which our deepest drives, fears, doubts, sense of unworthiness, and guilt are healed – unless we allow all of the structured ideas and perceptions we carry about ourselves, others, and life itself to be flushed up into awareness, there to be dissolved in a Love that far transcends the limits of 'reason.'

From *The Early Years* channelings, onto *The Christ Mind Trilogy,* the years of diving deep into, and creating with Him *The Living Practices*, discerning under Jeshua's guidance *The Aramaic Beatitudes*, living homeless, traveling the globe to share and learn from others (like you!), making eight pilgrimages to Israel and many other pilgrimages to sacred lands, ten years founding and living in an ashram in Bali, birthing The *Jewels of the Christ Mind* program and many other online courses, and so much more...Jeshua has led me throughout.

Could I have known any of this would unfold? Of course not! And, boy, did I ever put up a good fight attempting at times to resist every bit of it! And clearly, it was not "me" doing it. Rather, God was having His way with me, and I have learned from it all one crucial, essential, vital thing: we simply cannot unfold God's life for us, which is what our life really is. Only God can do this, and this life will unfold only when we have truly said "yes," when we have surrendered our need for control, and allow ourselves to BE unfolded – then, and only then.

The entire body of teachings that comprise *The Way of Mastery Pathway* are astounding in both depth and breadth. We remain free, however, to elect just how far along the steppingstones Jeshua has set before us we will walk at any time.

What I have seen now, very deeply in myself and in the journeys of the thousands I have been blessed to grow with (even when such growth seemed a torment for ego) has revealed for me this truth: together, we are the makers of the 'world,' which is a projection of fascinating 'frequencies' made by 'bending' Light into distortions, so that what we see, feel, and believe is the opposite of Reality. That is our remarkable creation, called by Him "the dream of separation." But separation does not – cannot – exist.

What, then, an astounding thing we have done, experiencing what cannot exist! And still, Love calls us home, and however real the dream may seem, still, only Love is real. Indeed, the dream exists only in what we project upon reality, veiling the shimmering, extraordinary, infinite, and astounding Presence of God from ourselves, then using our creations in an attempt to regain what we threw away without having to remove those veils!

While only loving thoughts are real, until we heal beyond thoughts themselves and come to rest in the field of Love itself, often our 'loving thoughts' merely veil what remains to be healed into wholeness; we are hallucinating, still lost in the dream. And yet, Love is shimmering and smiling at us through all that we see, and we can come to see this Love infinitely, if we choose to. The "problem," then, isn't out there, it is with the nature of the seer. Turn within, then, not to escape, but to discern the veils that color reality, bringing all to Love for healing and correction.

Once we do this, we no longer hold onto the belief that, "If I just 'wake up,' I can finally escape this damn world," because we no longer have a desire to escape.

Waking proves that we have been utterly wrong about awakening itself, for the result is just the opposite – it is not about escaping at all but about embracing and loving our 'enemies.' For as we are free to choose what we put our attention on, and thereby create our experience, we see that our true 'enemies' are merely the veils we have allowed to cloak our minds, express through our bodies, and warp our very use of life and time.

That even thought arises from a far more primary field of energy, of frequencies made of Light that can veil Light from operating not just as thought, but as feeling, as the true power and potential of Love—this profound realization is what sets the fullness of *The Way of Mastery Pathway* apart from most forms of spirituality.

We are 'the world.' And it changes only as we choose to change. Until we become conduits for the transfiguring power of Love exactly where we have thought we were trapped – like Dorothy in Oz – there is no completion in Christed Being.

As these realizations truly began to dawn for me as a result of my journey under His masterful guidance, Jeshua led me to a statement in *A Course In Miracles* that I had not heard anyone teaching the *Course* refer to, let alone emphasize: "Heaven and earth will pass away means only they will cease to exist as separate states." Yes. There is no room for the hope of getting 'beamed up,' or shirking total commitment to our own transformation and serving the healing of all, nor can we justify ongoing distraction (which most of the world is designed to be – just go shopping!) if our deeper desire is awakening to Truth, Love, and Reality!

Jeshua makes it clear: "Christ assumes responsibility for the whole of Creation."

The Christ Path is one of radical death to self, rebirth, *and* a call to see that 'there is no other, you see only your Self,' a call to fully participate in the very process of coming to experience heaven and earth as ceasing to exist as separate states.

All we need do is humbly, fully, devotedly, allow Love to guide our own unique journey from fear to Love, under all conditions. All the rest will unfold from there, exactly as the creations of 'my life' have unfolded from the willingness to be 'taken all the way, no matter what.'

The Way of Mastery Pathway is a vital part of such an unfoldment for many, and though we may never meet face to face, we journey on it together, and I want you to know I am grateful for each time you choose forgiveness, or are willing to look within and question the little mind, open to new revelations, and are moved to new creations and choices to extend Love to one and all.

What Jeshua says is true: "This we do together, until all of Creation is returned to being only the praise of God's Presence." Peace comes when, truly, this is seen and known, and we see that the bringing of fear to Love, and the bringing of illusion to Truth for healing and transformation, for seeing the remarkable, joyful journey that this includes, is the only truly worthwhile use of time.

Blessings to you!

Jayem
July 2021

The Way of Mastery Outline
Pathway of Enlightenment

The book you hold in your hands is part of a larger body of work, namely *The Way of Mastery*.

The Way of Mastery is a pathway offering a profound and comprehensive theology and lived experience of love via a progression of teachings, exercises, and *Living Practices*, all devoted to a genuine – and radical – depth of living enlightenment.

This depth goes beyond intellectual belief or the acceptance of certain concepts and ideas. It guides the student into their essential and eternal Heart, into a radical, transfigured gnosis, a 'knowledge by being that which is known.'

The purpose of *The Way of Mastery Pathway* is threefold:

~ To create a pathway that can support any student from their first steps all the way to truly awakening into 'Christ Mind'

~ To restore the original Teachings of Jeshua (Jesus) given to His followers

~ To 'birth a million Christs'

The Way of Mastery Pathway is comprised of four essential and interconnected parts:

~ The Jeshua Channelings: *The Jeshua Letters, The Early Years, The Way of the Servant, The Christ Mind Trilogy: The Way of the Heart, The Way of Transformation and The Way of Knowing and The Later Years.*

~ The Living Practices: a series of alchemical trainings and Aramaic teachings, including *LovesBreath, In the Name* meditation, *The Aramaic Lord's Prayer, The Aramaic Beatitudes, Radical Inquiry,* the seamless life and more.

~ Facilitated Teachings and Sacred Journeys: deepening into a spiritual path often requires support; private sessions, workshops, seminars, on-line classes, sacred pilgrimages and a host of classes and gatherings are led by *Pathway* teachers.

~ **Temple Canyon Sanctuary:** sacred land near Abiquiu, New Mexico, miraculously purchased in the early days of the Pathway, and meant for future steps of development, as given specifically by Jeshua during the time of its purchase.

In summary, *The Way of Mastery* is a Pathway of Enlightenment that re-establishes Jeshua's original teachings, and in doing so, it offers a profound, in-depth roadmap to support any soul from the first inkling to awaken all the way into knowing their most essential Self.

The *Pathway* aims at nothing less than a radical shift of identity from 'Ego' to 'Christ,' aiding students to increasingly live in and create from Christ Mind, itself. Through His *Pathway*, Jeshua seeks nothing less than the birthing of "a million Christs" on this planet and the transformation of the experience of humanity from fear to Love—the manifestation of Heaven on Earth that 'completes the very need for Time.'

Jayem is the channel of *The Way of Mastery*.

The Way of Mastery Pathway and its contents are copyright (c) Jayem.

Official Website: www.wayofmastery.com

Shanti Christo

'Shanti Christo' is a term mentioned often in *The Way of Mastery* texts. The meaning of Shanti Christo is 'Peace of Christ.' This term was first given by Jeshua to Jayem prior to the unfolding of the *Pathway* (as *The Way of Mastery Pathway* is often called) itself.

Shanti Christo was also the name given to the non-profit foundation that Jayem set up in the early years of his channeling with Jeshua. The Shanti Christo Foundation was established to disseminate *The Way of Mastery* teachings, and to steward the Temple Canyon Sanctuary land near Abiquiu, New Mexico, until time for it to be developed further.

In 2002, Jayem received guidance from the Holy Spirit related to the foundation and his role within it. Following this guidance, he resigned as its director and continued his own deep immersion with Jeshua. It feels important to share the portions of the guidance related to Jayem's role for you to read directly:

> *"First, you* [referring to Jayem] *must step aside completely. You have successfully completed the stage of vision. The twofold purpose of the entity* [Shanti Christo] *is fully revealed and given: the teachings, which began with* <u>The Jeshua Letters</u> *and ended with the three works entitled* <u>The Way of the Heart, Transformation, and Knowing</u>. *Second, the physical setting has been attracted, discovered, purchased, and its design features openly shared* [the land near Abiquiu].
>
> *"The next stage, implementation, is not your role or your concern.* [Jayem interjects at the time of the channeling: 'And frankly, this is a surprise to me in big doses.' The reading continues:] *Remember, you can only be what your Creator would make of you, not what you may perceive you should be."*

Holy Spirit later goes on to share:

> *"Your only role* [speaking directly to Jayem], *the essence of your existence, is to bridge vision and the teachings of Christ mind to others, thus fully learning them yourself."* ★

As a result of Jayem's continued immersion with Jeshua, further stages of the *Pathway* developed after his departure from the foundation – namely the *Living Practices* (*Love'sBreath* and *Radical Inquiry*) and *Facilitated Teachings*. Also included in this unfolding was what Jeshua states as a primary purpose *of* the *Pathway*: "to restore My original teachings." These unfolded under His guidance and are known as the *Aramaic Teachings*, which in themselves express the soul, depth, and heart of the entire *Pathway*.

Interestingly, this development was 'predicted' in Lesson 10 of *The Way of Knowing*. Jeshua revealed that much more would be coming forth after the completion of what came to be known as *The Christ Mind Trilogy*:

"...as we enter these last days of this *Way of Knowing*, we have come in this hour to share with you that we do not so much come to a culmination, or an end, but to a *springboard* for what shall be."

To this day, Jayem continues to develop teaching tools that provide valuable assistance to thousands as they engage *The Way of Mastery Pathway*. He has gone on to become a masterful facilitator and continues his dedicated servantship with Jeshua – holding His vision for the *Pathway* as sacred.

༄

Notably, after Jayem stepped away from the Shanti Christo Foundation, its board elected to publish only three of the five core teachings: *The Way of the Heart, The Way of Transformation,* and *The Way of Knowing*. Substantial sections of these texts were edited and removed, including the questions and answers that followed many lessons, and the trilogy was published within a single book entitled *The Way of Mastery* (referred to by many as the "blue book").

While this publication served to disseminate the teachings to many, identifying the trilogy under this title has also created confusion for many students who have come to equate *The Way of Mastery* with a single book. The *Pathway* is far from complete without *The Jeshua Letters* and *The Way of the Servant* texts (which the Shanti Christo Foundation chose not to publish), and the crucial experiential components that Jayem has continued to develop—*The Living Practices, Facilitated Teachings,* and *Aramaic Teachings.*

⌘

This series of books—the only authorized and complete version now in print—has been published to ensure that students understand the broader context in which *The Jeshua Letters, The Way of the Servant*, and *The Christ Mind Trilogy* were given, and that they are only one part of a comprehensive 'pathway that can carry anyone from the first inkling to awaken all the way to Christ mind.'

May *Shanti Christo*—the Peace of Christ—be with you.

* *The complete text of the 2002 Message is available on our website: wayofmastery.com*

Way of Mastery Pathway

The *Way of Mastery Pathway* offers a comprehensive road map if you have the desire to **grow,** to **heal** and to **know yourself**.

Find out more about what is available by visiting our website: www.wayofmastery.com

www.ingramcontent.com/pod-product-compliance
Lightning Source LLC
Chambersburg PA
CBHW020352170426
43200CB00005B/133